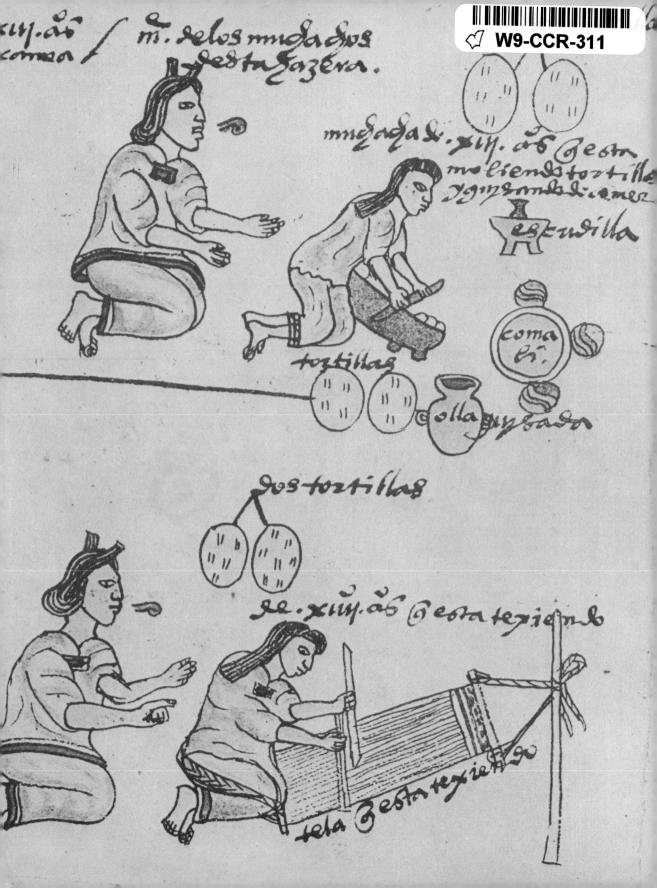

xiij. años / comen̄ m̄. delos m̄chados q̄esta hazera.

m̄chada d. xiij. años q̄ esta moliend̄ tortillas y q̄ya comed̄ vna escudilla

tortillas

comalj.

olla q̄ guisado

dos tortillas

de. xiiij. años q̄ esta texiend̄

tela q̄ esta texiend̄

THE CUISINES OF MEXICO

Symbol of Abundance

THE

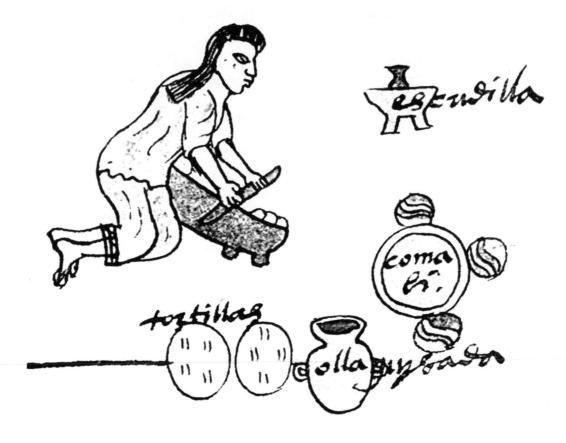

escudilla

comal

tortillas   olla hirviendo

CUISINES OF
Mexico

Diana Kennedy

Foreword by Craig Claiborne

Drawings by Sidonie Coryn

HARPER & ROW, PUBLISHERS

New York, Hagerstown, San Francisco, London

Photograph opposite page 171, Jon Naar; photographs opposite pages 42, 43, 74, 75, 138, 139, 170, Francis Stoppelman. Dishes and ornaments courtesy of the Museo de Artes Populares, Mexico, D.F.

Detail on page iii from *Codex Borbonicus* (Paris, 1899) courtesy Rare Book Division, The New York Public Library (Astor, Lenox and Tilden Foundations).

STANDARD BOOK NUMBER: 06-012344-3

LIBRARY OF CONGRESS CATALOG CARD NUMBER: 72-79677

79 80 81 10 9 8 7 6

TO MY BELOVED PAUL,
WHO WAS MY REASON FOR BEING IN
MEXICO IN THE FIRST PLACE

Contents

Illustrations

Color Plates

Drawings

Scenes from the Mexican Codices

The Mexican codices were the ancient manuscripts—colored pictograms, ideograms, and phonograms on bark paper or deerskin parchment—depicting the religious ceremonies, myths, and history of the Mexican tribes. They date back to pre- and early post-Columbian periods; some are post-Columbian copies of earlier manuscripts.

The illustration on page iii is the Symbol of Abundance taken from Plate 32 of the *Codex Borbonicus*. Plates 31 and 32 together represent a fiesta in honor of the Mother Goddess, to fecundity. The asterisk-like marks on the symbol depict the bark papers splashed with liquid rubber to represent rain that were presented to the deities.

The illustrations on the endpapers, title page, and pages 1, 57, and 353 are scenes from the *Florentine Codex*, which forms part of Fray Bernardino de Sahagún's *Historia General de las Cosas de Nueva España* (del Paso y Troncoso edition). Fray Bernardino was among the second group of Spanish friars to arrive in Mexico in 1529, sent to convert the Indians to the Catholic faith. In order to do this, he not only learned their language but became conversant with their history and customs through the picture writings of the Aztec elders. The *Florentine Codex* is made up of these picture writings.

Acknowledgments

No book of this kind can be written without a great deal of help, at every step of the way, from friends and acquaintances—and there is a long list of them. I should like, therefore, to thank most sincerely:

Elizabeth David, who was, unwittingly, my inspiration, for when I first went to Mexico I read and cooked from her books avidly.

Katherine Canaday and Craig Claiborne, whose help and encouragement launched me into writing and teaching in New York.

Frances McCullough, my editor at Harper & Row, who loved the idea of this book from the beginning and helped me convince other people about the cuisines of Mexico.

Eleanor and Bob Corkery, whose eternal house guest I was for three consecutive summers. Ted Shepherd and his wonderful crew, for whose hospitality I am also most grateful.

Thelma Sullivan, who so generously made her library of published and unpublished material available to me, and supplied ideas, definitions and translations for the book.

Shana Conron, who helped me set up the recipes in the first place and who, with Judy Suratt, taught me to have more respect for the English language and those elusive punctuation marks.

Gladys Delmas, who suggested the opening quote from Guanajuato and was that Christmas *mole* broadcaster.

The staffs of the Mexican Government Tourism offices and Peter Celliers of the Mexican Tourist Council for their help, especially for putting me in touch with my "cooks" all over the Republic.

Paula Krotzer, who suggested the title of this book to me.

Lothian Lynas of the New York/Bronx Botanical Gardens library, who patiently checked and corrected my identifications of plants.

Botanists Dr. Antonio Marino, Helen O'Gorman, Evelyn Bourchier, and the late Pepe Roldán, who helped me identify herbs and chilies collected in all parts of Mexico.

John E. Fitch, research director of the Department of Fish and Game Marine Resources; Tom and Lilia Lee; and Don Amando Farga.

Joann Andrews in Mérida, who helped me check out many questions on Yucatecan food.

The people who have come to my classes and contributed suggestions and ideas, particularly Grayson Hall, Ann Swint, and Roberta Schneiderman.

Margery Tippie, my splendid copy editor, who did so much for this book; and Sidonie Coryn, for her infectious smile and quick hand.

And the following Mexican friends who have contributed recipes for this book:

Sra. Alicia Castro de Alcaraz, Sra. Elsa de Anaya, Sra. Maggie Anderson, Sra. Ana de Andrea, Don Miguel Armijo Ramos, Sra. Maria B. de Bárcena, Sra. Maria de los Remedios Broca, I. Howard Brown, Sra. Maria Carlo de Carlín, Sra. Godileva de Castro, Sra. Luz de Cruz, Sra. Beatriz V. de Dávalos, Sra. Julia Romay de Duarte, Sra. Maria Emilia de Farías, Sra. Jovita de Figueroa, Sra. Angela de Galindo, Sra. González, Sra. Alicia Ferrer vda de González, Srta. Lic. Maria Concepción Hinojosa, Srta. Arq. Adriana Jeffrey, The late Sra. Dora Larralde, Sr. Fidel Loredo, Sra. Loreta Mediz de Loret de Mola, Sra. Consuelo M. vda de Martínez, Sra. Maria Luisa de Martínez, Sra. Rosa Margarita N. de Mejía, Sra. Berta López de Marrufo, Sra. Rosa Maria Casas vda de Merlo, Sra. Lilia de Nájera, Sra. Isabel Marín vda de Paalen, Sra. Cantú Peña, Srta. Rufina, Sra. Olga Silva de Rubio, Srta. Margarita Sánchez, Sra. Luz Maria Morales de Santiago, Sra. Agustina Murguia de Silva, Sra. Victoria Marín de Trechuelo, Sra. Elizabeth Borton de Treviño, and the many others who spent hours patiently answering my questions and contributing toward my knowledge of Mexican food.

Foreword

It is a long time between an idle remark, a casual wish, and a much desired reality.

I first met Diana Southwood Kennedy more than a decade ago in her home on the Calle Puebla in Mexico City. I was food news editor and restaurant critic for *The New York Times* and her husband Paul, a gentle, effusive soul with a lust for life, was the *Times* correspondent for Central America, Mexico, and the Caribbean. During his lifetime—he died in 1967—their home was an international gathering place, a crossroads where men and women from many of the world's more interesting milieus came to discuss art, politics, revolutions here and there, and the state of the world in general. And—foremost, perhaps—to eat Diana's food.

But the thing that I most vividly recall about our first meeting was her offer to buy me a Mexican cookbook. "No," I demurred, "I'll wait for the genuine article. The day you publish one."

I have always had a passion for the Mexican table since as an infant I ate hot tamales sold by a street vendor in the small town where I lived in Mississippi (there were dreadful rumors about what that meat filling consisted of but, poof, I couldn't have cared less). Never have I eaten such glorious Mexican food as I have in Diana's home, and with good reason. I know of no one with her dedication to the pursuit of great Mexican cooking. (If her enthusiasm were not beautiful, it would border on mania.)

Although Diana lives in a New York apartment and teaches Mexican cooking there, she spends her summers traveling the Mexican provinces, visiting local markets, studying the seemingly endless varieties of chilies used in cooking, talking to and learning from local cooks. And cooking. She was a friend of the late Agustín Aragón y Leiva, considered to be the greatest Mexican gastronome and authority on his country's cuisine, and spent many hours in research in his library. She may have the finest collection of Mexican cookbooks north of the border, including many antique volumes, among which is her "bible," *Nuevo Cocinero Mejicano: Diccionario de Cocina,* published in Paris, of all places, in 1878. Diana found that one in the flea market in Lagunilla and paid about sixteen American dollars for it.

Diana introduced me to and taught me to make what I consider one of the greatest drinks (Is it a cocktail? I've never been able to decide) in the world, the *sangrita* (not *sangría*). It is made with sour orange and the juice of crushed fresh pomegranates. Drunk, of course, with tequila. But beyond that, her food! Good lord, where is there anything to equal her *papa-dzules,* that Yucatecan specialty made with the pulp of *pepitas,* eggs, and tortillas; or her pork in chili sauce, or squash in cream, or tamales fixed in any of a dozen fashions.

No wonder that Diana's kitchen smells better than most kitchens.

One of the intriguing things about her cooking is her talent at improvisation. "These tamales," she was saying recently, "are Veracruzana style, with pork and chilies and wrapped in a softer *masa.* I didn't find an herb they use in Veracruz, so I used an avocado leaf. It tastes very much like it." And I remember her search some years ago when she first moved to Manhattan. She had trouble finding a typical and quite common herb used in Mexican cookery, *epazote.*

"For months I searched the local markets with no success. And then, one day in the autumn, I took a stroll in Riverside Park and found it growing wild at my feet." She harvested enough for a year's supply, dried it, and stored it away.

Long ago, she and I agreed on the merits of Mexican food. It is, we decided, earthy food, festive food, happy food, celebration food. It is, in short, peasant food raised to the level of high and sophisticated art. If this book is a measure of Diana's talent, it will probably rank as the definitive book in English on that most edible art.

CRAIG CLAIBORNE

A Culinary Education

Although I have always loved good food, it was in Wales during the war years, when I was doing my service in the Women's Timber Corps, that I first savored food I can still remember today.

In the Forest of Dean we would toast our very dull sandwiches over the smoldering wood fires and roast potatoes and onions in the ashes to help eke out our rations on those frosty, raw mornings. Later, in the Usk Valley, as we cycled for pleasure through the country lanes and walked the Brecon Beacons, we would stop for the farmhouse teas: thick cream and fresh scones, wedges of homemade bread spread thickly with freshly churned butter, wild damson jam, buttery cakes that had been beaten with the bare hand. From there I moved to an even more remote village in Carmarthenshire. To supplement the strict rationing, there was salmon trout fished from the river that ran within a few hundred yards of the cottage; when fishing wasn't good there was a steaming bowl of cowl, a soup made from stinging nettles, or just a plate of green beans—picked fresh from the garden and doused with butter from the big earthenware crock that stood by the kitchen door. The butter was soft and yellow, with perceptible grains of salt and globules of water—hand-churned butter from the farm next door. On summer evenings, when everyone from the village would go up to the hillside farms to help bring in the hay, the ham that had been strung up to the rafters by the fireplace months earlier was cut down. It was a feast to us then with bread, onions, and creamy local cheese. Thursday was baking day, and as we cycled wearily home from the woods the smell would waft toward us as the bread was being taken, very crusty, from the brick wall ovens.

After the war there were occasional trips to France, and memories flood back of the first *belons*, and *moules* along the Côtes du Nord; rice cooked with minute crabs that had to be sucked noisily to extract their sweet juice; the *ratatouille*, and refreshing Provençal wines in a Saint-Tropez bistro. I can't forget the lunchtime smell of olive oil in northern Spain as we walked up through the oleander bushes from the beach, and the never-ending meals in the Ramblas restaurants in Barcelona, or beef *à la tartare* after a day's skiing in the Austrian Alps. It was then that I really learned to cook, to reproduce what had been eaten with such pleasure.

I soon wanted to travel further afield, so I emigrated to Canada. I had never before eaten such crusty rye bread as that of the Spadina Road market in Toronto, or cheeses, summer sausage, and sugar-cured ham quite like the ones the Mennonites made. There was a wonderful breakfast of freshly caught fish on the banks of Lake Louise after an early morning hike through pine forest on a sparkling and pine-scented day. Later in our journey it was followed by poached West Coast salmon in Vancouver, the minute Olympia oysters, and further south in San Francisco the sand-dabs and rex sole.

When I traveled back to England via the Caribbean, everything was new and had to be tried: callaloo, lambie stew, and soursop ices; salt fish and ackee in Jamaica, where, too, you had to see the famous Blue Mountain coffee growing and buy the syrupy sugarloaf pineapples. I ate my first mango, a huge Bombay, conveniently standing up to my neck in crystal-clear water on a small island off the Kingston harbor.

And that was the summer I met Paul Kennedy in Haiti, where he was covering one of the many revolutions for *The New York Times*. We fell in love and I joined him in Mexico later that year.

And so life in Mexico began. Everything was new, exciting, and exotic. Luz, our first maid, loved to cook. One day she brought her corn grinder to the house and we made *tamales*: first soaking the dried corn in a solution of unslaked lime, washing the skin of each kernel, and then grinding it to just the right texture. It seemed to take forever, and our backs ached from the effort. But I shall never forget those *tamales*. She introduced us both to the markets and told us how to use the fruits and vegetables that were strange to us.

Finally Luz had to go, and Rufina came from Oaxaca; it was her first job. She was young and moody, but she was a really good cook and my apprenticeship continued as she taught me how to make her rather special *albóndigas,* rabbit in *adobo,* and how to draw and truss a hen.

But I suppose it is Godileva to whom I am most indebted. I always loved the evenings she would stay to do the ironing; we would chat about her life when she was a young girl on her father's small ranch in a remote area of Guerrero. They had lived well, and she loved good food. She would pat out our tortillas, and before lunch would make us *gorditas* with the fat of marrow bones to enrich them, and as we came in the door would hand us, straight from the comal, *sopes* smothered with green sauce and sour cream. We would take turns grinding the chilies and spices on the *metate,* and it is her recipe for *chiles rellenos* that I have included in this book.

I had other influences as well.

My friend Chabela, on several trips into the interior, taught me almost all I know about the handicrafts of Mexico; together we visited craftsmen in remote areas and on those journeys we would try all the local fruits and foods. It was she who spent many hours in my kitchen showing me, accompanied by meticulous instructions, the specialties of her mother's renowned kitchen in Jalisco.

At last our stay had to come to an end. Paul had been fighting cancer courageously for two years, and it was time to return to New York. By then we had traveled extensively together, and on my own I had driven practically all over the country, seeing, eating, and asking questions. I started to collect old cookbooks and delve into the gastronomic past to learn more for the cookbook that I hoped some day to write.

Paul died early in 1967, and later that same year Craig Claiborne suggested that I start a Mexican cooking school. I suppose I wasn't ready to start a new venture; I was too saddened and worn by the previous three years. But the idea had planted itself, and in January 1969, on Sunday afternoons, I did start a series of Mexican cooking classes—the first in New York. A wintry Sunday afternoon is a wonderful time to cook, and the idea caught on.

The classes expanded beyond those Sunday afternoons, and the work for the book went on as well. But while the classes continue to flourish and grow, the research and testing have come at least to a temporary halt—if only to allow the book to be published at last. For I find myself involved in a process of continual refinement, due both to the frequent trips I make to Mexico to discover new dishes and to refine old ones, and to the constant dialogue between myself and my students and friends who try these recipes with me.

DIANA KENNEDY

New York
April 1972

En pobres trastos, servía
A su Hijo y Esposo amados,
Manjares bien sazonados
La Puríssima María.

In humble dishes,
the Most Holy Mary served
to her beloved son and husband
well-seasoned food.

—Words written by the curate
on the wall inside an eighteenth-century
country church in Guanajuato

PART ONE

Ingredients and Procedures

The Mexican Kitchen

The first summer after my husband died I spent traveling through Latin America looking at archaeological sites and searching for local dishes. I certainly found many interesting foods throughout Latin America, but nowhere was there such variety as in Mexico. It made me wonder more and more about the coincidences of history and topography that brought about such a combination of cultures to produce such fascinating cuisines—for in Mexico it can hardly be called *one* cuisine.

The title for this book came from an archaeologist working on some excavations—actually unearthing kitchen floors, which brought the subject up—in Teotihuacán (which was probably the largest urban development of the New World). Indeed there are many cuisines that have grown up and flourished from pre-Columbian times to the present day. The regional dishes of Sonora, or Jalisco, have practically nothing in common with those of Yucatán and Campeche; neither have those of Nuevo León with those of Chiapas and Michoacán; in Oaxaca certain chilies are grown and used that are found nowhere else in Mexico.

The reasons for these great differences can be seen in part in the topography of the country. Two great ranges of volcanic mountains with peaks up to seventeen thousand feet run from north to south: the Western Sierra Madre, near and parallel to the Pacific coast, and the more broken Eastern Sierra Madre following the Atlantic coast. Between them are mountainous areas and plateaus ranging from five thousand to eight thousand feet above sea level. Where the mountains fall off steeply to the coastal plains, within relatively few miles there are constantly changing vegetation, crops, and foodstuffs.

European influences played their part as well, beginning of course with the Spanish. From Cortés himself and one of his soldiers, Bernal Díaz del Castillo, have come the first accounts of the splendors of Moctezuma's court and the tremendous variety of foods prepared for him daily; in Fray Bernardino de Sahagún's massive work *Historia General de las Cosas de la Nueva España,* which records the life, myths, and history of the ancient world, accounts of the food of the rulers, their feasts, and rituals are described in amazing detail; Hernández left us a record of the plants found there. But early in the colonial period the cuisine began to change. The nuns, especially, began to use local products—among them tomatoes, chilies, wild turkeys, sweet potatoes, cacao—mixing them with those that had been introduced by the Spaniards—including almonds, citrus fruits, dairy products.

French influences came in the 1860s during the time of Maximilian's reign, and Mexican cookbooks of the late nineteenth century included recipes for Italian pastas. Today *sopa de fideo* (vermicelli soup) and dry pastas in tomato sauce (*sopas secas*) are a firmly established part of the cuisine of central Mexico. In the capital you can eat European-type cheeses, breads, pork products, and pastries of excellent quality, all made in Mexico.

Yet today in the United States, a country that shares a 2,000-mile border with Mexico, and where there is a yearly interchange of tourists from both sides that runs into millions, far too many people know Mexican food as a "mixed plate": a crisp taco filled with ground meat heavily flavored with an all-purpose chili powder; a soggy *tamal* covered with a sauce that turns up on everything—too sweet and too overpoweringly onioned—a few fried beans and something else that looks and tastes like all the rest. Where is the wonderful play of texture, color, and flavor that makes up an authentic, well-cooked Mexican meal?

It has been said that the Chinese cuisine is based upon four thousand recipes and the Mexican on two thousand. Choosing a mere hundred and seventy from those two thousand for this book became a very difficult task, which finally devolved upon two criteria: those recipes I knew and liked best of all, and those which are practical to reproduce outside Mexico *without losing their essential characteristics.*

I have cooked all the dishes on both sides of the border so I would be able to reproduce faithfully the texture and balance of flavors, which seem so important to me and to which virtually no notice has been paid by most writers on Mexican food, who have compromised it beyond the point of authenticity. I have kept wherever possible to the original cooking methods (although not to the grinding methods, which are impractical) as they were demonstrated or told to me, for Mexicans generally have a wonderfully intuitive sense about food. Nowhere else, except perhaps among the Basques, do you find a businessman unashamedly extolling the virtues of a rustic sauce at the local *taquería* or a cab driver singing the praises of a simple pot of beans. And well they might, for here are foods at their basic best, and like their country, bursting with life, energy, and color.

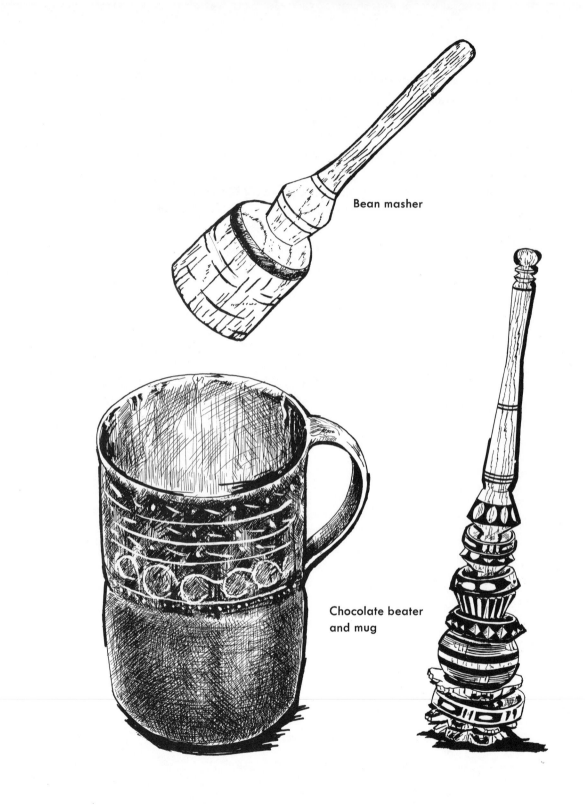

Bean masher

Chocolate beater
and mug

Cooking Equipment

BEAN MASHER: If you cannot find the wooden Mexican bean masher as illustrated, then an ordinary wooden potato masher will do, but the metal mesh mashers are not as efficient.

BLENDER: It is useful to have two blender jars and sets of cutters or blenders, for in some of the recipes you will be blending two different mixtures. This is certainly not essential, but it helps if time is a factor.

CHOCOLATE BEATER: The *molinillos* of Mexico are delightfully carved and make a useful and decorative addition to any kitchen.

COMAL: This is a thick cast-iron griddle for making tortillas and *antojitos*. There is a double comal that sits conveniently over two burners, and you can make up to four small tortillas at one time on it. It is available in New York at Casa Moneo (see page 356). Do not wash it unless absolutely necessary, and wipe with a good coating of vegetable oil before putting it away.

COOKWARE: It is most useful in Mexican cooking to have dishes that can be put straight onto the flame and serve the dual purposes of cooking and serving. I find that those I use most are round and about 3½ inches deep. One is 7½ inches in diameter at the bottom and 10 inches across at the top. It does for rice, for Budín Azteca (page 81), and also for Chilaquiles (page 67), among other things. The other, 8½ inches at the bottom and 12 across the top, is useful for Carnitas (page 112), Chongos Zamoranos (page 324), Pollo en Pipián Rojo (page 206), Puerco en Mole Verde (page 171), and so forth. Another very useful dish is an 8½ × 13 ×

7

Flan mold

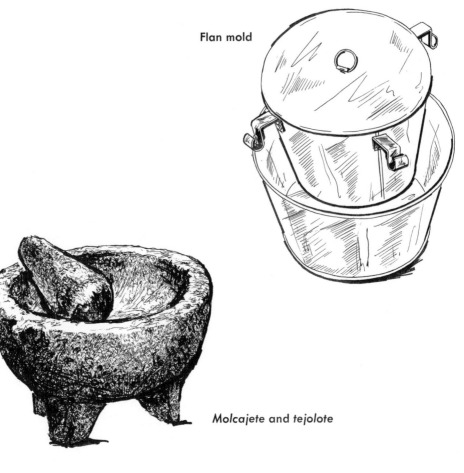

Molcajete and *tejolote*

Metate and *mano*

1½ Pyrex or ovenproof dish for cooking fish dishes, heating up *enchiladas,* etc.

DUTCH OVEN: For braising turkey and duck for *mole,* for Cochinita Pibil (page 169), Birria (page 185), etc.

FLAN MOLD: The Mexicans are the only ones I know who make a compact unit for cooking a flan in a water bath in the oven. They are made of a light tin, in three parts: the water bath, the mold, and the lid. They look primitive and flimsy, but I have had mine for ten years. Always dry them off well in the oven after washing, and grease lightly, or they will rust.

The flan mold will probably leak when you first put some water in, so before attempting a flan put the mold, with water about a third of the way up the outer pan, into the oven and heat at 300° for about two hours. That should seal it. If you are unlucky and the mold isn't cured, then have the leaks soldered. I used to be able to find flan molds all over Mexico but now there is only one place that seems to stock them, in the lower level of the huge Merced market—stand number 20. Since at the present time they are not available in this country, a charlotte mold in a water bath or any other pan used for making custard will be an excellent substitute.

FOOD MILL: A food mill is indispensable for many of these recipes, and I have found the French Mouli, with its 3 graded disks, to be the most efficient.

FRYING PANS: Two cast-iron frying pans are useful, 8 and 10 inches in diameter.

LIME-SQUEEZER: Limes are used in such abundance in the cooking of the Latin American countries that there are juice squeezers designed just for them. There are no more practical lime-squeezers than those made in Mexico. They look rough and ready, but they are very efficient.

METATE: Although I am not suggesting you get one, I must mention the *metate* and its grinding stone, the *mano* or *metlapil.* The *metate* is of the same material as the *molcajete* (see entry for *Mortar and Pestle* below). It is a sloping, rectangular piece of volcanic rock supported on three stout legs, and is still used in the villages for grinding corn, chilies, and cacao and all the ingredients for making sauces, like *mole* sauce. The men who were packing our household goods when we left Mexico were astounded that I should want to take a *licuadora azteca* (an Aztec blender) to New York—my *metate.*

MOLCAJETE AND TEJOLOTE: See following entry.

MORTAR AND PESTLE: Or, better still, a *molcajete* and *tejolote*, their Mexican counterparts of black basalt. These are indispensable pieces of kitchen equipment for all serious Mexican cooks and, I would go so far as to say, for all those who love the kitchen. A small amount of spices is never ground very efficiently in a blender or spice grinder; in the *molcajete* they are pulverized in no time, and much more easily than in the standard mortar.

The *molcajete* is also excellent for making sauces. A sauce that calls for some texture—a good example is Salsa de Tomate Verde Cruda (page 297)—loses its character, to say nothing of its savor, if blended, and becomes one of those all-purpose frothy mixes; and the aroma that rises as the onion, garlic, chilies, and coriander are being ground together in the *molcajete*—after all, isn't this part of what the joy of cooking and pleasing the senses is all about? The *molcajete* looks solid and rustic in the kitchen, and after a sauce is made in it, it can be carried straight to the table.

The *molcajete*, which has truly proved its classicism and efficiency since its first use in the Mexican kitchen about 3,500 years ago, is made of the same material and in practically the same form as today's. It is a thick bowl of porous volcanic rock supported by three short legs. The most useful size for the average kitchen is 7 to 8 inches in diameter and 4 to 5 inches high. The size of the cylindrical, pointed *tejolote* (pestle) varies quite a bit, but it is usually 1½ to 2 inches in diameter and 3½ to 4 inches long. The very best quality, not easy to come by these days, is heavy black basalt, with very fine pores. The next best is a dark grayish-black stone: it must be heavy, and not coarsely pitted. Scratch the surface with the *tejolote* or, better still, a nail. If it leaves a chalky mark in the stone, go on to the next. It should last a lifetime, unless, of course, you drop it. It will break easily, like any brittle, porous stone.

The very fine black *molcajetes* can be used almost right away after a preliminary scrub and grinding. But most of them have to be "cured" a little more thoroughly. First of all, wash the *molcajete* out well under running water and scour it with a stiff brush. Then grind a handful of rice in it until the rice is pulverized. Wash the *molcajete* again and grind some more rice. The first lot of rice will be a dirty gray color; the second grinding should be lighter. Repeat the process at least twice again and the *molcajete* should be ready to use. Take care, as there are many thoroughly bad ones around that will become thinner and thinner as you grind. Give up, and use them as decorative pieces.

In some areas of Mexico, especially along the coast, ceramic *molcajetes* are used. The wet clay at the bottom of the bowl is scored or cross-hatched before it is fired. However, they are not as durable, or as efficient for grinding chilies, but they are good for grating onion, for instance.

SCALE: I emphasize elsewhere that weighing ingredients provides better results than measuring them does; needless to say, then, I consider a good kitchen scale indispensable. Any type is fine, so long as it is accurate, although I have found a scale marked in both pounds and kilos especially valuable.

SPICE/NUT GRINDER: The small Moulinex grinder is useful and efficient. It will grind pumpkin seeds, sesame seeds, and whole spices much more quickly and much finer than the average blender.

TORTILLA BASKET: The *chiquihuite* is the traditional tortilla basket made of woven reed grass. It is lined with a cloth, which must completely cover the tortillas and keep them warm.

TORTILLA PRESS: A 6-inch tortilla press is indispensable unless you know how to pat tortillas out by hand. Tortilla presses are carried by many gourmet stores throughout the country, by some Chinese stores—they sometimes use them for their pancakes—and Casa Moneo in New York (see page 356).

12-INCH RULER: Since I have purposely been so geometrical.

Ingredients

ACHIOTE

Achiote is the small red seed of the annatto tree (*Bixa orellana*) which is indigenous to tropical America and the Caribbean. The seed is used for both coloring and flavoring food. In Yucatán and the southern part of Mexico up to Mexico City, you can buy achiote ground to a paste ready for use. It may even be imported to certain parts of the United States in this form, but I have never seen it in the New York area. However, the seeds, labeled *annatto,* are available in the Latin American food sections of most supermarkets and in Latin American and Caribbean food markets. They are extremely hard and have to be softened before they can be ground. Just cover them with a little water and bring them to a boil. Let them simmer for about 5 minutes; leave them to soak for as long as possible. Crush them roughly in a *molcajete* or mortar, and then grind them in the blender as fine as possible.

Achiote is used mainly as a base for the seasoning pastes (*recados*) of Yucatán and Campeche, which are used for meats and fish. If you go into any Yucatecan market you can always find stands selling huge mounds of colored pastes. Instead of the earth-colored *moles* and *adobos* of central Mexico sold in exactly the same way, you have the green of the ground pumpkin seeds, the red achiote—alone or with other spices—the dark brown pepper and spice seasonings for beefsteaks or *escabeche oriental* and the jet-black paste of burned, dried chilies for the famous *pavo en relleno negro.* Of course, the more fastidious cook may not be happy about the balance of flavors in the prepared or commercially packaged *recados* and will want to blend her own, adding spices and seasoning to the ground achiote paste.

ACITRÓN

Acitrón is candied biznaga cactus (the huge cushionlike *Echinocactus grandis*), and is used a great deal in the central part of Mexico in meat stuffings (*picadillos*). It is usually sold in bars about 1 inch square, and is available in supermarkets and grocery stores in Mexico City. It is also very conveniently sold in the candy stores at the Mexico City airport. It really doesn't have any particular flavor, but with the almonds it contains lends a very interesting texture to the soft meat stuffings. You can substitute any candied fruit, therefore, that is not too strong—not citron—and I have on occasion used candied pineapple or sweet potato, which were very good.

It will keep for several months if stored in a cool, dry place.

AVOCADOS

Most of the following remarks do not apply to cooks living in areas where avocados are grown; they are based on the experience of buying them in New York, after living many years in Mexico.

Never wait to buy an avocado until the day it is going to be used. Avocados come very green to the markets—unless you find them when they have been around for a while—and you will have to buy one when it is hard and let it mature in a warm kitchen for about three days. A good, ripe avocado should be tender, but not too soft to the touch; the pit should not move about inside as you shake it; and the outside skin should not have parted from the flesh. The flesh itself should be compact and creamy, like firm butter, and have the rich flavor of hazelnuts and anise. (I am explaining all this because all too often those of us who live in New York and other parts of the country where the avocado is not grown get the thin edge of the wedge, and even armed with this knowledge I have wasted a great deal of time and money on avocados. More often than not the flesh is sweet, watery, and tasteless, which, while it will just about do for a garnish, ruins a soup or guacamole. For the past few years I have not been able to find those superb black, knobbly-skinned ones from California, the best of all for texture and flavor.)

The avocado is indigenous to Mexico and, of course, a great deal has been written through the years about it and its properties, medicinal and otherwise; the early botanists described them in great detail and recommended them for dysentery, to stop hair from falling out, and as a cure for rashes and scars among other things.

In Mexico I always liked to buy the little speckled black avocados. The skin was thin, and tasted strongly of anise; it was ground and eaten with the flesh.

AVOCADO LEAVES

Avocado leaves are used quite often in Mexican dishes in the region south of Mexico City and Puebla. They can be used fresh or dried, sometimes ground and sometimes whole, and it is usual to toast them slightly on the comal first. They are not essential, but they do add a delicious flavor and authentic touch. Friends in California and Florida keep me supplied. I have even used the leaves of a plant grown in a Manhattan apartment, but they are not as strong in flavor, and you have to double, at least, the amount used. To find out just how strong your leaves are, grind them to a powder in a *molcajete* and smell them. There should be a lovely anisey–hazelnut odor, just like the taste of a good avocado. Avocado leaves can be used in Pollo en Pipián Rojo (page 206), as a substitute for *hoja santa* in Tamales estilo Veracruzano (page 101) and Puerco en Mole Verde (page 171), and ground and sprinkled on Frijoles Refritos (page 282).

BANANA LEAVES

If you live in a warm part of the country and just happen to have a banana tree in the garden—it may not bear fruit but adds an exotic and decorative touch—you can use the leaves fresh from the tree. Remove the stalk and center vein—but do not throw them away, as they can be used to tie up *tamales* or a Muk-bil Pollo (page 103). Just before you use the leaf, pass it quickly over the bare flame of a burner—at least 6 inches above, as the leaf is delicate and will easily burn and be mottled with dark brown patches (although it can still be used). This warming makes them flexible for wrapping *tamales,* etc.

You can buy fresh banana leaves in the Latin American markets of many cities, where they are in great demand at Christmas and Easter for the festive *tamales* of the Latin Americans and the *pasteles* of the Puerto Ricans and Dominicans. They look rather decrepit and discolored, since they are seared for easier packing, but they are usable and full of flavor. They will keep for about three months if they are covered completely in a polyethylene bag and stored at the bottom of the refrigerator. Just before using them, rinse off the white, filmy mold that may have formed on the surface of the leaf, dry them with paper toweling, and don't forget to pass them over the flame.

BEANS. See pages 278–286.

CHAYOTE

The *chayote,* or vegetable pear, is thought to be indigenous to Mexico, and there are usually three types found in the markets there: the small, light-green ones, the creamy-white ones, and the large, dark-green *chayotes* covered with long thin spines like a porcupine. The latter are considered the best of all as they have more flavor and are not as watery as the others. A friend with whom I often stay in Cuernavaca has a decorative *chayote* vine almost covering the back wall of her garden. I love to pick them when they are just about the size of a large egg. They are so delicate and sweet, particularly good boiled and made into a salad.

The ones available—in New York, at least—in Spanish American and West Indian markets nearly all the year round, weigh about one pound each and are rather tasteless and watery; they are pale green or whitish in color. They need a rather heavy hand with seasoning and cheese, as you see by the two recipes I have included for them: Chayotes Rellenos (page 273) and Chayotes Empanizadas (page 274). However, they make an interesting change from the usual vegetables.

CHEESE

The Spaniards introduced dairy cattle into Mexico around 1530, and the Indians very soon learned how to make the cheeses for which Spain was so renowned. They immediately adopted them into their cuisine. Cheese has such an affinity to chilies and corn, and one cannot think of the *antojitos,* soups, and *tamales* without it.

I watched the cheese-making industry grow rapidly during my years in Mexico, and now every supermarket has a large counter devoted to dozens of varieties: *manchego,* San Fandila, *asadero,* Chihuahua, and the little cream cheese of Chalco alongside very creditable copies of the European Port Salut, Gruyère, Chester, blue cheese, and Camembert. It seems a pity that many more restaurants do not serve a typical Mexican cheese board, which I am always advocating—I have come across only one, in the very elegant Virreinal Restaurant in San Luis Potosí.

The most generally used cheeses for the recipes in this book are the *quesillo de Oaxaca, queso añejo,* and *queso Chihuahua.*

Quesillo de Oaxaca is a soft, braided, slightly acid cheese, very popular for cooking as it strings nicely—a Mexican requisite—and particularly suitable for *quesadillas,* the stuffing in chilies, and for some vegetable dishes. The fresh Italian mozzarella looks right, but it is not acidy enough, and the packaged mozzarellas that I have tried are not adequate, so I substitute a Muenster. I see no point in searching for and paying the higher price for Monterey Jack unless you happen to live in California. The block Muenster from Wisconsin is a very good product, which is more than I can say of many of the smaller packages that go under the same name. (A good test is to heat some cheese gently: if it becomes rubbery, or exudes some milky liquid and has a residue like chewing gum—there are, unfortunately, several on the market that do that—then throw it away and find a better variety.)

Queso añejo is an aged (as its name implies), salty, and crumbly cheese used for *enchiladas* and *antojitos.* I have yet to come across a product that comes reasonably near to it. There are indeed *quesos blancos* and *añejos* sold for the Latin American market that I cannot recommend. I use instead a good, fresh farmer cheese, which makes a delicious filling for *enchiladas,* if it is well salted. I have not found a truly acidy cream cheese like those made on the ranches of Sonora, Chihuahua and San Luis for using in soups, and it seems too ridiculous to pay the price of an imported French cream cheese to use in cooking.

The original *queso Chihuahua* was, and still is, made in the Mennonite communities around Chihuahua City. It should be a porous, spongy cheese, slightly acid, and with a good creamy flavor. Needless to say, in Mexico there are many poor, some fair, and a few good imitations—I always try and look for the stamp on the top of the wheel of cheese, for the Mennonites proudly stamp the name of the community on it. This cheese is used for stuffing chilies, is grated and sprinkled over dishes to be gratinéed, and sometimes just melted like a fondue and served as *queso asado*. A mild Cheddar is a suitable substitute.

CHILIES. See pages 32–40.

CHOCOLATE. See pages 347–349.

CINNAMON

It is advisable to buy the softer cinnamon bark from Ceylon, since it has a more delicate flavor than the harder, stronger bark from Malabar (India).

COFFEE. See pages 350–351.

COOKING FAT

For frying *antojitos* and many Mexican dishes you really need a good pork lard, which is becoming daily more difficult to find—most commercial brands are deathly white and tasteless.* If you care about the flavor, and have the time and patience, you can always render your own from scraps of pork fat (see below). For certain dishes, however, you do not want the strong flavor of lard—e.g., Arroz a la Mexicana (page 288) or Chiles Rellenos (page 263)—and for these I suggest peanut or safflower oil (corn oil has far too strong a flavor). When I lived in Mexico everybody used sesame seed oil, but now, of course, safflower oil is all the rage. Cooking

---

* If there is a pork butcher in your area, he may carry a homemade lard such as I found in a small pork store on Ninth Avenue in New York—the *masa* of *quesadillas* fried in this lard is unbelievably good.

oil can always be used again as long as it is strained through a fine-mesh strainer and refrigerated.

Home-Rendered Lard

About 1½ pounds

A meat grinder	Cut the fat into pieces and pass it through the coarse disk of a meat grinder.
2 pounds pork fat	
A large bowl	Pour the water over the fat in the bowl and mix it in well. Set aside to soak for at least 6 hours.
1 cup cold water	
3 8-ounce jars	Sterilize the jars.
	Preheat the oven to 350°.
A heavy iron pan	Transfer the fat and water to the pan, place on the top shelf of the oven, and cook until the fat starts to render out—about 15 minutes. **The fat must not start to color.**
The fat and water	
The prepared jars	Reduce the oven heat to 225° and continue cooking for 2 to 2½ hours. Pour off the drippings from time to time, straining them into the prepared jars.
	Set the jars aside for about 36 hours and then seal and store in a cool, dry place.

The rendering could be done on top of the stove but I find the steady, indirect heat of the oven more satisfactory—the fat is less likely to catch you unawares and start to color.

CORIANDER

Both the dried seeds and the fresh green leaves of this plant are used in Mexican cooking, mostly in fresh sauces, with fish, and as one of the main herbs in *mole verde.* Also known as Chinese parsley (*Coriandrum sativum*), it is now widely available in Latin American, Caribbean, Indian and Chinese markets. It is called *cilantro* by the Mexicans, but to the Puerto Ricans and Dominicans it is *cilantrillo,* and if you ask them for *cilantro* you will end up with a rather coarse herb with a pointed, serrated leaf with very much the same flavor—*Geringium foedidum* (I have only come across this once before, in Tabasco in southern Mexico, where it is confusingly called *perejil,* or parsley).

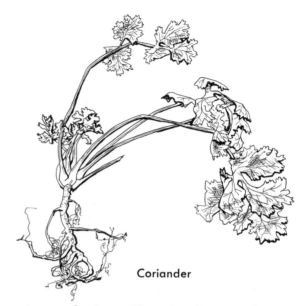

Coriander

If you are not going to use all your fresh coriander right away, it is better to buy it with the roots on so that it will keep fresh very much longer. Remove any leaves that are dead or yellowing and place the fresh ones in an airtight plastic container with a little moisture in the bottom. Store in the bottom of the refrigerator. Coriander does not freeze successfully, and there is no substitute. If you can't get it, leave it out—parsley will change the flavor.

Once used to it you can become addicted—although many can't stand even the smell of it. Its name is derived from the Greek word for bedbug—*koris*—as it was said to resemble that insect's fetid odor.

CORN

Wild corn and squash were probably the first plants to be cultivated in the Valley of Mexico, and domesticated ears have been found in the caves of San Marcos dating as far back as 5000 B.C. All the ancient civilizations devoted ceremonies to their gods and goddesses of corn, vestiges of which still exist today.

Nothing is wasted of the plant: the young, tender ears and husks are used for *tamales* and *atole;* the corn silk is made into a medicinal tea, said to be good for the kidneys; and in ancient times the corn tassel was made into *tamales* with amaranth seeds. When it is dried the kernels are used for *masa* and the husks for *tamales;* nothing is wasted.

For tortilla *masa,* ears of corn are left to mature and dry out on the stalk. When harvested the dried kernels can be stored ready for use. When they are needed they are brought to a boil and left to soak in a solution of unslaked lime and water until the kernel has been softened slightly and the little transparent skins loosened; it is then washed well and ground wet. If too much lime has been used the *masa* will be a dirty yellow color and have a bitter taste, just as if you had added too much baking powder to the biscuits.

CORN HUSKS. See page 90.

CREAM

Many recipes from central Mexico call for cream. It should be slightly sour, like the *crème fraîche* of France. I suggest that you make your own, which is far more satisfactory than using the commercial brands. The recipes are given below.

Thick Sour Cream

About 1 cup

A glass bowl or jar
½ pint heavy cream
2 tablespoons buttermilk

Put the cream and buttermilk into the jar and mix them well together.

Cover with plastic wrap and set the mixture aside in a warm place, but not too warm (a strong pilot light is too warm; the cream will taste "cooked" and a skin will form) until it is set, about 6 hours (see note below).

Put the cream into the refrigerator overnight; it will thicken and become more solid.

Some creams will sour more quickly, and some become thicker than others. The milk experts inform me that these are uncontrollable factors depending on the culture of the buttermilk, the amount of light and heat to which the cream was exposed before it was used, and even the bacteria in one's own kitchen.

Thin Sour Cream

Chilaquiles (page 67) require a thinner sour cream. For this you can substitute light for heavy cream.

EPAZOTE

Epazote (*Chenopodium ambrosioides*) is known in English as Mexican tea or wormseed. It is a pungent herb with pointed serrated leaves, a native to tropical America, but it grows in profusion in Central and Riverside parks and backyards in New York City, as I have found, and throughout many other parts of the country as well. It is very much an acquired taste, but after a while to cook black beans without it is unthinkable. In this climate it does not have such a strong flavor as that grown in Mexico, but it seems to reach its peak in the fall (the very lush plant in damp spring weather has a most uncharacteristic flavor). The plants here will start appearing toward the end of April and last sometimes well into December if the frosts are not too severe. It is undoubtedly best used fresh. You can easily uproot a plant, or grow one from seed, and it will flourish throughout the winter indoors if planted in a large, deep pot and kept moist. However, if this is too much trouble, you can gather a quantity of it, dry it, and store it away, out of the light.

Epazote is used a great deal in central and southern Mexico but not so much in the north and northwest. It is used to flavor black beans, soups, certain fillings for Quesadillas (page 120), Muk-bil Pollo (page 102), etc. There is no substitute.

The name of the herb, like that of coriander, is disparaging. It comes from the Nahuatl words *epatl* and *tzotl*, an animal with a rank odor like a skunk and something unclean.

GREEN TOMATOES. See *Mexican green tomatoes*.

GUAUZONCLES. See page 275.

HERBS

The most commonly used fresh herbs are usually sold with the vegetables in the market, but there is always a stand where nothing but dried plants, flowers, roots, and bark are sold for remedies, infusions, and poultices. I once saw bunches of them laid out on a sidewalk in Oaxaca and given such very convenient labels as "tapeworm," "acidity," "tired vision," "varicose veins," "reducing without dieting," "ringworm," and "dandruff," among many others.

Epazote

Mexican green tomato

I have great faith in the infusions of flowers and leaves that our maids in Mexico introduced us to: boldo leaves (*Boldoa fragrans*) to dispel that liverish feeling; manzanilla or chamomile (*Matricaria chamomilla*) to calm the stomach; orange leaves to sleep peacefully; cinnamon bark to sweat out a fever; and the fragrant teas made of lemongrass (*Cymbopogon citratus*) and Mexican balm (*Cedronella mex.*). They were such a pleasure to drink as well as soothing to the stomach—and they all did what was promised of them; little wonder that I scorn the commercial antacids and sleep inducers.

HUITLACOCHE

Huitlacoche is the fungus that forms on the ears of corn (*Ustilago maydis*) and produces big, swollen, deformed kernels, black inside and covered with a silvery-gray skin. As the fungus cooks it exudes a black juice. It is perfectly delicious, with an inky, mushroomy flavor that is almost impossible to describe. It is not available commercially; it can only be obtained from the corn itself.

Apart from being the most sought-after filling for *quesadillas* (see Huitlacoche para Quesadillas, page 123), *huitlacoche* is made into soup —or, more elegantly, stuffed into thin crêpes, which are then covered with cream.

MEXICAN GREEN TOMATOES

The fruit generally called the Mexican green tomato is not an unripe ordinary tomato but a variety of *Physalis*, the family of the Cape gooseberry and ground-cherry. They are known in Mexico as *tomates verdes, tomates de cáscara,* or *fresadillas* and are canned there and in the United States under the names *tomatillos enteros, tomatitos verdes* (import regulations have called for a revision of labeling, and some are now being called, rather misleadingly, "peeled green tomatoes"). They turn yellow when they are ripe, but they are usually used in their unripe state, which gives a lovely green color to sauces. It is hardly likely that you will find fresh ones for sale in the eastern part of the United States, but they do grow well—some students of mine have planted them and report good crops from Pennsylvania, Maryland, and New Jersey. If you are lucky enough to find them fresh, they will keep for about three weeks in the bottom of the refrigerator, if they are wrapped in paper.

To use them, remove the papery husk around the outside, rinse them, and barely cover them with water. Bring them to a boil, lower the flame and simmer them for about 10 minutes. By this time they should be soft. If you cook them over too high a flame they will burst. If they do, just drain off some of the liquid and grind the debris with the remaining water. If they remain whole, as they should, drain them and grind them with their skins and seeds, and a little of the cooking water, to a smooth sauce. They can then be used immediately or stored in one- or two-cup containers in the freezer for future use.

Some Mexican recipes specifically call for fresh green tomatoes, but I have not included any here, although the Puerco in Mole Verde from Jalapa (page 171) would definitely be better cooked with the fresh ones.

The canned green tomatoes are distributed widely throughout the United States. There is no substitute, since ordinary unripe tomatoes do not have the same characteristics.

NOPAL CACTUS

Hedges of nopal cactus interspersed with weeping *pirule* trees form a typical central Mexican landscape. The oval, fleshy joints of several varieties (*Opuntia*) are edible. Always buy the smallest and thinnest joints; the thicker and darker in color, the less delicate they are to eat. Scrape off the thin, sharp thorns from around the rim and sides of the nopal but do not remove all the green outer layer. Cut them into small pieces, less than ½ inch, and cook them in well-salted water until they are tender. Drain and rinse them thoroughly under cold, running, water for a few minutes to wash away the slimy substance they exude—just like okra.

Cactus pieces, as the *nopales* are called when they are canned, are widely distributed and are an adequate substitute for the real thing, at least for the two recipes given here, Ensalada de Nopalitos (page 312) and Huevos Revueltos con Nopales (page 245). The imported ones seem to come off best: the other varieties that I have tried have too acrid and salty a canning liquid. Be careful not to buy them *en escabeche* for these recipes.

ONIONS

Purple onions are used for pickled fish in Yucatán, and in garnishing *antojitos* in Jalisco, Sinaloa, and other parts of the country, but generally a sharp, white onion is used. The so-called sharp, small yellow onions here so often turn out to be sugary sweet and spoil the whole balance of the dish— I am sure many of you have ruined an onion soup with them. There really is no way to tell unless you pierce the onions with a small knife blade and try, but, of course, the usual vegetable stand owner neither understands the problem nor approves the test.

OREGANO

When I asked at the Botanical Garden at the National University of Mexico about the different types of oregano that I had found around the country, someone very kindly listed the Mexican varieties for me; there were thirteen. In Monterrey they prefer a long-leafed variety, *Poliomintha longiflora,* in Campeche and Yucatán, apart from a small-leafed oregano, used dried, they use a fresh one with a large leaf, *Coleus amboinicus.* There the dried oregano is toasted before it is used, and the flavor is delightful.

PINE NUTS

Available in Latin American markets and many supermarkets throughout the country.

PLANTAINS

Plantains resemble green bananas and are available throughout the country in Spanish American markets the year round. But you have to be careful how you choose them for Mexican dishes. Not only must the skin be almost black, they should be soft to the touch—many have black skins and are still hard. The most common way of using them is to cut them lengthwise into slices about ½ inch thick and fry them in oil until they are a deep golden brown. When Mexican white rice is served as a *sopa seca,* a course on its own, then it is usually accompanied by some slices of fried plantain. They can be used as a thickening agent for some chili sauces (see Enchiladas de Mole, page 79), and cut up as a vegetable in stews and soups. Only in Tabasco do plantains really come into their own. There, to mention only two of many recipes, they make a *budín* of plantains, and more unusual still, they mash cooked plantain, mix it with tortilla dough and lard, and pat out rather thick tortillas. These can be filled with cheese or a *picadillo* and fried until crisp. But then Tabasco has the best plantains of all, the *dominicos*, which are thin and pointed, with a sweet and fruity flesh. They are delicious. The name is rather confusing, since the very tiny banana about 2 inches long is also called *dominico* in the capital.

PUMPKIN BLOSSOMS. See *Squash blossoms.*

PUMPKIN SEEDS

Ground pumpkin seeds have been used since pre-Columbian times as a base for sauces. There are many types used; the very small ones in Yucatán, for instance, are toasted unhulled, and ground together with the husk. But however carefully they have been ground or the sauce strained, there remains a slightly grainy-gritty texture.

Pumpkin seeds are available here in health food and specialty food stores, but remember to buy the hulled, unsalted pumpkin seeds or *pepitas.* The best ones are long, thin, and dark green in color. They can be kept indefinitely providing they are stored in a cool, dry place; if not, they will become rancid. They are used in Pato en Mole Verde de Pepita (page 204), Mole Poblano de Guajolote (page 199), and Papadzules (page 70).

RICE

For all the recipes in this book use a long-grain white, *unconverted* rice.

SALT

Measurements for salt can only be approximate, and mine are given for ground rock salt, sold in any supermarket or hardware store under the name of melting crystals. I have always used it, both here and in Mexico—the grayish appearance may put some people off, but once you have used that or sea salt you cannot return to the kosher or the normal commercially packed salt.

Rock salt can be ground in a *molcajete,* mortar, or salt mill.

SESAME SEEDS

Sesame seeds are used in some Mexican sauces, *mole poblano, pipián,* etc. Buy the white ones—not the gray, uncleaned ones that are also available—

which are sold in health food and specialty food stores. They are often sold, too, in small jars in the Latin American food sections of supermarkets. They will keep indefinitely if stored in a cool, dry place.

They are nearly always toasted to a golden color before they are used. They are very oily and burn readily, so stir them constantly over a medium flame.

SEVILLE ORANGES

The Seville orange is called *naranja agria* in Mexico. In the United States they are generally available on order from the leading fruiterers in February and March for making marmalade, but they can be found the whole year round in Latin American markets. In the northern part of the Caribbean—Cuba, Puerto Rico, and the Dominican Republic—as well as the southeast of Mexico, they are used instead of vinegar to season meats and sometimes to make vinegar. (If you live in New York and can find them nowhere else, then try the Puerto Rican *botánicas*—small stores selling all types of herbs and cures—in Spanish Harlem, but they are expensive.)

For those not familiar with them, they have a rough, thick skin, and are generally rather soft. I have kept a supply of them for about two months, separately wrapped in several layers of paper—they must be kept dry. An alternative way to have some juice always on hand for Yucatecan dishes is to squeeze and strain the juice of 2 oranges, say, blend it with the grated rind of half an orange, and freeze it. In this way you do not lose the flavor and astringency of the oil in the peel. As a substitute you could use a fruit vinegar, or a mixture of lime juice, orange juice, and a little grated peel of grapefruit, which also has an astringent quality. The actual flavor of the Seville orange can never be quite captured with substitutions, but the nearest mixture is, for ½ cup of blended juice:

1 teaspoon finely grated   Combine all the ingredients.
grapefruit rind
3 tablespoons orange juice
3 tablespoons grapefruit
juice
2 tablespoons lemon juice

SHRIMPS, DRIED

Available in most Latin American, Chinese and Japanese groceries. In this country they are sold cleaned, with heads and tails removed, ready for use.

SPICES

I much prefer to use whole spices, as they do in Mexico, and grind my own. The flavor is so much fresher and better.

SQUASH BLOSSOMS

I personally have never seen squash blossoms on sale in Italian markets in New York, although the Italians use them in their cuisine, but they may be available in some areas. If not, and you have a garden, the plants grow rapidly and you can cultivate your own blossoms for Flor de Calabaza para Quesadillas (page 124) and Sopa de Flor de Calabaza (page 149). Both male and female flowers grow on the same plant, and the male flowers tend to appear a little before the female ones. If you want the plant to yield squash, then leave about one in every twenty-five male blossoms to ensure fertilization. Remove the stems from the flowers and strip off the rather stringy sepals. Then chop the flowers ready to cook.

Pumpkin blossoms are interchangeable with squash flowers, and can be cultivated the same way.

TOMATOES

Mexican tomatoes must be among the best in the world. They are picked ripe and come to the markets fat, juicy, and sweet. They are imported on a large scale into the United States in the spring, and what a joy it is for city dwellers to suddenly find them on the vegetable stands instead of the low-quality, tasteless ones usually available.

It is interesting to think of all the cuisines that rely heavily upon tomatoes, and to know that they were only introduced into Spain in the sixteenth century. A native plant of Mexico and South America, at that time they were considered by many to be unhealthy and by others an aphrodisiac, therefore forbidden to women. But by 1740 they had become firmly established and were being included in recipes written down by the nuns in Spain. But it was not until a century later that they were introduced to France and called *pommes d'amour*.

I have indicated in each recipe if canned tomatoes can be substituted for fresh. But be careful in choosing the brand. For instance, plum tomatoes in a thick, soupy sauce are entirely too strong. I have found Contadina peeled, round tomatoes to be consistently good for most of the recipes. However, canned tomatoes always give a much stronger flavor and care should be taken with the measurements.

If your tomatoes are not too ripe or sweet I would normally suggest that a little sugar be added to compensate. However, always allow for the fact that the onions usually used with the tomatoes, our normal sharp yellow onions, taste these days as though they have been grown in sugary earth, and have disastrous effects on such things as onion soups and sauces.

TORTILLAS

Fresh tortillas are ideal, of course, especially if you can make them yourself (pages 62–67). I cannot recommend canned tortillas. The frozen ones that are available in most supermarkets across the country these days are quite satisfactory for *tacos, enchiladas, chilaquiles, budín azteca,* and *totopos,* but I do not like them heated through to serve with a meal, nor do I agree with the method suggested for heating them through. These remarks, of course, only apply to areas where there is no large Mexican community, for there you can always rely upon a regular supply of freshly made tortillas or well-prepared *masa* so you can make them yourself.

For more information on tortillas see pages 59–61.

VINEGAR

In many of the recipes a mild vinegar is called for. It is very easy to make your own from the skin of a pineapple (see below), or buy a Japanese rice vinegar or a very mild white vinegar.

Vinagre de Piña [*Pineapple Vinegar*]

About a quart

A 3-pint glass jar
Peel of half a pineapple
¼ cup dark brown sugar
A small segment of the
    pineapple flesh
1 quart water

Put all the ingredients together into the jar and stir them well. Cover the jar with plastic wrap and set it in a warm spot on the stove or in the sunlight.

(continued)

In a few days the mixture will begin to ferment. Remove some of the peel. As the liquid starts to change color and become more acid, remove the flesh and rest of the peel.

It will then become a pale honey color and very acid; the process will probably take from 2½ to 3 weeks. Strain the vinegar and store it.

Basic Store of Ingredients

DRIED CHILIES

1 pound chiles anchos
½ pound chiles cascabel
1 pound chiles guajillos

½ pound chiles mulatos
1 pound chiles pasilla

CANNED CHILIES

2 4-ounce cans, 2 7-ounce cans, and 1 27-ounce can peeled green chilies (preferably Ortega) or chiles poblanos (*Del Fuerte*)
2 small cans chiles serranos en escabeche

4 small cans chiles jalapeños en escabeche
2 small cans chiles chipotles en vinagre *or* en adobo

SPICES (*small quantities of the following*)

achiote
allspice
aniseed
cinnamon bark
cloves, whole

coriander seeds
cumin seeds
peppercorns
paprika (sweet and *hot)*
vanilla bean

HERBS

avocado leaves (optional; see note
    page 14)
bay leaves
coriander

epazote
marjoram
oregano
thyme

NUTS AND SEEDS

½ pound almonds
1 pound pumpkin seeds (pepitas),
    hulled and unsalted

½ pound sesame seeds
½ pound pine nuts (optional)

MISCELLANEOUS

2 5-pound bags Quaker masa harina
1 pound Quaker Quick Grits
1 5-pound bag long-grain rice
4 small cans tomatitos verdes or
    tomatillos enteros (Clemente
    Jacques have had to change their
    label and now call them "peeled
    green tomatoes")
4 large cans whole, round tomatoes
1 ½-gallon bottle peanut oil
2 pounds lard
1 quart mild white vinegar

1 large bag rock salt
1 package Mexican chocolate (Ibarra,
    Carlos V, or Morelia Presidencial)
1 bottle large capers
2 jars small, pitted green olives
1 1-pound package raisins
2 packages dried corn husks
¼ pound dried shrimps
small and large polyethylene storage
    bags
paper toweling

Chilies: Fresh and Dried

Description of the market in Zacatecas in the 1820s: "The quantity of chile disposed of was really prodigious: waggons laden with it, drawn each by six oxen, were arriving hourly from Aguas Calientes, yet their contents rapidly disappeared, piles of capsicum sufficient to excoriate the palates of half London vanishing in the course of a few minutes."

—FROM *Ward's Mexico*

Chilies are indigenous to Mexico and played an important part in the cuisine long before the Spaniards arrived. No definitive study has yet been made of the chilies in Mexico, since such a study would be long and costly: chilies are air pollinated and cross easily; the local names change from place to place; and some are grown in remote mountainous areas where climatic conditions can vary enormously within a few miles, producing many different varieties. The Mexican authority on the subject, Dr. Antonio Marino, says there are roughly two hundred different types of chilies in existence, over a hundred of which are to be found in Mexico. He also believes that they are all varieties of the *Capsicum annuum*, with the exception of the *chile habanero*, which is a *Capsicum sinense*.*

From my own experience, wandering through the markets of the Bajío alone—where many chilies are grown—I soon became confused by the

* C. B. Heiser, "Name for the Cultivated Capsicum Species," *Taxon* 18 (June 1969).

numerous types, shapes, and colors, all almost alike but not quite, many of which I had seen before. And when you think you have got the chilies in central and northern Mexico straightened out, you then go to Oaxaca and see a completely different and wide variety: the *chilcostles*, the *amarillos*—for the famous dish of the same name—and the *chilhuacles negros* for the unique black *mole* of Oaxaca; and then there are the white chilies of Chiapas and Tabasco. And chilies range in size from the huge *chile de agua* from Oaxaca to the tiny, round *chile piquín*, less than ¼ inch in diameter, which grows wild on the river banks of Tamaulipas (there is another *piquín* sold green in the markets of Mérida, elongated and slender, less than ½ inch long). Each chili has its own character as well, a definite flavor and a degree of piquancy—from the large, mild green chili from Magdalena in Sonora to the most fiery of all, the *chile habanero* of Yucatán. And chilies on the same plant can vary from mild to hot.

Many chilies can be used fresh or dried, although when they are used fresh, the flavor of the green (unripe) chili is generally preferred.

Descriptions follow of those most generally used. See also the photographs opposite pages 42 and 43 . For notes on cleaning and cooking fresh and dried chilies, see pages 44–47.

FRESH CHILIES

Chile Serrano

The *chile serrano* is a small, smooth mid-green chili, mostly rounded but sometimes pointed at the end, with an average size of 1½ inches long and just under ½ inch wide. The flesh has a strong, fresh flavor, and the seeds and veins are very *picante*. They are used fresh, and boiled or toasted: fresh for such dishes as Guacamole (page 113), Salsa Cruda Mexicana (page 297), Salsa de Tomate Verde Cruda (page 297), and toasted or boiled for Salsa de Tomate Verde Cocida (page 299), Salsa Ranchera (page 299), or other cooked sauces.

When they are fresh they will keep for several weeks if they are kept dry and stored at the bottom of the refrigerator, but they will become a little wrinkled and lose a little of their fresh flavor. Before storing them, remove any that are becoming soft or turning color and set aside for immediate use. Put a line of them across a paper towel and roll them up, just a few at a time—in paper to absorb any moisture and a few at a time because as they ripen they exude moisture, which will spread to the others. On no account use a polyethylene bag, which will keep in heat and moisture. Look them over about once a week and remove any that are ripening or becoming soft.

For use in cooked sauces you can store them more easily. Toast them on a warm comal until the skin is blistered and brown and they are soft; or boil them in water for about 10 minutes. Then freeze them, a few together, in small polyethylene bags. For some reason they remain separate as they freeze, so one or two can be taken out as they are needed. *Do not freeze them in their raw state,* or they will lose their flavor and piquancy. A ripened, dried *chile serrano* is sold as *serrano seco* or *chile japonés.*

In parts of the United States where there are large Mexican communities you will always find fresh supplies of these chilies. (If not, a substitute is the fresh long, thin *chile cayenne*—anywhere from 3 to 4 inches long and about ⅜ inch wide—which are available all the year round.) I have occasionally seen them in greengrocers here in Manhattan and quite often on stand 499 in La Marqueta, 114th Street and Park Avenue. (For other sources, see pages 355–357.)

Chiles serranos are also canned in a pickle (*escabeche*), with onions, carrots, and herbs, which is distributed widely under many different labels.

The recipes will specifically indicate if canned or fresh chilies are to be used.

Chile Cayenne

This is a mid-green, 3-inch long, ⅜-inch-wide chili that is widely available throughout the year and all over the country. Use as a substitute when fresh *chiles habaneros, jalapeños,* and *serranos* are not available.

Chile Jalapeño

The *chile jalapeño* is a mid- to dark-green chili with a smooth surface and more often rounded at the tip than pointed: an average one measures 2½ inches long and ¾ inch at its widest part. Their seeds and veins can vary from hot to very hot.

In Veracruz they are often called *chiles gordos* ("fat chilies") and in Mexico City they are called *cuaresmeño* (there is always disagreement whether in fact they are the same chili, but this has been confirmed by the expert Dr. Antonio Marino). Stuffed with fish or cheese, they are used a great deal in the central part of Mexico and Veracruz, during the Lenten period. They are also ripened and smoked, at which point they become *chiles chipotles.*

Only two recipes here call specifically for fresh *chiles jalapeños:* Puerco en Salsa de Jitomate (page 118), to which the fresh chilies give a very special flavor; and Jaibas en Chilpachole (page 152), for which they are first roasted.

Chiles jalapeños are sometimes to be found in the stores that sell *serranos* —and they can be stored and frozen in exactly the same way.

They are canned, either whole or in strips, in *escabeche* and distributed under various labels. There are now some seeded *rajas* (strips) on the market that are, naturally, milder and have a very good flavor—they are extremely good with cold cuts. *Chiles jalapeños en escabeche* are probably the most ubiquitous condiment on the Mexican meal table, used as they are to accompany *enchiladas, antojitos* of all types, *frijoles;* and they are cooked in the sauce of such dishes as Huachinango a la Veracruzana (page 223).

There is no real substitute for *chiles jalapeños.* If you cannot get them, you will have to use any available fresh chili, either *serrano* or *cayenne.*

Chile Poblano

Chiles poblanos can vary in shape, color, size, and flavor depending on where and when they are grown. They are at their most typical in the markets of central Mexico at the height of the rainy season. They have an undulating, triangular shape—wide at the top and center and suddenly tapering off to a point at the bottom (3 × 5 inches). They have a deep ridge around the base of the stem and a dark- to almost black-green, shiny skin. It is when they are in this condition that their flavor is so rich and inky and is complemented so deliciously by cream, corn, squash flowers, and cheese. They vary from almost mild to *picante.*

In the central part of Mexico this chili is known as *chile poblano;* further north as *chile para rellenar;* and in Baja California, very confusingly, *ancho* or even *pasilla*—yes, the fresh ones.

Chiles poblanos are roasted and peeled before using—though there are some minor exceptions to this in the cuisine of Sinaloa—so it is easy to prepare and store them for future use in the freezing compartment of the refrigerator (see pages 44–45 for preparation). After a few days, if they are left fresh, they begin to get wrinkled and lose their flavor. They are stuffed with cheese or *picadillo* for Chiles Rellenos (page 263), cut into strips (*rajas*) and used in many vegetable dishes and casseroles, blended into soups and sauces, and used in other ways.

In the United States, they are imported where there are large Mexican communities but are generally unavailable elsewhere, although I did find them once in Manhattan, at La Marqueta (the stand owners have tried, so far without success, to get a regular supply of them).

Some years ago a Mexican brand of canned *chiles poblanos* was imported, but they were unskinned and too acidy to be of real use in the normal recipes calling for them. Another product has just come out: whole shells with stalk and top complete and ready for stuffing—the flavor is not quite as rich as the fresh ones, and in the canning process that lovely dark-green color is lost; nevertheless it is a good product. I have not yet heard whether or not they will be distributed in the United States. I think frozen ones, if promoted properly, would be a great hit here.

The canned, peeled green chilies (Ortega brand) are the nearest substitute. They are flame peeled and not lye peeled, which makes all the difference to the flavor.

The *chile poblano,* when ripened and dried, becomes the *chile ancho.*

Chile Chilaca

This is a long, slim, black-green chili with an average size of 6 inches long and 1 inch wide, and its surface is ridged horizontally. It has a real bite to it, and a deep, inky flavor.

Chiles chilacas are used mostly in central and northwestern Mexico—Jalisco and Baja California, although not in Sonora and Sinaloa. They are toasted and skinned before using, and often torn into thin shreds, which is how they got the name in Morelia of *chiles para deshebrar.*

There are only two recipes in this book that call for them if they are available—I have seen them fresh in markets in Los Angeles, but they are unavailable elsewhere—Carne de Puerco con Uchepos (page 179) and Tamales Dulces de Elote Fresco (page 97). *Chiles poblanos* make a passable substitute and canned chilies a poor one.

When ripened and dried, *chile chilaca* becomes the blackish-brown *chile pasilla.*

Chile Güero

As its name implies, *chile güero* is fair—a pale-yellow chili that can vary tremendously in size, but an average one would be about 4 to 5 inches long, and 1 inch wide. Pointed at the end with a smooth, small-ridged undulating surface, it can vary from quite hot to hot and has a delicious and distinctive flavor. In Yucatán it is a pale green color rather than yellow, and it is called *x-cat-ik*.

It is toasted and cleaned and used as a salad; it is pickled and canned and used unskinned in stews. It is almost always toasted and added, unskinned, to such sauces as that for Bola de Queso Relleno (page 133) and Pollo en Escabeche Oriental (page 209).

It is not available in this country, and while there is no real substitute from the point of view of flavor, for appearance's sake a large, toasted *cayenne* or a pale-green Italian pepper could be used.

Chile Habanero

The *habanero* is shaped like a small lantern. It is light green, and has a smooth, undulating surface, and is fiercely *picante*, probably the strongest of the lot. It is used fresh or toasted in the sauces of Yucatán and Campeche; fresh in *x-ni-pec*, the sauce for Cochinita Pibil (page 165), and Frijoles Colados y Refritos a la Yucateca (page 284); and toasted for the tomato sauce of Yucatán, Salsa Picante a la Yucateca (page 306).

It is the one chili in Mexico that is not of the *Capsicum annuum* group but *Capsicum sinense*.

For the recipes in this book that call for *chile habanero*, substitute *chile cayenne* (fresh, of course), because the *habanero* is unavailable here.

DRIED CHILIES

Chile Ancho

The *chile ancho* is probably the chili most commonly used in Mexico. It is the ripened and dried *chile poblano*, wrinkled and a deep reddish-brown color. After soaking, it becomes a brick-red color. A large, good-quality *ancho* is about 5 inches long and 3 inches wide, and it ranges from almost mild to *picante*. It is often stuffed. Toasted lightly and torn into small pieces, it is used as a table sauce, or relish, but more often it is ground to make the base of a cooked sauce. In Morelia it is confusingly called *pasilla,* and I have seen it labeled *pasilla* in California.

Chile Mulato

The *chile mulato* is the same shape as the *ancho,* but the skin is tougher and slightly less wrinkled and it is a brownish black when dried. Sometimes it is difficult to tell the difference between the two chilies. Open them up and hold them up to the light—the *ancho* will have a reddish tone, and the *mulato* a dark, rich-brown hue. It has a sweeter flavor than the *ancho.* The Mole Poblano de Guajolote (page 199) is the only recipe using this chili in the book. A first-class-quality *mulato* will be a little larger than the *ancho.*

Chile Pasilla

The *chile pasilla* is a long, slender, brownish-black chili—the *chile chilaca* dried. It has a wrinkled appearance, and an average one would be 6 inches long and 1 inch wide. It is very *picante* and rich tasting, toasted and ground dry for either a table sauce or a cooked sauce to eat with seafood.

One has to be careful when buying, for in Oaxaca what is called a *chile pasilla* is entirely different, and this is called *pasilla de México;* on the West Coast and in Baja California it is called *chile negro.*

Chile Guajillo

This is a long, pointed, slender chili with a smooth, brownish-red skin. It can sting with a vengeance and is referred to as the "mischievous" (*travieso*) chili. The average good-quality *guajillo* is about 4½ inches long and 1¼ inches wide.

In the Bajío area of Mexico it is often called *cascabel,* because it resembles the tail of and sounds like a rattlesnake. This name has also carried over into the United States, so when ordering *chiles cascabel* be absolutely sure that you specify that you want the round ones or you will find yourself with more *guajillos* than you need.

Chile Chipotle

This is a light-brown chili, with a wrinkled skin that smells distinctly of smoke. It is in fact the *chile jalapeño,* ripened, dried, and smoked. (I am told that it is smoked under banana leaves, but I have not yet found anyone who can confirm this.) Its name comes from the Nahuatl *chil-* ("chile") and *poctli-* ("smoke"). It can also be spelled *chilpotle* or *chilpocle*—all forms are used. The average *chile chipotle* is 2¼ inches long and just less than ¾ inch wide.

It is very often used whole to season soups and stews, but is probably most popular of all canned in vinegar or a red *adobo* sauce. The canned ones are imported and available in all specialty stores carrying Mexican foods.

There is no substitute for it.

Chile Cascabel

The *chile cascabel,* as its name denotes, sounds like a rattle as you shake it. It is a small, round chili with a brownish-red, smooth skin, just like that of the *guajillo.* A good-sized one measures about 1 inch in diameter. Not as *picante* as the *guajillo,* it has a very pleasant nutty flavor when toasted and ground for sauce (see page 303). You may come across some that appear to be the same but are triangular—they are *chiles catarinas* and are interchangeable with the *cascabel.*

See also under *chile guajillo* (page 38) about the confusion of name.

Chile Catarina. See *Chile cascabel.*

Chile Seco

The only dried chili that I know of used in the Yucatecan and Campeche cuisines is the small, bright red *chile seco.* I have ground some of them and found that they taste very much like a hot paprika, which makes an easily available substitute. Many cooks in Yucatecan households where *picante* food is not particularly liked prefer not to use *chiles secos* in the seasoning pastes, but to grind and serve them separately so that each person can season his own *tacos* for Cochinita Pibil (page 169), for instance.

Note the following general information on dried chilies:

1. All dried chilies will keep indefinitely provided they were in good condition in the first place—that is, properly dried, free from insects and maggots—and stored in a cool, dry place. Even so it is a good idea to go over them every two months and remove any that may appear to be deteriorating.

2. For obtaining supplies of dried chilies turn to page 355. Dried chilies are often incorrectly labeled, so become thoroughly familiar with them and be very specific or send samples if you are ordering by mail.

3. Each dried chili has its own quality, piquancy, and flavor. To become familiar with them, take one sauce as a base and make it with the different chilies.

4. It is very difficult to give exact measurements for chilies, as they vary enormously in size, depending often on the quality of the chili. If you go by weight, they become lighter as they dry out. (In Mexico, when buying in bulk you have to watch, since the vendors quite often dampen the chilies so they will weigh more, and if they are not used immediately they will start to rot.) The only thing to go by is the number of chilies given in the recipe, and until you become very familiar with sizes, check them against the average size mentioned in the descriptions on pages 37–39. Then make up for any small ones you may happen to have.

Cooking Methods

The actual cooking of Mexican food requires no frighteningly precise techniques, like those of the French cuisine, for example. There is a great deal of detailed preparation and cutting, but from then on it is a matter of becoming accustomed to the simple cooking methods and following the rules. Don't let it defeat you after one or two tries so that producing a good, authentic Mexican meal becomes too tiresome. It is a matter of organization. Use these points as a guide:

1. Keep your basic store of ingredients up to date (see list pages 30–31). I remember a last-minute panic when I could not find sesame seeds in any of the specialty stores, supermarkets, or health food stores in the area.

2. When planning a meal, shop well ahead for the more specialized fresh ingredients, like coriander and chilies, or Seville oranges; allow time for avocados to ripen; order fish of a special size several days in advance.

3. Prepare all that can be done a day ahead.

4. When planning a menu, remember not to choose too many things that must be cooked at the last moment—*antojitos* fall into this group.

5. No matter how simple or complicated your menu, make yourself a detailed timetable.

6. If you are making your own tortillas, always overestimate the time. I have been caught out on this far too many times, greeting guests red-faced and breathless.

7. Cooking times can only be approximate, since much depends on what the cooking utensils are made of—metal pans cook faster than those of earthenware, and so on.

8. I always try and persuade people to weigh ingredients instead of mea-

suring them. It is so much more accurate, especially when you are trying to learn a new cuisine and want the dishes to be as near the original as possible. A cupful of flour, for example, can vary by 6 tablespoons, depending upon the way it is packed into the cup. The only time I do not weigh is when I am dealing with dried chilies (see page 40).

9. I think one of the secrets of the wonderful flavor of a well-prepared Mexican sauce is that it is cooked fast in a very concentrated form, with very little liquid, and all the flavors "explode." That is why what I often stress when blending chilies and other ingredients is not to add any more liquid than is absolutely necessary. It will take more time and more patience, as you have to keep stopping and releasing the cutting blades, but after years of talking to and watching Mexican cooks, and experimenting on my own, I am sure this is an important point to watch.

FRYING ONION AND GARLIC

Fry onion and garlic gently, without browning, until soft: as the Mexicans would say, *acitronar* the onion and garlic. In any recipe it is essential to have them cooked through well before adding the rest of the ingredients.

SHREDDING MEAT FOR PICADILLOS, TACOS, AND OTHER DISHES

Many cooks now use ground meat for *picadillos*, for stuffing chilies, and so forth, but to me it always seems hard and indigestible. I therefore go along with the old school, who say that the consistency and flavor are better when the meat is first boiled and then shredded fine or roughly chopped.

The basic method is to cut the meat into large squares; cover it with water; add salt, onion, garlic, and peppercorns and simmer until it is just tender. Let the meat cool off in the broth—it will be quite tender by then. Drain and shred. Meat prepared this way is used for *tacos,* and other *antojitos,* with the notable exceptions in this book of Enchiladas de Jalisco (page 75) and Garnachas Yucatecas (page 128).

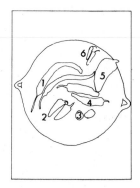

SOME OF THE MORE COMMONLY USED FRESH CHILIES
1 *chiles chilacas;* **2** *chiles jalapeños;* **3** *chiles habaneros;*
4 *chiles güeros;* **5** *chile poblano;* **6** *chiles serranos*

TOASTING

In several of the recipes—Mole Poblano de Guajolote (page 199), Pollo en Escabeche Rojo (page 209), and many of the Yucatecan dishes—you will see that seeds, spices or other ingredients are toasted or fried to enhance their flavor. Take, for example, the recipe for Bola de Queso Relleno (page 133): the meat is cooked with salt, toasted garlic, and toasted oregano; these simple ingredients make a fragrant delicious broth.

GARLIC

You can toast garlic by placing the unpeeled cloves of garlic on a hot comal and letting them cook through on both sides for a few minutes. Peel; the charred skin will come away easily from the soft flesh.

HERBS

For herbs, just shake the oregano or other herb in a small pan over the burner. Very soon you will be able to smell its real flavor.

FRESH CHILIES

To toast chilies, place the chili on a warm comal and turn it from time to time until the skin is charred and the flesh soft. (See also pages 44–45.)

SEEDS

To toast sesame, pumpkin, or other seeds, heat an ungreased frying pan and toast the seeds very lightly, stirring them all the time—they should barely turn color. (Keep a lid handy for pumpkin seeds, since they pop around explosively.) Set them aside to cool a little before grinding.

TOMATOES

SKINNING AND SEEDING

Plunge the tomatoes into boiling water to cover and leave them for 15 seconds. Remove and put them into cold water to stop the cooking process.

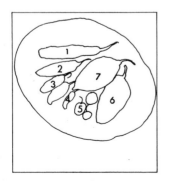

SOME OF THE MORE COMMONLY USED DRIED CHILIES
1 chile pasilla; **2** chile guajillo; **3** chiles chipotles;
4 chile mora; **5** chiles cascabels; **6** chile mulato; **7** chile ancho

They can then easily be skinned. Remove the core, cut the tomatoes across into halves, and squeeze out the seeds. Push the seeds through a strainer to extract the juice. Then mash or chop in the usual way.

BROILING

Many Mexican recipes call for tomatoes to be *asados* (roasted). Traditionally they are put onto a hot comal and cooked until the skin is wrinkled and brown and the flesh is soft right through—this takes about 20 to 25 minutes for an 8-ounce tomato. However, since this method is very messy, it is best to line a shallow metal pan with foil and put the tomatoes in it. Place them under a hot broiler—do not have the flame too high or the tomato will burn without cooking through—and turn them from time to time so that they cook through evenly—the skin will be blistered and charred. A medium tomato will take about 20 minutes. Blend the tomato, skin, core, and seeds to a fairly smooth sauce. The skin and core give both body and flavor to the sauce. And never mind if the skin *is* charred: that adds character, too. If the skin is very badly blackened and hard in places, then remove a little of it.

This method of cooking tomatoes makes for a very rich-flavored sauce.

BOILING

In parts of the west of Mexico, recipes require tomatoes to be boiled—for 5 minutes only—and then blended. In these recipes the tomatoes have to be skinned after they are cooked and before they are blended.

GRATING

In Sonora, tomatoes for sauces are grated raw. Remove a thin slice from the top of tomato. Put the tomato in the palm of your hand and rub it against a coarse grater. In no time at all the flesh will be reduced to a fine pulp and only the skin will be left in your palm.

This is one of the easiest and quickest ways of reducing them to a pulp without the skin.

FRESH CHILIES

ROASTING AND PEELING

First choose good-quality chilies or bell peppers. They should be smooth —not wrinkled with age—and firm, thick fleshed, and therefore heavy.

Place the chilies directly onto the flame of an open burner and let the skin blister and char slightly. Turn them from time to time—so that the flesh does not become burned through—until they are evenly charred. Place them immediately into a damp cloth or polyethylene bag and let them "sweat" for about 20 minutes. While the skin will be ready to come off long before that, this steaming process will also help to cook the chili a little more—but not overcook it. You could also roast the peppers under a broiler, if you wish—although I like to keep a constant eye on them on top of the stove. Do not do them in the oven, for by the time the skin is blistered and loose the flesh will be too soggy. Besides, you lose that lovely burned flavor that enhances the taste of the chilies.

The skin will peel off easily. Slit each chili down the side, leaving the top ridge intact. Carefully cut out the core under the base of the stem; wash out the seeds and remove as much as you can of the veins without tearing the flesh of the chili. By this time you will know how *picante* the chili is—and some *poblanos* can be very *picante*. If it is too strong, leave it to soak in a mild solution of vinegar, salt and water for about 30 minutes to an hour. Dry the chili well with paper toweling before using it. If you are using the chili for Chiles Rellenos (page 263) and you find that it is rather tattered after all this, don't worry too much, because the batter, light as it is, seals up the chili and filling quite efficiently.

PREPARING RAJAS

Many recipes call for *rajas* or strips of fresh chilies. Roast and peel the chilies in exactly the way described above and then cut them into strips about ⅜ inch thick and about 2 inches long. If you are using the canned chilies, already peeled, then just cut them into strips. Remember that they have undergone a certain amount of cooking in the canning process, so never cook them for as long a time as you would cook strips of fresh *chiles poblanos*.

For information on further cooking of *rajas*, see page 260.

DRIED CHILIES

CLEANING

Remember when cleaning chilies that the seeds and veins are the hottest parts. If you are not used to them, wear thin rubber gloves when handling; otherwise you may have stinging fingertips for some hours—and if you forget and rub your eyes or skin you will feel quite a burning sensation. To avoid this, scrub your fingertips well, especially under the nails, with plenty of soapy water, then soak them for a few minutes in strongly salted water. If you do rub your eyes, wash them immediately with water.

If the chilies you are using have dried out and are brittle, heat them for a few minutes on a warm comal; they will then become pliable, and you will be able to clean them easily without breaking them into a hundred pieces.

GENERAL PREPARATION

When you toast chilies for any length of time, the flesh will start to blister. Turn them before they burn or the sauce you're using them in will have an acrid taste. The chilies with a smooth hard skin, like the *guajillo* and *cascabel,* burn very easily, so make sure the flame under the comal is not too high.

If the chilies are to be ground dry, toast them well, clean them while they are still flexible, and then let them cool. They should be quite crisp, and will grind down in no time at all to a fine powder (the Moulinex grinder does a very efficient job).

Chilies are treated in different ways, depending on how they are going to be used or in what region the recipe originates:

1. Clean them and leave them to soak.
2. Clean them and boil them in water for a few minutes.

(Speaking very generally, in the west of Mexico the food is not as *picante,* so these two methods are used. The chilies become much milder, but they do lose something in flavor.)

3. Toast lightly, clean, and soak. This is a generally accepted method for many sauces. The toasting enhances the flavor and the soaking makes the chilies soft and fleshy so they can be ground very easily to a thick sauce.

4. Toast the chilies well, clean them, let them cool, and grind them dry. This method is used for rustic table sauces, as in Salsa de Chile Cascabel (page 303) and Salsa de Chile Pasilla (page 304), where, in fact, seeds and veins are left in.

For the filling of Tamales Norteños (page 94) and Mole de Olla (page 160), the chilies are cleaned and ground dry and then the powder is fried for a few seconds in lard—the smell is unbelievable.

Many real *poblano* cooks would never dream of soaking chilies for *mole:* they toast them and grind them on the *metate* with green tomatoes and the other ingredients. But the sauce takes longer cooking to get the body a soaked chili sauce has.

5. Fry the cleaned chilies and then soak them, as in Mole Poblano de Guajolote (page 199) and Camarones en Escabeche Rojo (page 237). The flavor of the chili is greatly enhanced, and the sauce will be thick from the start.

6. When you are going to cook a sauce of ground chilies, make sure that the fat is not too hot or the sauce will burn immediately. This rule applies when you are frying *enchiladas* that have been dipped into an uncooked sauce as well, as in, for example, Enchiladas de Plaza (page 73).

7. Burn the chilies black. For the *relleno negro* (black stuffing) for a turkey in Yucatán, the chilies are actually burned black before they are used. Now most cooks buy their seasoning—*chilmole*—already prepared and packaged. Not only is it a time saver, but it means that their families and neighbors will not choke and cry from the effects of the burning chilies. And for the *chichilo* of Oaxaca (a type of *mole*) I watched a friend burning the *chile chilhuacle* seeds until they were completely black before grinding them with the rest of the ingredients.

Menus

The full Mexican *comida* can be a wonderful meal if you have all the time in the world and come to it very hungry, ideally about two-thirty on a Sunday afternoon; it makes me nostalgic to write about it. While you are sipping your tequila there would be some *antojitos,* and then some of the wonderful Mexican beer as the meal goes along. By about five o'clock you would have finished and be very ready to sink into a siesta. It is not a meal recommended for eating late in the evening, however, and in any case I think most people without help in the kitchen would welcome some modifications. I have given some suggestions on the following pages. I have broken the main dishes up into groups, with regard to their character, adding groups of first courses and desserts that seem most appropriate for them. This scheme gives you endless variations.

LA COMIDA MEXICANA [*An example of a typical Mexican meal*]

Antojitos (appetizers): *guacamole, carnitas, sopes,* or *salsa de tomate verde* with tequila and *sangrita*

Sopa (soup): *Caldo tlalpeño* or *caldo de pollo*

Sopa seca: Arroz a la Mexicana or *arroz blanco con plátano macho*

Entrada: Chiles rellenos, tortitas de calabacitas, pescado a la Veracruzana

Platillo fuerte (main course): *Mole poblano de guajolote* or *pato en mole verde de pepita* or *carne asada a la tampiqueña*

Frijoles (beans): *de olla* or *refritos*

Postre (dessert): *chongos* or *flan* or *ate de guayaba con queso*

Café (coffee): *café de olla*—or you may need a calming *té de manzanilla,* a great digestive that calms the stomach

48

DINNER SUGGESTIONS

1. With fish as a main dish:

TO START

Tacos of Cochinita Pibil (page 169)

Tacos of Birria (page 185)

Tacos of Carnitas (page 112)

Tacos of Bola de Queso Relleno
  (page 133)

Burritos of Chilorio (page 132)

Chilaquiles (page 67)

Papa-dzules (page 70)

FISH

Huachinango a la Veracruzana
  (page 223)

Pámpano en Salsa Verde estilo
  Campeche (page 229)

Pescado en Cilantro (page 224)

Pescado Alcaparrado (page 227)

Pescado Relleno (page 226)

The fish could be accompanied by Arroz Blanco, either plain (page 290) or cooked with kernels of corn (page 291), or a *budín* of vegetables (pages 276–277), or Torta de Elote (page 272) with sour cream, or Tortitas de Papa (page 270).

DESSERT

Cocada Imperial (page 339)

Cajeta de Celaya (page 331)

Torta de Cielo (page 321)

2. For the main dishes that have a rather thick and heavy sauce, it is better to start with something light and refreshing:

TO START

Cebiche (page 231)

Sierra en Escabeche a la Yucateca
  (page 232)

Pescado en Cilantro (page 224)

Jaibas Rellenas (page 236)

MAIN COURSE

Pollo en Pipián Rojo (page 206)
Mole Poblano de Guajolote (page 199)

Pato en Mole Verde de Pepita (page 204)
Estofado de Lengua (page 187)

White rice is a good accompaniment to all of these dishes, but serve "Blind" Tamales (page 92) with the *mole poblano.*
They could be followed with Ensalada de Nopalitos (page 312).

DESSERT

Huevos Reales (page 326)
Flan a la Antigua (page 337)

Guavas Rellenas con Cocada (page 322)
Mangos Flameados (page 328)

3. For the drier or plainly broiled meats:

TO START

Caldo de Queso (page 146)
Sopa de Tortilla (page 143)
Sopa de Lima (page 144)

Camarones en Escabeche Rojo (page 237)

MAIN COURSE

Carne Asada a la Tampiqueña (page 181) with its garnishes
Chuletas de Puerco Adobadas (page 173) with Frijoles de Olla (page 282) and Calabacitas con Crema (page 259)

Plainly roasted or broiled meats with any of the *raja* or *calabacitas* dishes, Budín de Elote (page 277) or Torta de Elote (page 272) with Salsa de Jitomate del Norte (page 301)

DESSERT

Chongos Zamoranos (page 324)
Flan a la Antigua (page 337)
Queso de Nápoles (page 338)

4. For the simple stew-type dishes with plenty of sauce I would suggest:

TO START

Ensalada de Chiles Rellenos (page 311)
Tacos de Salpicón de Jaiba (page 114)
Pescado en Tikin Xik (page 234)

MAIN COURSE

Bisteces Rancheros (page 182)
Carne Claveatada (page 183)
Albóndigas (page 191)

All of these could be accompanied by a green salad.

DESSERT

Cajeta de Piña y Plátano (page 334)
Guavas Rellenas con Cocada (page 322)

5. For a very light and refreshing main course you could start with something a little more substantial:

Chilaquiles (page 67)
Arroz Verde con Chiles Rellenos (page 291)
Torta de Calabacitas (page 254)

Pescado Alcaparrado (page 227)
Sopa Tarasca (page 150)
Sopa de Elote (page 154)

MAIN COURSE

Pollo en Escabeche Oriental (page 209)
Fiambre Potosino (page 188)

These could be followed by Frijoles de Olla (page 281) or Refritos (page 282).

DESSERT

Huevos Reales (page 326)
Dulce de Camote (page 323)
Torta de Cielo (page 321)

6. **There are the peasant stews with plenty of sauce and vegetables, which I think go very well after the drier** *antojitos* **like:**

Sopes (page 115)
Quesadillas (page 120)
Enchiladas del Sanctuario (page 130)

MAIN COURSE

Puerco en Mole Verde (page 171)
Guiso de Puerco (page 177)
Mole de Olla (page 160)

DESSERTS

Cajeta de Leche Envinada (page 333)
Cajeta de Celaya (page 331)
Torta de Cielo (page 321)

7. **Finally we come to the richer, more filling dishes that need a light opening to the meal:**

Cebiche (page 231)
Jaibas Rellenas (page 236)
Sierra en Escabeche a la Yucateca (page 232)

MAIN COURSE

Pechugas de Pollo con Rajas (page 211) and Arroz Blanco (page 290)
Budín Azteca (page 81)
Muk-bil Pollo (page 103)

Enchiladas de Jalisco (page 75)
Enchiladas de Plaza (page 73)
Chiles en Nogada (page 267)
Chiles Rellenos (page 263)

The chilies should be followed by Frijoles Refritos (page 282) and the rest of the dishes served with or preceding a plain green salad.

DESSERTS

Cajeta de Piña y Plátano (page 334)   fresh fruit
Guavas Rellenas con Cocada   Mangos Flameados (page 328)
   (page 322)

SUPPER SUGGESTIONS

1. The hearty soups with all their trimmings and hot tortillas make very satisfying supper dishes and are very Mexican, especially when followed by Tamales de Dulce and hot chocolate.

Pozole estilo Jalisco (page 162)
Menudo estilo Norteño (page 159)
Gallina Pinta (page 161)

2. Or you might start with some *antojitos*:

Quesadillas (page 120)
Sopes (page 115)
Enchiladas del Sanctuario (page 130)

and follow that by a vegetable dish like:

Torta de Calabacitas (page 254)
Calabacitas Rellenas de Elote (page 256)
                    or
Jaibas en Chilpachole (page 152)

LUNCH SUGGESTIONS

MAIN COURSE

Enchiladas (pages 73–81)   Crepas de Camarón (page 239)
Papa-dzules (page 70)   Camarones en Escabeche Rojo
Budín Azteca (page 81)   (page 237) with Arroz Blanco
Chilaquiles (page 67)   (page 67)

All of these can be served with any mixed green or spinach salad.

DESSERT

Guavas Rellenas con Cocada (page 322)
Cajeta de Piña y Plátano (page 334)
fresh fruit

* * *

MAIN COURSE

Corn soup (any of the three, pages 154–157)
Sopa Tarasca (page 150)
Sopa de Apatzingán (page 151)

FOLLOWED BY

Jaibas Rellenas (page 236) and a green salad
Pámpano en Salsa Verde estilo Campeche (page 229)
Sierra en Escabeche a la Yucateca (page 232)

DESSERT

Chongos Zamoranos (page 324) or fresh fruit

BRUNCH SUGGESTIONS

1. You could start with fruit, followed by one or two of the following:

Huevos Motuleños (page 248)
Huevos en Rabo de Mestiza (page 247)
Higaditos (page 249)
Huevos Revueltos de Rancho (page 242), with Frijoles de Olla (page 281)
plain omelet with Salsa de Tomate Verde Cruda (page 297), or Salsa Mexicana Cruda (page 297) and Frijoles Refritos (page 282)

Machacado de Huevo (page 244) with Frijoles Refritos (page 282)
Huevos Revueltos a la Mexicana (page 241) or
con Chorizo (page 245) and Frijoles Refritos (page 282)

and finish up with Tamales de Dulce (pages 95–96) and *café con leche.*

2. **If you have a real hangover, you might think about the Mexican way of curing it:**

Pozole estilo Jalisco (page 162)
Menudo estilo Norteño (page 159)
Huevos Rancheros (page 246) with
a very *picante* sauce

Chilaquiles (page 67) with plenty
of *guajillos*

with fruit and coffee.

PART TWO

Recipes

Tortillas and Tortilla Dishes

"What is it that goes along the foothills of the mountains patting out tortillas with its hands? A butterfly."

—FROM *Nahuatl Proverbs, Conundrums, and Metaphors*
COLLECTED BY SAHAGÚN; TRANSLATED BY THELMA D. SULLIVAN

The haunting smell of wood smoke or charcoal is always the first thing that you are aware of as you near a Mexican village, and then, if it is early in the afternoon, you can hear from every household the rhythmic clapping of hands as the tortillas are patted out and smell the unmistakable, comforting smell of maize cooking quickly on the comal.

At the same time in the cities, long lines are forming outside the *tortillerías*. Not so long ago, each little business had its group of women and young girls standing around a high drum of a stove with a large circular metal top heated by huge gas jets, chatting and joking as they patted out hundreds upon hundreds of tortillas daily. But now things have changed, and the machine has taken over from start to finish. The art of *torteando* is dying fast, and more and more people are buying them ready made.

The ground *masa* is fed into a large hopper and pushed out at the bottom through a press, which stamps the tortillas out onto a narrow conveyor belt. The tortilla goes on its way as the belt jiggles over jets of hot flame; the belt goes just so far and then doubles back in such a way that the tortilla is flipped over, and as it cooks through it starts to puff and dance, and very soon it is thrown onto a fast-growing pile in the cloth-lined basket on the floor below.

In Tuxtla's market you can still find the smallest disks of crisp tortillas—about 2½ inches across—ready for use with their famous *botanas* (see page 111), and with your meals in Oaxaca you pull away at tortillas about 8 inches across.

The corn used for tortillas is also affected by population growth and automation. I have bought the little fat cakes, *gorditas*, of a bluish-green corn from Indians in the street, and there are tortillas made of yellow, red, and variegated corn. Sahagún mentioned a lion-colored corn—and there is purple corn—but while white is considered best for tortillas, only in the provinces will you find the white, light, and floury tortillas that never seem to harden or become really stale, for in the cities no one can spare the time to clean the corn so meticulously and still provide tortillas for the ever-increasing population.

It is often a surprise to visitors to discover that Mexico produces tortillas of wheat as well as of corn. The most important wheat-growing area in Mexico is the flat, irrigated land in Sonora and the northern part of Sinaloa. Tortillas of wheat flour (*tortillas de harina de trigo*) are common all over the north of Mexico, but they really come into their own in Sonora. There are the sweet ones, thicker and shorter, more like pastry; there are those in the recipe below, usually called *tortillas de manteca* (lard tortillas); and then the largest tortillas in Mexico, *tortillas de agua*, as thin as tissue paper and about 18 inches across. When served with a meal these come to the table folded into four and wrapped in a napkin. Folded just like that they are often used for *burritos*—rolled around a filling of meat or *machaca* (note: the *machaca* of Sinaloa is the equivalent of *machacado* in the rest of the north).

Most people buy them ready made, since it takes skill to produce them without a great deal of practice, but Sr. Colores, a restaurant owner in Hermosillo, has them freshly made for his restaurants daily, and I went there to see them prepared.

An older couple who have worked for him for years were making them. They rolled the dough into 2-inch balls and let them sit a while. To make the tortilla they rolled and stretched the dough until it was translucent—this has to be done with lightly greased hands. Then they cooked it on a comal over a hot wood fire. After a few seconds it ballooned up and had to be flattened back onto the comal. They flipped it over, just a few seconds more, and then stacked it on top of the others, wrapped up in a cloth to keep them moist and warm.

The recipe they told me was "a handful of lard to a kilo of flour, salt, and water. Hot water if the weather is cold; cold water if the weather is hot." Later on I had one toasted crisp with the biggest piece of meat, cooked over the wood fire, that I have ever seen on any plate.

Notes on Making Tortillas

1. The recipes using tortillas throughout this book are for corn tortillas unless noted in the recipes themselves.

2. Freshly made tortillas are, of course, the best to serve with a meal.

3. Stale tortillas can be cut up and used as Totopos (page 139) or Chilaquiles (pages 67–71) or they can be eaten in truly rustic Mexican fashion—thrown onto the bare flame of the burner to heat through for a few seconds on either side—a little burned, a little crisp round the edges, and delicious; or they can be toasted crisp on a wire toaster over the flame, or on a comal.

4. For use in Tacos (page 116), if it is a plain, unfried taco, then the tortilla has to be freshly made and hot. If the taco is going to be fried, then the tortilla does not have to be hot and flabby, but neither must it be allowed to get leathery or it will not roll up neatly.

5. For Enchiladas (pages 73–81), the tortillas should be made the same day, but do not have to be hot and flabby. They will soften up the moment they are immersed in the hot fat.

6. You will need a 6-inch tortilla press and one or two cast-iron griddles or frying pans (in Mexico they use a comal, of thin earthenware for charcoal fires or of tin or cast iron for gas stoves). A double comal that sits over two burners is now being imported here; it is extremely convenient because you can very soon get accustomed to making two or three tortillas at one time.

7. Quaker brand *masa harina* is the only satisfactory product that I have come across for making tortillas.

The tortilla dishes in this chapter are only a representative selection. For the many more that are included throughout the book, see the index.

TORTILLAS

16 small tortillas about 5 inches in diameter

I must confess that I was never able to pat out tortillas by hand, although I tried at least a hundred times; the ball of *masa* always became dirtier and dirtier as I dropped it on the floor for the umpteenth time. Finally I gave up. And when I first came to New York, I tried to apply all the rules that I had learned about cooking tortillas and the proper consistency of the dough. It didn't work, of course, because dough made of *masa harina* has an entirely different character. But I asked around among the Mexicans who are now living here and practiced some more.

It will take some practice for you, too, before you can make a batch of tortillas without wishing you had never begun.

2 cups masa harina
1⅓ cups warm water (or
    less in very humid
    weather)
2 cast-iron griddles or
    frying pans
A 6-inch tortilla press
2 sandwich-sized
    polyethylene bags

Mix the flour and water together to a soft dough.

Meanwhile, heat the griddles, one over a low flame, the other over a rather high flame.

Place one of the bags on the bottom part of the opened tortilla press. Roll a piece of the dough into a ball about 1½ inches in diameter. Place the ball *almost* on the center of the bag —a little more toward the hinge of the press. Place the second bag on top of the ball of dough. Close the press and push the handle down hard, then open up the press and peel the top bag off the flattened dough, starting at the side opposite the handle, since the dough nearest the handle is too thin to pick up easily. If the dough is still rather thick and has a grainy uneven edge, then it is too dry. Add some more water to the dough and knead it well.

Pick up the second bag, together with the dough, and place the dough on your fingers—not your palm. Carefully peel the bag off the dough—do not try to peel the dough off the bag. If the dough does not come away easily from the bag, or if it sticks to your hands, it is too wet. Add some more flour and knead the dough again well, and lightly grease your hands to make it easier to handle.

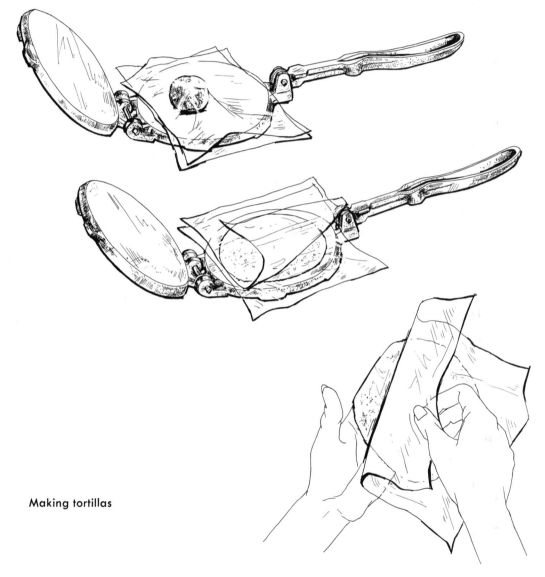

Making tortillas

(*continued*)

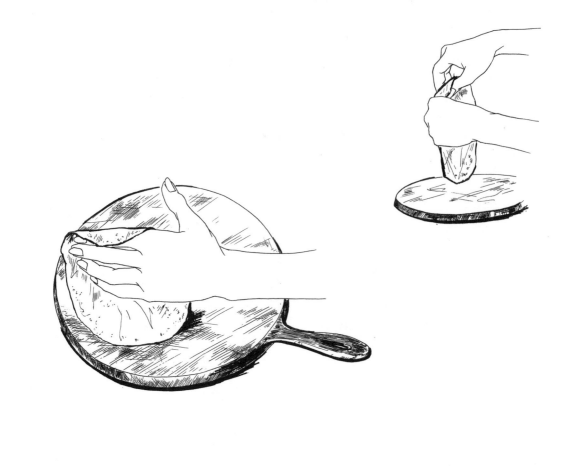

Place the tortilla on the cooler of the two griddles. After a few seconds, the dough will begin to dry out at the edge. Do not wait for it to curl up, but flip the tortilla over into the hotter pan and let it cook until it is speckled with dark-brown patches. Flip it back onto the first side, still in the hotter pan, and let it cook further and color a little. The total cooking time for each tortilla is about 2 minutes.

The second side, which is now on top, is the "face" of the tortilla. It will probably puff up, indicating that the tortilla will be light and nicely cooked through.

The puffing is not absolutely necessary unless you are making Panuchos (page 126) or Enchiladas de Jalisco (page 75), but you can encourage it by pressing the tortilla just before it finishes cooking with a piece of cloth or paper towel—Mexican cooks use their fingers and say they are "tickling" the tortilla. Much will depend on the heat of the pans, however. From time to time you will have to adjust it, especially under the hotter of the two, which is apt to burn after a while.

As each tortilla is cooked, stack it on top of the others in a dry cloth, which must cover them completely. In this way they will keep warm and moist. To conserve the heat even more, cover the cloth with foil.

Tortillas can be made about 2 hours ahead of time and warmed up, in their package, for about 20 minutes in a low oven.

Wipe the tortilla press with a dry cloth or sponge, and store it away with some paper toweling between the plates.

Tortillas are traditionally served out of a *chiquihuite*, a square-shaped basket, woven from a reed-grass, that is always lined with a cloth so the tortillas will remain hot and soft. Never, never leave them uncovered when you help yourself to a tortilla at table.

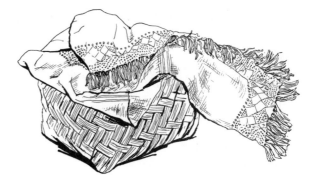

TORTILLAS DE HARINA DE TRIGO [*Wheat-flour tortillas*]

24 6-inch tortillas

A mixing bowl
¼ pound lard or shorten-
ing (½ cup)
1 pound all-purpose flour,
sifted
2 teaspoons salt
1 cup warm water (not
lukewarm and not
hot)
A cast-iron griddle or
frying pan
A rolling pin

Using the fingers, rub the fat well into the flour.

Dissolve the salt in the water and add it to the flour mixture. Knead the dough well for about 3 minutes. Set it aside, covered, for at least 2 hours. Do not refrigerate.

Heat the griddle over a medium flame.

Knead the dough again for a minute or so, then take a piece of the dough and roll it into a ball roughly about 1½ inches in diameter. Press the ball out evenly on a floured board or pastry cloth—you are trying to roll it out to a paper-thin circle about 7 inches in diameter. With each press of the rolling pin turn the dough around slightly to keep it circular.

Place the tortilla on the griddle—if it is the correct heat there should be a slight sizzling sound as the dough touches it. Leave it for 20 seconds, by which time bubbles will appear on the surface and the underside will be speckled with dark brown. (If it puffs up, press it back onto the griddle.) Turn the tortilla over and cook it for a slightly shorter time on the other side.

Place the tortillas, one on top of the other, in a polyethylene bag. They should be thin, light, and flexible.

You can make the tortillas several hours ahead and simply warm them up, one at a time, on a hot griddle—just a few seconds on each side will warm them through sufficiently and make them soft and flexible. The tortillas can be stored for several days in the refrigerator, or frozen as long as they are kept flat. Warm them through on a hot griddle. There is no need to defrost the frozen ones before reheating.

For the best results, take special care with measurements and the type of ingredients used:

1. Sift the flour and weigh it, if possible. Measuring flour in a cup is inaccurate and can vary as much as 6 tablespoons, depending on how you fill the cup.

2. Weigh the fat at room temperature. Fat cold from the refrigerator does not attain the correct weight.

3. Use all-purpose unbleached flour.

4. After much experimentation, I decided that Crisco produced the lightest and thinnest tortilla.

Don't worry if the first few batches of tortillas you make don't turn out absolutely round. You will most probably be using them rolled around a filling, and the shape will not be noticed.

CHILAQUILES [*A casserole of tortillas in chili sauce*]

6 servings

The word *chilaquiles* comes from *chil-a-quilitl,* meaning "herbs or greens in chili broth"—colloquially, "a broken-up old sombrero." It is, in fact, one of the many recipes devised to use up stale tortillas. The purists say that the tortillas must be torn up into large pieces, but the dish is easier to serve and eat if they are smaller.

Like so many other recipes in Mexico, every cook has her own way of preparing them. In Sinaloa *chilaquiles* are sometimes cooked in a white sauce; then there is a version where you cut tortillas into quarters, stuff them with cheese, and cook them in a sauce of *chiles anchos.* To me they are all equally delicious.

A day or two ahead make 24 4-inch tortillas (page 62), cut them into strips about 3 × ¾ inches, and leave them on a wire rack to dry out.

(continued)

Have ready:

A flameproof dish at least 3 inches deep and ideally about 10 inches across

½ pound farmer cheese, crumbled, or mild Cheddar, grated (about 1⅓ cups)

1 cup *Thin Sour Cream* (page 20)

2 chorizos, crumbled and fried

1 medium onion, thinly sliced into rings

2 limes, cut into wedges

THE SAUCE

A griddle or comal

12 chiles guajillos

Heat the griddle and toast the chilies lightly on both sides. Be careful—they burn very quickly. When they are cool enough to handle, remove the seeds and veins.

A bowl

Hot water to cover

A blender

⅓ medium onion, roughly chopped

2 cloves garlic, peeled

½ teaspoon salt

¼ teaspoon cumin seeds

½ cup chicken broth or water

Cover the chilies with the hot water and leave them to soak for about 20 minutes, then transfer with a slotted spoon to the blender jar. Add the rest of the ingredients and blend to a smooth sauce.

THE CHILAQUILES

A small frying pan

2 tablespoons peanut or safflower oil

½ cup chicken broth

Heat the oil and cook the sauce until it darkens in color and is well seasoned—about 3 minutes.

Add the broth and let the sauce cook over a high flame for a few minutes longer. Set aside.

A frying pan

Peanut or safflower oil (½ inch deep)

The tortilla strips

Paper toweling

Heat the oil and fry the tortilla strips until they are a pale gold, but not too crisp. Remove and drain on the toweling.

The flameproof dish
The cheese
The sauce

3 to 3½ cups chicken
    broth

2 large sprigs epazote

The sour cream
The chorizos
The onion rings
The lime wedges

Cover the bottom of the dish with one-third of the tortilla pieces. Cover them with a layer of one-third of the cheese and a layer of one-third of the sauce. Repeat the layers twice more.

Add the broth and bring to a boil. Lower the flame and continue cooking the *chilaquiles* at a brisk simmer, until most of the broth has been absorbed—about 15 minutes. Add the *epazote* a minute or so before the *chilaquiles* have finished cooking.

Pour the sour cream around the edge of the dish, then garnish with the *chorizos* and the onion rings.

Serve in small deep bowls with lime wedges on the side.

This was our maid Godileva's recipe, a real peasant version and wonderfully robust. It is a very versatile dish and could be used for brunch—it is said to be very good for a *crudo,* or hangover—as an accompaniment to plainly broiled meat, or as a supper dish.

The tortillas here—either homemade or frozen—start to disintegrate much more easily in the broth than the Mexican ones, and I have had to modify the original recipe enormously with regard to cooking time and the amount of broth added. If you do not want to go to the bother of making your own, then frozen ones can be used quite satisfactorily. Let them defrost, cut them into pieces, and leave them to get stale for a day or two. About 18 will be needed—1 pound in weight.

You could always make the sauce ahead of time and even fry the tortilla pieces, but do not assemble the dish until you are ready to start cooking.

CHILAQUILES EN SALSA VERDE [*Chilaquiles in green sauce*]

1 serving

Have ready:

3 small stale tortillas cut into pieces
1 cup Salsa de Tomate Verde Cocida
    (page 299)
An individual flameproof serving dish
⅓ cup poached and shredded chicken,
    warmed

2 tablespoons Thick Sour Cream
    (page 20)
2 tablespoons crumbled farmer cheese,
    or grated mild Cheddar

A small frying pan
Peanut or safflower oil
    (¼ inch deep)
The tortilla pieces
Paper toweling

Heat the oil and fry the tortilla pieces lightly —do not let them become too crisp. Remove from the oil and drain.

A saucepan
The sauce
The tortilla pieces
The serving dish
The shredded chicken
The sour cream
The cheese

Heat the sauce, and when it is bubbling add the tortilla pieces and cook them for about 3 minutes.

Pour the *chilaquiles* into the dish, cover with the shredded chicken, and sprinkle with the sour cream and cheese. Pass under a hot broiler for a moment or two until the cheese melts, then serve.

PAPA-DZULES [*Tortillas in pumpkin-seed sauce*]

6 servings

Papa-dzules are tortillas dipped in a pumpkin-seed sauce, filled with crumbled hard-boiled egg, rolled, and covered with more sauce. The dish is then garnished with a tomato sauce and decorated with the green oil squeezed from the pumpkin seeds.

I really think this is one of the most beautiful dishes in the Mexican cuisines: the rich red of the tomato sauce, and the deep-green pools of oil sprinkled over the pale-green pumpkin-seed sauce. It is said that the Mayas prepared *papa-dzules* for the Spaniards and that was how it got its name, which is said to mean "food for the lords."

They make a delightful, if rather filling, first course.

Have ready:

A large serving dish
12 freshly made tortillas (page 62)
1 cup Salsa de Jitomate Yucateca
*   (page 300)*

5 hard-boiled eggs, crumbled and
*   mixed with salt to taste*

A small saucepan
2 large sprigs epazote
2½ cups water
1½ teaspoons salt, or to
*   taste*

Put the *epazote* into the water with the salt and let it boil for about 5 minutes. The water should be well flavored with the *epazote*. Set aside and keep hot.

A spice grinder or blender
½ pound hulled, unsalted
*   pumpkin seeds (about*
*   1⅔ cups), toasted*
*   (page 43)*

Grind the toasted, cooled pumpkin seeds as finely as possible.

A shallow dish
¼ cup very hot epazote
*   broth, strained*

Put the ground seeds into the dish and sprinkle them with the broth. Then, as soon as you can do so without burning your hands, knead the ground seeds together. They will become a darker color. Start to squeeze the paste; almost immediately drops of oil will start to exude from the mixture. Prop the shallow dish up at one side so that it is slightly inclined and the green oil will begin to collect at the lower edge. Transfer it to the small dish. In a short time there will be sufficient oil—about 3 to 4 tablespoons—to decorate the *papa-dzules*.

A small glass dish

A saucepan
The remaining epazote
*   broth*

Transfer the paste to a saucepan and gradually stir in the rest of the epazote broth, pressing out the lumps as you do so until you have a smooth, pale-green sauce.

(continued)

Set the pan over a low flame and heat the sauce through, just a little, so that it will begin to thicken slightly. *Stir it continuously,* scraping the bottom of the pan well. Remove from the heat.

The tortillas
The crumbled eggs
The serving dish

Dip each tortilla into the sauce—it should just coat them very lightly—sprinkle some of the egg across the tortilla and roll it up loosely. Place the tortillas side by side on the serving dish and mask with the remaining sauce.

The tomato sauce
The green oil

Heat the tomato sauce and pour it over the *papa-dzules*. Sprinkle the oil decoratively over the green sauce and serve immediately.

The sauces can be prepared a day ahead, if necessary, but the dish must be assembled with freshly made tortillas just before serving. *Papa-dzules* are always served lukewarm, not hot.

Some points to watch when you are making the sauce:

Toast the seeds very lightly or the sauce will be a golden yellow instead of pale green.

Let the seeds cool off after toasting or the blades of your blender or grinder will clog. (I find that the Moulinex spice/coffee grinder does a more efficient job of grinding than the normal blender.)

Grind the seeds as finely as possible, and be sure that the *epazote* broth is very hot when you add it to the ground seeds because it will heat them up and enable the oil to come out more easily.

Measure the broth carefully. The oil will not start to come out if you do not add enough, and if you add too much you will get a whitish-looking paste that will take a lot of kneading to get back to the proper consistency. The oil is just about to come out when the paste is dark green and shiny and squelches just a little as you squeeze it.

If the sauce looks rather grainy and lumpy after you have added the remaining broth, put it into the blender and blend at high speed for a few seconds until it is very smooth.

It is well worth the trouble of extracting the oil. It adds a very rich flavor to the sauce and it looks so beautiful. I had to go to Yucatán myself to find out how to do it. Sra. Berta, who taught me so much about the Yucatecan kitchen, told me exactly how to do it—and to prove that I had finally learned, I had to do it in front of her.

ENCHILADAS DE PLAZA

6 servings

As dusk falls, the archways around the cathedral square in Morelia begin to fill up with benches, tables, and improvised stoves for the brisk supper trade of *enchiladas de plaza.*

Have ready:

12 freshly made tortillas (page 62)
½ pound farmer cheese, crumbled and lightly salted
1 medium onion, finely chopped
A large serving dish, warmed

A 3-pound chicken, poached and cut into serving pieces
Strips of canned **chiles jalapeños en** *escabeche*

THE GARNISH

A saucepan
½ pound red bliss or waxy new potatoes (3 small ones), unpeeled
½ pound carrots (3 medium)
Boiling water to cover
1 teaspoon salt
2 tablespoons red wine vinegar
A colander

Wash the potatoes well and cut them into quarters; scrape the carrots and cut them into smaller pieces (so they will cook in the same time as the potatoes). Cover the potatoes and carrots with boiling water, add the salt, and cook them for 10 minutes only.

Add the vinegar to the vegetable water. Let the carrots and potatoes cool off in the water and become slightly acidy. Drain, peel the potatoes and cut them, with the carrots, into small cubes. Set aside.

THE SAUCE

A griddle or comal
2 chiles anchos
2 chiles guajillos

Heat the griddle and toast the chilies lightly, turning them constantly so that they do not burn. Slit them open and remove the seeds and veins.

(continued)

A small bowl
Hot water to cover
A blender
2 cloves garlic, peeled and
    roughly chopped
¼ medium onion, roughly
    chopped
¼ teaspoon salt
1 cup water

Cover the chilies with the hot water and leave them to soak for 20 minutes, then transfer with a slotted spoon to the blender jar. Add the rest of the ingredients and blend to a smooth sauce.

THE ENCHILADAS

A frying pan
6 tablespoons lard
The tortillas
The sauce
Water, if necessary
The farmer cheese
The chopped onion
The serving dish

Melt the lard, and when it is hot, but not smoking, dip each tortilla into the sauce, which should just lightly cover it—if the sauce is too thick dilute it with a little water—and fry it quickly on both sides.

Remove from the frying pan and put about 1 good tablespoon of the cheese and ½ tablespoon of the onion across each tortilla. Roll them up loosely and set them side by side on the serving dish. Keep warm.

The chicken

In the same fat, fry the pieces of chicken until they are golden brown. Arrange them around the *enchiladas.*

The cubed vegetables

In the same fat, fry the vegetable cubes and scatter them over the *enchiladas.*

The remaining sauce

In the same fat, cook the remaining sauce for a few moments and pour it over the *enchiladas.* Garnish with the chili strips and serve immediately.

The chili strips

SOME MEXICAN ANTOJITOS AND THEIR INGREDIENTS
1 an ordinary *taco* about to be rolled; **2** *tacos dorados* (fried *tacos*); **3** *chalupas* (filled tortilla "boats");
4 *salsa de tomate verde* (green tomato sauce);
5 *salsa cruda* ("fresh" sauce); **6** *guacamole*;
7 a tomato; **8** *chiles serranos*; **9** fresh coriander leaves;
10 *tomate verde* (Mexican green tomato or *fresadilla*);
11 an avocado

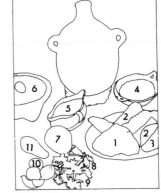

ENCHILADAS DE JALISCO

6 servings

In preparing this dish I have followed word for word the cooking methods of Sra. Victoria, a marvelous cook and daughter of one of the most distinguished cooks in Jalisco, because behind very step there is a reason, to enhance either the flavor or the texture of every ingredient in it.

In Mexico, *queso añejo* would be used, and the dish would be served with *frutas en vinagre*—such vegetables as carrots, beans, zucchini, onion, and chilies preserved in a fruity vinegar.

Start the day before to prepare the tortillas. Make 24 4-inch tortillas (page 62). Try to make them puff up on the comal so that while they are still warm you can remove the thin, loose layer of dough on top, which is then discarded. Wrap them in a cloth in the usual way and store them overnight in the refrigerator.

The reason for removing that thin layer on top is because the tortillas for this recipe must be as thin as possible.

Have ready:

An ovenproof serving dish just large enough to hold the enchiladas in 2 layers
¼ cup grated Cheddar cheese

½ medium onion, finely chopped
Shredded lettuce
Thinly sliced radishes
Strips of chiles jalapeños en escabeche

(*continued*)

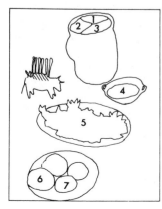

SOME MEXICAN BEANS AND WAYS THEY ARE USED
1 *frijoles bayos,* very like California pink beans;
2 *flores de mayo,* very much like pinto beans;
3 *frijoles negros* (black beans); **4** *frijoles de olla*
(a basic bean dish); **5** *brazo de frijoles refritos* (well-fried bean roll); **6** *tostados* (crisp-fried tortillas);
7 *garnachas*

THE FILLING (OR PICADILLO)

A large saucepan
*1 zucchini squash (about
    ¼ pound)*
*2 small carrots (about
    ¼ pound)*
*3 small red bliss or waxy
    new potatoes (about
    ½ pound)*
Boiling water to cover
2 teaspoons salt, or to taste
½ pound ground pork
½ pound ground beef
*2 large tomatoes
    (1 pound)*

Trim the squash and leave it whole. Trim and scrape the carrots and cut them into quarters lengthwise. Peel the potatoes and cut them into halves. Cover the vegetables with boiling water, add the salt, and let them cook for 5 minutes.

Press the meat tightly into two large balls and add them, with the whole tomatoes, to the vegetables in the pan. Cover and cook all together over a medium flame until the vegetables are just tender—do not overcook—and the meat balls are almost cooked through. Drain and reserve the broth.

When the vegetables are cool enough to handle, chop them into small cubes and set aside.

A blender
The cooked tomatoes
A frying pan
3 tablespoons lard
*½ medium onion, finely
    chopped*
The cooked meats
*1 tablespoon finely
    chopped parsley*
The tomato puree

Skin the tomatoes and then blend for a few seconds. Set aside.

Melt the lard and cook the onion, without browning, until it is soft.

Crumble the cooked meat balls into the pan, add the parsley, and fry for about 5 minutes over a medium flame.

Add the tomato puree and cook over a brisk flame until some of the juice has evaporated.

*⅓ cup reserved meat
    broth*
The chopped vegetables
Salt as necessary

Add the broth and vegetables and continue cooking the mixture until it is well seasoned —about 10 minutes. Add salt as necessary. Set aside.

THE CHILI SAUCE

A griddle or comal
10 chiles guajillos
   (*about 2 ounces*)

A bowl
Hot water
A blender
2 whole cloves
¼-inch stick cinnamon
½ teaspoon salt
1 cup reserved meat broth

A small frying pan
2 tablespoons lard

Heat the comal and toast the chilies lightly, turning them constantly, since they burn very quickly. Slit them open and remove the seeds and veins.

Cover the chilies with hot water and leave them to soak for about 20 minutes, then transfer with a slotted spoon to the blender jar. Add the rest of the ingredients and blend to a smooth sauce.

Melt the lard and cook the sauce until it is well seasoned and a rich, dark-red color—about 8 minutes. Set aside.

THE ENCHILADAS

Preheat the oven to 350°.

A small frying pan
¼ cup lard
The tortillas
Paper toweling
The sauce

The picadillo

The ovenproof serving
   dish
The remaining sauce

The grated cheese
The chopped onion
The shredded lettuce
The thinly sliced radishes
The rajas

Melt the lard and fry the tortillas quickly—they should just soften and heat through in the hot fat. Pile one on top of the other between sheets of the toweling and keep warm.

Dip the tortillas into the sauce, which should lightly cover them (if it is too thick, then add a little more broth).

Place some of the *picadillo* across each tortilla and roll up.

Put one layer of the *enchiladas* in the bottom of the dish. Pour a little of the remaining sauce over them. Then place another *enchilada* layer on top and pour over the rest of the sauce.

Heat the *enchiladas* through, covered in foil, in the oven for about 15 minutes, then serve immediately, sprinkled with the cheese and chopped onion and garnished with the lettuce, radishes, and canned chilies.

(*continued*)

I have prepared this dish of *enchiladas* at least 3 hours ahead, taking care that the filling was not too juicy or it would make the tortillas soggy, and that the extra chili sauce was poured down the sides and over the top of the *enchiladas* just before they were put into the oven.

The chili sauce and tortillas can be done the day before, but the *picadillo* really has to be prepared the same day or the potato gets that warmed-over taste. To heat the *enchiladas* through, cover tightly with foil so that the top layer does not get dried up. It is quite important, too, that they just fit snugly into the dish used.

ENCHILADAS SENCILLAS [*Simple enchiladas*]

6 servings

Preheat the oven to 350°.

Have ready:

12 freshly made tortillas (page 62)
7 large eggs, scrambled with plenty of
    salt, or 1½ cups cooked and
    shredded chicken, well salted

1 onion, finely chopped
A shallow ovenproof dish
1 cup grated Cheddar cheese

THE TOMATO SAUCE

A blender
1 pound tomatoes, broiled
    (page 44)
1 clove garlic, peeled
2 fresh chiles serranos,
    toasted

Blend the ingredients to a smooth sauce. (Makes about 2 cups.)

A frying pan
2 tablespoons peanut or
    safflower oil
½ teaspoon salt

Heat the oil and fry the sauce for about 5 minutes, or until it has reduced and thickened. Add the salt. Set aside to cool a little.

½ cup Thick Sour Cream
    (page 20), at room
    temperature

Stir the sour cream well into the sauce and just heat it through gently. **Do not let the sauce come to a boil after the cream has been added or it will curdle.**

THE ENCHILADAS

A small frying pan
Just under ½ cup peanut
    or safflower oil
Paper toweling

Heat the oil and fry the tortillas quickly, one by one, without letting them become crisp around the edges. Place them, one on top of the other, between sheets of paper toweling and keep them warm.

The tomato sauce
The scrambled eggs or
    shredded chicken
The chopped onion
The ovenproof dish

Dip the tortillas into the warm sauce—they should be just lightly covered—put about 2 tablespoons of the scrambled egg or shredded chicken across each tortilla, and sprinkle it with a little of the onion. Roll the filled tortillas up loosely and set them side by side on the ovenproof dish.

The grated cheese
The remaining chopped
    onion

Cover the *enchiladas* with the remaining sauce and sprinkle with the cheese and remaining onion. Put the dish into the oven and just heat them through for a very short time, no more than 10 minutes, in a 350° oven. Serve immediately.

A good alternative would be to use Salsa Tomate Verde Cocida (page 299) and fill the *enchiladas* with chicken or farmer cheese. Like all *enchiladas*, they go rather soggy if left to stand around after they are prepared.

ENCHILADAS DE MOLE

6 servings

Have ready:

12 freshly made tortillas (page 62),
    kept warm
1½ cups cooked and shredded chicken
    or pork (about 1½ pounds)

A shallow serving dish
¾ cup grated mild Cheddar cheese
    (3 ounces)
1 large onion, thinly sliced into rings

(*continued*)

THE SAUCE

A griddle
3 large chiles anchos

Heat the griddle and lightly toast the chilies, turning them from time to time so that they do not burn.

A bowl
Hot water to cover

While they are still pliable, slit them open and remove the seeds and veins. Cover them with hot water and let them soak for about 15 to 20 minutes.

A small frying pan
2 tablespoons lard
8 almonds, unskinned
A blender

Meanwhile, melt the lard and fry the almonds until they are well browned, stirring them so that they do not burn. Crush the almonds slightly and transfer to the blender jar.

½ very ripe plantain
    (about ½ pound)

Skin the plantain, slice it thin lengthwise, and fry it until golden on both sides. Transfer to the blender jar.

2 medium tomatoes
    (about ¾ pound),
    broiled (page 44)
Water if necessary

Add the tomatoes to the ingredients in the blender and blend to a smooth puree—add a little water if necessary. Set aside.

The soaked chilies
½ cup water
¼-inch stick cinnamon
2 whole cloves
⅛ teaspoon oregano
1 large clove garlic,
    toasted (page 45)

Separately, blend the chilies with the water, spices, oregano, and garlic to a smooth puree.

A frying pan
3 tablespoons lard
The plantain-tomato
    mixture

Melt the lard and cook the chili puree over a high flame for about 5 minutes.

Remove from the flame, add the plantain-tomato mixture, and continue cooking the sauce for about 5 minutes over a medium flame, stirring all the time so that it does not stick. Keep a lid handy, as it will splatter about fiercely.

1 cup pork or chicken broth *A food mill or coarse sieve* *¼ teaspoon salt, or to taste*	Stir the broth gradually into the sauce and continue cooking it for a minute or so, then push the sauce through the medium disk of a food mill or coarse sieve. Return the sauce to the pan, add the salt, and continue cooking it for about 15 minutes over a low flame.

THE ENCHILADAS

A small frying pan *6 tablespoons lard* *The warm tortillas* *The shredded chicken or pork* *The serving dish*	Melt the lard—but do not let it get too hot—and place each tortilla, face down (see note page 65), into it for a few seconds. Then remove and cover the face with a thin layer of the sauce. Put some of the shredded meat across the tortilla, roll it up; place the tortillas side by side on the serving dish.
The remaining sauce *½ to ¾ cup hot pork or chicken broth* *The cheese* *The onion rings*	Thin down the remainder of the sauce a little with the broth and pour it over the *enchiladas*. Garnish with the grated cheese and onion rings and serve immediately.

Once the *enchiladas* are assembled they should be used right away. The sauce can be made ahead of time—it freezes very well, too.

BUDÍN AZTECA [*or Moctezuma Pie*]

6 servings

A rich casserole of layers of tortillas, chilies, chicken, cheese, and cream, this makes a very substantial main course and is best served simply with a green salad.

(*continued*)

Preheat the oven to 350°.

Have ready:

22 *fresh small tortillas (page 62),*
about 4 inches across

An ovenproof dish at least 3½ inches
deep and ideally 10 inches in
diameter

2 *cups poached and shredded chicken,*
well salted

1 *cup Thick Sour Cream (page 20)*

1¾ *cups grated Cheddar cheese*
(about ½ pound)

THE GREEN TOMATO SAUCE

A blender

2 *cups* tomate verde,
drained

2 *small cloves garlic,*
peeled

¼ *teaspoon granulated*
sugar

½ *teaspoon salt*

½ *cup water*

Blend the *tomate verde* with the rest of the ingredients to a smooth sauce.

A small frying pan

2 *tablespoons peanut or*
safflower oil

Heat the oil and cook the sauce over a high flame for about 8 minutes, by which time it will have thickened a little and be well seasoned.

THE RAJAS

7 *chiles poblanos or 10*
canned, peeled green
chilies (2 4-ounce
cans)

⅓ *medium onion, sliced*

¼ *teaspoon salt*

3 *tablespoons peanut or*
safflower oil

Cook the *rajas,* with the onion and salt, in the usual way (see page 260).

THE BUDÍN

A small frying pan
⅓ cup peanut or safflower
  oil
The tortillas
Paper toweling
The ovenproof dish
The shredded chicken
The rajas
The sauce
The sour cream
The grated cheese

Heat the oil and fry each tortilla in it for a few seconds—they should not get crisp or hard. Drain them on the paper toweling.

Spread one-third of the tortillas over the bottom of the dish. Then spread, in layers on top of them, half the chicken, half the *rajas,* and a third each of the sauce, sour cream, and cheese. Repeat the layers and finish off with a layer of tortillas, sprinkled with the rest of the sauce, sour cream, and cheese.

Bake the *budín* for about 25 minutes, or until it is well heated through and the cheese has melted.

This dish is a great favorite in Mexico City and among those to whom I have introduced it. You can vary the recipe with ordinary tomato sauce, add some corn kernels, use shredded pork, anything—you have carte blanche.

It could be assembled about 2 hours ahead of time but it would be best not to add all the sauce. Just use half of it between the layers, and then, at the last moment before putting the dish into the oven, pour in the sauce around the edges. Be careful not to cook it for too long or the tortillas will disintegrate—they should be soft but keep their shape.

If you use the commercial frozen tortillas, allow 17 or 18 cut into halves, and another ½ cup sauce and ½ cup sour cream. The frozen tortillas seem to absorb much more liquid.

This pie does not freeze successfully.

Tamales and Tamal Dishes

"They also ate many kinds of tamales, like pellets they are white and roundish, though not completely round nor exactly square, and on top they have a snail designed by the beans with which they are mixed. Other tamales are white and delicious as, shall we say, a fluffy, light biscuit. Another type, white but not as fine as the aforementioned and somewhat tougher. Another kind were red and have a snail on top; they turn red because after the dough is made they keep them in the sun or over the fire for two days, mixing it, and thus it becomes red. Another which means simple, not very white but middling in color."

—FROM *"Historia General de las Cosas de Nueva España 1547–1582"*
BY SAHAGÚN; UNPUBLISHED TRANSLATION BY THELMA D. SULLIVAN

TAMALES

You may not be able to tell at first that *tamales* are being cooked except perhaps by the steamy windows—but later on a rich, subtle smell of corn husks, *masa*, and good lard, all intermingled, fills the house and gets stronger and stronger as the cooking nears completion. After their allotted time, you open one up to see if it is done. You heave a sigh of relief as a soft, spongy, white *tamal* rolls quite easily away from the husk. It could so easily have been heavy and damp.

Tamales are made for an occasion, and an occasion is made of making them. Men, women, children, and servants all join in with good humor, shredding, chopping, stirring, and cleaning the husks, until all is prepared.

Then everyone converges to form a real assembly line, some daubing the husks with *masa* while others add the filling, fold, and stack into the steamer. And there is nothing quite so delicious as that first *tamal,* straight from the steamer.

Tamales are fiesta food, the Sunday night special in many restaurants, the ceremonial food prepared in honor of the dead on All Saints' Day—and they were eaten by the Mexican rulers long before the Spaniards came to the New World.

Those early inhabitants of Mexico also had *tamales* of corn tassels mixed with amaranth seeds and the meat of ground cherries. And they made them of tender corn, like the *uchepos* of Michoacán today.

And what an enormous variety there is today, from the smallest *norteño* to the three-foot *sacahuil* from the Huastec country, which lies roughly where the extremities of the states of Veracruz, San Luis Potosí, and Tamaulipas converge.

I had often read about this giant *tamal,* and yet I could find no one who had eaten it or seen it prepared until I went to Tampico, where I seemed at last to be closing in on it. At the river town of Pánuco, about forty miles away, the favorite breakfast fare, I was told, was *sacahuil.* All you had to do was catch an early bus to be there before it all disappeared.

The day before I went I stood in line to reserve my ticket on the early bus. Then the next day I got up at the crack of dawn and braved torrential rains and hurricane winds to get to the bus station on time. We were late in going out because the downpour was so bad, but we finally got off, and after cruising along in a leisurely fashion, arrived at last in Pánuco.

The town itself was almost dead, and the air was hot and heavy as I made my way from one little restaurant shack to another. I was met by shaking heads and pitying glances, and then it finally dawned on me that Sunday was the only day for the *sacahuiles*—and this was only Friday. But I also learned that they were made en masse by someone in the town, and I was able to find her without too much difficulty.

Srta. Chanita was a strikingly handsome woman, tall, dark skinned, and white haired. We talked and talked, and finally got to the point. Could she make me a *sacahuil* for tomorrow morning, but a reduced one, say only two feet?

This was only Friday, she argued. How could they get all the ingredients? But after a while we had it all smoothed out.

Back at Tampico I started making negotiations for a car the following morning, one with good brakes and a steady driver and one that would leave extra early, since I had to catch a midday plane on to Monterrey. We did indeed leave early, but no sooner had we reached the halfway mark than the engine began to falter. I swear that the driver was so scared by my ranting and raving that he coaxed the car to the edge of Pánuco, where it finally stopped dead. But we were not too far behind time, and as I neared the house I could smell the *sacahuil* on the sultry air and see Chanita opening up her huge mud-brick and earth oven, which had been built in the garden just behind the porch of the house.

The night before, a wood fire had been lighted on the wide floor of the oven, and when the bricks were sufficiently hot the glowing embers had been pushed aside and the *sacahuil,* wrapped first in a banana leaf and held stiff in a frame provided by a palm leaf, which was tightly secured with strips of palm, had been left to cook all night. I don't think I shall ever forget the aroma as it was opened up. The dough was very soft and textured with pieces of corn kernels that had been roughly crushed—*maiz martajado.* The loin of pork that had been set down the center of the dough was succulent and falling off the bone, and was seasoned with a sauce made of *chiles anchos* and spices.

What a breakfast we had! I even relented and dragged the driver from under the car to come and join us. We ate the *sacahuil* hungrily, along with little earthenware mugs of steaming *café huasteco*—locally grown coffee boiled with raw sugar and cinnamon sticks. Then we learned of the previous day's crisis; no meat could be found in the town, until finally some kind person was prevailed upon to slaughter a pig especially for the occasion.

My friends in Tampico got an unexpected lunch that day, and I flew off on my journey feeling quite contented. And I think that may perhaps be the most expensive *tamal* in all history.

Probably the most surprising members of the *tamal* family are the shrimp ones from Escuinapa in Sinaloa. Small unskinned shrimps are used, and their little spines and feelers stick out through the dough. Of course you have to know where to eat them or you will find yourself with a mouthful of spines and debris. In Sinaloa, too, they make large *tamales* like elongated bonbons. They are filled with the usual pork and tomato sauce, but added to it are all sorts of vegetables cut into little strips—zucchini, potatoes, green beans, plantains, and *chiles serranos.*

Chiapas seems to have more than its share of varieties. On the coast there are those of iguana meat and eggs, and inland around Tuxtla Gutiérrez the Indians make countless varieties. I was told of at least ten kinds, of different herbs, beans, *chicharrón* (the crisp-fried pork rind), and those called *cuchunuc,* to which small pink flower buds are added. But probably the best known of all are the *tamales de bola,* with the corn husk tied on top making them round, as their name implies, and inside a rib of pork, a prune, and a small dried local chili called *simojovel.*

You will have to persevere to find the *tamales colados* in Campeche and Mérida. They are cooked in banana leaves, with a wonderfully savory filling seasoned with *achiote* and *epazote.* The *tamal* itself is made of uncooked tortilla dough that has been diluted in water, strained, and thickened over the fire; as one Campeche cookbook says ". . . the dough must be almost transparent and so delicate that it trembles at a touch." There are small *tamales* whose dough is studded with little beans called *espelón,* the skin of which turns black when cooked, and the completely pre-Columbian *dzotobichay,* which is a large *tamal* of *masa* flecked with cooked *chaya* (tastes rather like Swiss chard) and formed like a jelly roll, with a filling of well-toasted pumpkin seeds. It is then steamed in a banana leaf and served with a tomato sauce.

Michoacán, too, is famed for its *tamales:* the fresh corn *uchepos* and the *corundas*—the bread of the Tarascan Indians—made of maize dough leavened with wood ash and wrapped cunningly into rhomboid shapes with the long leaf from the corn stalk. There are those, cooked in banana leaves, of wild cherries and raw sugar from the low, hot Río Balsas country, and the *tamal agrio* of fermented *masa.* And there is a sweet *uchepo,* too, called *uchepo de leche* or *chuchara.* The corn is ground very finely, mixed with milk, and strained through a very fine strainer. The liquid is then cooked with sugar and cinnamon sticks until thick, like a *cajeta.* The fresh leaves are boiled very briefly, cooled off, and then filled with the corn paste. These are left some hours to set and then eaten with a spoon, accompanied by a glass of cold milk.

Throughout Mexico there are *tamales* filled with fish, pumpkin, pineapple, and peanuts, and those made of black and purple corn and rice. Wherever you go you will find something different. You will have to get up early and go into the marketplaces and breakfast there. For instance, there is Puebla on a Sunday morning. For a few cents you can eat steaming *tamales,* with a mug of thick, hot *atole* and fortify it with some freshly barbecued lamb from the stands opposite. When I last went to Uruapan, we would go very early to the *portales* around the central plaza and eat *tamales* of blackberries growing wild in the surrounding hills and *atole* of freshly picked corn brought in by the Indians from the surrounding villages.

And just when I had decided that there could be no more *tamales,* the servants in a friend's house in Cuernavaca made me some *tamales del campo* (country *tamales*) of tortilla *masa* beaten with lard and salt and cooked between avocado leaves. The steamer was lined with leaves and the whole air around was perfumed with them. We ate them up that day with a dish of pork in green tomato sauce and tender zucchini squash.

The *tamales* from central Mexico have a white, spongy dough that bears no resemblance to the rather soggy, grayish dough of most commercial *tamales* available here. Today the Mexican housewife has a choice of many first-class flours prepared especially for *tamales* (Nabisco puts out an excellent one there, but so far it is not available in the United States.) The best is made of large white corn kernels called *cacahuazintle,* just like hominy, in some places called *pozole.* (*Pozole* is more generally known as a soup in which the large corn kernels are cooked.) The corn is boiled for a short time only and left to soak in a lye solution until each particle of the outside skin and little husky base can be removed. The corn must be cleaned with meticulous care before it is ground for the *tamal* dough or dried to be ground into flour.

Except for places where there is a large Mexican community in the United States or in special stores in New Mexico and Arizona, you will probably not be able to find the right type of corn. I have experimented a great deal with substitutes and find that the only satisfactory one is the Quaker product, Quick Grits, ground as fine as possible. It lacks a certain special flavor, but the texture is very good.

It is very important to have a good, pure lard for *tamales.* Since the only good natural lard that I could find in New York, Marhoefer, seems to have gone off the market, I have gone back to rendering my own (page 18). I absolutely refuse to buy the pallid white, tasteless stuff, full of stabilizers, that has flooded the market.

BASIC TAMAL DOUGH

About 3 dozen medium tamales about 3 inches long

A blender or spice grinder
1 pound Quaker Quick
  Grits
2 teaspoons salt

Grind the grits as fine as possible and add the salt.

An electric mixer
½ pound pork lard, at
  room temperature

Beat the lard in the mixer for 5 minutes.

The grits
1½ to 1¾ cups strong,
  lukewarm chicken
  broth

Gradually beat the grits, alternately with the broth, into the lard, beating well after each addition. (Take care that the broth is not too warm or it will melt the lard; see note.) Continue beating for about 3 minutes longer.

1 cup cold water

To test to see if the dough is ready, *put* (do not drop) a small piece of the dough onto the surface of the water. If it floats, the dough has been beaten sufficiently; if it sinks, continue beating and test again.

½ teaspoon baking powder

Mix the baking powder in well.

The dough made with the grits will appear to be very loose and almost watery. The broth must be added very gradually—I let it trickle down the rim of the mixing bowl while the mixture is being beaten. If the broth has melted the lard too much, then put the mixture into the refrigerator to cool off for a few minutes before you continue beating.

After you prepare the dough, follow the notes below on how to prepare and cook the *tamales*.

Notes on Making Tamales

1. *The corn husks.* It is usual for corn husks bought here to be trimmed and flattened ready for use. But if by chance you have some in their rough state—just as they were when removed from the ear—cut off the cupped part at the bottom of the leaf and trim off the pointed tip. When you get them the husks will be dried out and papery. To soften them ready for use, pour plenty of very hot water over them and leave them to soak for several hours. Shake them well to get rid of excess water and pat them dry with a towel.

2. *Making the tamales.* Smear a thin coating of the *tamal* dough over the broadest part of the husk, allowing for turning down about 1½ inches at the bottom broad part of the leaf and about 3 inches at the pointed top. Let us say, for a good-sized *tamal* spread the dough over an area approximately 3 inches wide and 3½ inches long.

Spread the filling down the middle of the dough. Fold the sides of the husk together firmly. Turn up the pointed end of the leaf and fold the broader end over it. Tear some of the husks lengthwise into narrow strips, and use one for tying each *tamal* across the top flap. The husks are water repellent, and since the dough is to be steamed, the idea is to form a water-tight package so that when the dough is cooked through it will be light and spongy. If moisture gets in it will be soggy.

3. *Cooking the tamales.* The most convenient way to cook *tamales* is a conventional steamer. You can, of course, improvise, but improvisations are not usually as efficient—a lot of good steam escapes and the cooking is not as even.

Fill the bottom of the steamer with water up to the level indicated and bring it to a boil. Line the top of the steamer with corn husks, covering the bottom and sides well. Stack the *tamales* upright, with the tied-down flaps upwards. For the best results, they should be packed firmly but not too tightly, because the husks swell out as the dough cooks. (I always find that a small batch of *tamales*, not firmly packed in the steamer, do not cook as well or as quickly and are more likely to absorb the condensed steam.)

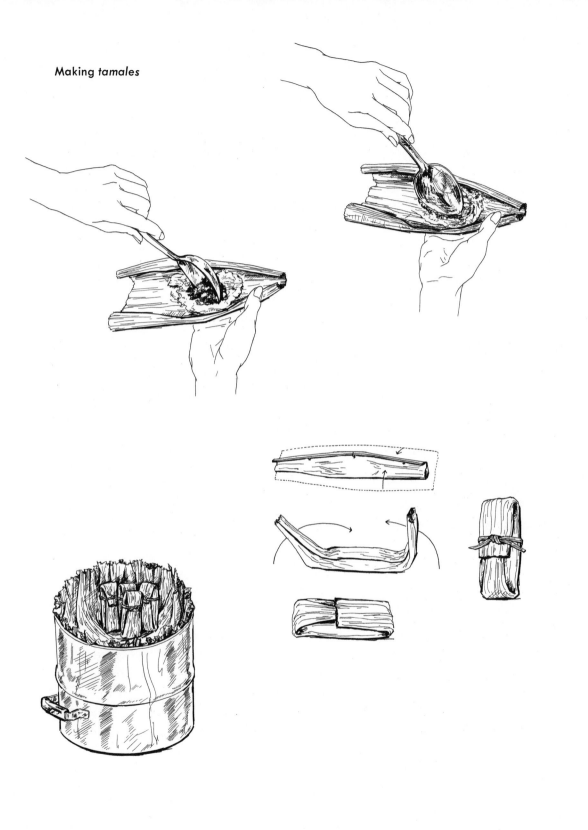

Making *tamales*

Cover the *tamales* with more corn husks. Cover the top of the steamer with a thick cloth—a piece of old toweling is best—to absorb the condensation from the lid of the steamer. Cover the steamer with a tightly fitting lid.

As the water in the bottom part comes to a boil, put a coin into it, put the top part of the steamer on, and let the *tamales* cook for about 2½ to 3 hours over a medium flame. Keep the water bubbling, but not boiling violently. That is the reason for the coin. You will be able to hear it dancing about, and it will tell you if the water goes off the boil or is getting dangerously low. If the water is allowed to go off the boil the *tamales* will be heavy. Keep a kettle of water simmering so that you can refill the steamer when necessary.

To test the *tamales* for doneness, remove one from the center, and one from the side of the steamer. As you open the husks, the dough should come away easily from the husks and be completely smooth. To make doubly sure, open up the *tamales* and see if they are spongy and well cooked throughout.

4. *Serving and storing the tamales.* Once cooked, *tamales* are very good tempered. They are wonderful eaten right away, straight out of the husks, but after they cool off they are also extremely good heated through very gently in their husks in an ungreased heavy frying pan, or on a griddle. Just keep turning them so that they heat through evenly and the husk gets slightly browned but does not burn. They can be refrigerated, and will keep well stored that way for about a week. It is best, however, to freeze them. To reheat, they can be wrapped in foil, put into a 350° oven still frozen, and heated through for about 30 minutes.

"BLIND" TAMALES

"Blind," or plain, unfilled *tamales* are served with Mole Poblano de Guajolote (page 199). Make them with the recipe for basic *tamal* dough. Spread the husks with a layer of dough about ¼ inch thick—about twice as thick as for filled *tamales*—then cook in the usual way.

TAMALES CON RAJAS Y QUESO
[*Tamales filled with chili strips and cheese*]

One of the most delicious yet simple fillings for *tamales* is a strip of the creamy white local Mexican cheese and roasted and peeled *chile poblano* or *chilaca*. As a substitute, use a thick strip of Muenster cheese and canned, peeled green chili.

TAMALES DE MOLE [*Tamales filled with mole poblano*]

If you have any *mole poblano* left over from making Mole Poblano de Guajolote (page 199) it makes a rich and savory filling for *tamales*. Put a tablespoonful of the sauce, together with some poached, shredded chicken, onto the dough.

TAMALES DE PICADILLO [*Tamales filled with meat*]

Fill the *tamales* with the *picadillo* used for Chiles Rellenos (page 263).

TAMALES DE PUERCO Y SALSA [*Tamales filled with pork and sauce*]

Fill the *tamales* with the taco filling on page 118.

PASTEL DE TAMAL [*Tamal pudding*]

With any "blind" or filled *tamales* left over you can make a very good *pastel* or *budín*—the same principle as a Budín Azteca (page 81), but using *tamales* instead of tortillas. When the *tamales* are cold, cut them into halves lengthwise and put a layer in the bottom of a casserole. Add the filling, then another layer of *tamales;* repeat, and top with a little tomato sauce and some strips of cheese.

Shredded chicken and *rajas,* with some corn kernels, make a very good filling. I have also had a delicious one with the same ingredients but an added layer of pumpkin flowers cooked with corn, *rajas,* and cream:

TAMALES NORTEÑOS [*Northern tamales*]

About 6 dozen tamales

The smallest *tamales* of all are the *norteños* from Coahuila and Chihuahua. They are as thick as a very fat finger and about 2½ inches long. The northerners express contempt for the large, fluffy white ones of central Mexico, which to them are all dough and very little else—which is true of the commercially made ones. The dough in these is almost overcome by the filling of pork in a sauce of *chiles anchos* strongly flavored with cumin.

FILLING

A saucepan
1¼ pounds pork shoulder
¼ onion, sliced
1 clove garlic, peeled
½ teaspoon salt
4 peppercorns
Water to cover

Cut the meat into 1-inch squares—it should have a little fat on it—and put it into the saucepan with the rest of the ingredients. Barely cover the meat with water and bring to a boil. Lower the flame and simmer the meat until it is tender—about 40 minutes.

Set the meat aside to cool off in the broth. Strain the meat, reserving the broth, and chop it roughly.

A griddle
3 chiles anchos (about 1½ ounces)

Heat the griddle and toast the chilies well, turning them from time to time so that they do not burn. Let them cool a little. When they are cool enough to handle, slit them open and remove the seeds and veins.

A blender or spice grinder
½ teaspoon cumin seeds

When the chilies have cooled off they should be crisp. Crumble them into the blender jar or spice grinder and grind them with the cumin seeds to a fine powder.

A frying pan
2 tablespoons lard
The chili powder
The chopped meat

Melt the lard, add the chili powder, and cook it for a few seconds, stirring it all the time. Add the meat and, continuing to cook, let it season for a minute or so.

1 cup reserved pork broth

Add the pork broth and let the mixture cook for about 5 minutes over a medium flame so that it reduces a little—there should be quite a bit of sauce left. Add salt as necessary.

Salt to taste

THE TAMALES

Basic Tamal Dough
(page 89)
2 teaspoons chili sauce
from the filling
6 dozen small corn husks,
soaked (page 90)

Make the basic dough but **do not add any baking powder.** Mix the chili sauce into the dough to give it a little color.

Using the smallest husks or the large ones cut in half, spread a scant tablespoon of the dough thinly over each husk, covering an area about 2 × 2 inches. Put a little of the meat with plenty of sauce into the center of the dough and fold the husk as you would for ordinary *tamales.*

A steamer

Stack the *tamales* in the steamer and cook for about 2 hours. Test to see if they are done (page 92).

TAMALES DE DULCE I [*Sweet tamales I*]

About 2 dozen tamales

Sweet *tamales* are very popular in Mexico, at breakfast or supper time with a cup of hot chocolate or *atole.* Do not attempt to serve them as a dessert. Their delicate flavor is completely lost after a meal.

They are exceptionally good heated through gently on a comal or iron frying pan until the husk is slightly browned and they are hot and spongy inside.

This is a recipe given to me by my friend Adriana, a fastidious cook from whom I have learned so much about the finer points in preparing Mexican dishes.

(*continued*)

½ recipe of Basic Tamal
    Dough (page 89),
    made with ½ butter
    and ½ lard and only
    ½ teaspoon salt (see note below)

1 tablespoon powdered   Mix the cinnamon, sugar, and nuts into the
    cinnamon   *tamal* dough. Spread a thin layer of dough
½ cup granulated sugar   onto the husks and fill each one with about 1
⅔ cup pecans, roughly   teaspoon of raisins.
    chopped
¾ cup raisins
2 dozen corn husks
A steamer   Steam as for ordinary *tamales* (page 90),
                             about 2 to 2½ hours.

TAMALES DE DULCE II [*Sweet tamales II*]

About 2 dozen tamales

½ recipe Basic Tamal
    Dough (page 89), made
    with ½ teaspoon
    salt only (see note below)
½ cup granulated sugar   Mix the sugar and syrup into the dough; it
2 tablespoons grenadine   should be a pale pink color.
    syrup
Approximately 2 dozen   Spread the husks with a thin layer of the
    corn husks   dough and fill each with a few raisins, *acitrón*
⅔ cup raisins   squares, and pine nuts. Steam as for ordinary
½ cup acitrón or candied   *tamales* (page 90), about 2½ hours.
    fruit, cut into small
    squares
½ cup pine nuts or blanched
    and slivered almonds
A steamer

Note: Even though these *tamales* are sweet, the chicken broth should
still be used for the dough.

TAMALES DULCES DE ELOTE FRESCO [*Sweet fresh corn tamales*]

About 2 dozen tamales

I had my first lesson on fresh corn *tamales* from my friend Chabela Marín from Jalisco. One morning we set out at promptly 5 A.M. and drove down to the big wholesale market in Jamaica (a part of Mexico City). For one square block there was nothing but mounds and mounds of fresh corn, and it was still coming in from the countryside around. It took at least an hour to choose twenty-five ears of just-right *cacahuazintle* corn, going from one pile to another and choosing one here and one there to meet Chabela's very high standards.

Once home again, she told me how to cut the cob at exactly the right spot to unravel the leaves without tearing them; to shave the kernels off as near to the core as possible, and to grind them to just the right texture on the *metate*. We then ground *piloncillo* (cones of raw sugar) with aniseeds and cinnamon, and gently melted the butter and lard so that it did not overheat. The most difficult of all was filling the fresh husks and folding them in just the right way to hold the loose, pasty dough firmly in place. It seemed like an endless process, but finally the *tamales* were cooking and that wonderful smell of fresh corn mixed with spices was filling the apartment.

This is an adaptation of one of the several Marín family recipes included in this book.

6 or 7 fresh, unhusked ears of corn, or enough to yield 4 cups kernels

Cut through each corn cob at the thickest part, just above the base. Unwrap the leaves very carefully, trying to keep them whole. Trim off the points. Rinse the leaves and set them aside to drain.

Cut the kernels from the cobs as near to the core as possible. You should have 4 cups of kernels.

A blender
½ cup water

Blend the kernels with the water, in two lots, until you have a rough-textured puree. You will have to keep stopping the blender and releasing the blades; but **do not add more water.** Set aside.

(continued)

A blender or spice grinder   Grind the spices to a fine powder.
2½ teaspoons aniseeds
    (3½ teaspoons
    ground)
8-inch stick cinnamon (4
    teaspoons ground)
1⅓ cups Quaker Quick   Mix the ground spices with the grits, sugar
    Grits (8 ounces),   and salt and stir into the corn puree.
    finely ground (as for
    Basic Tamal Dough,
    page 89)
The corn puree
1 cup dark-brown sugar
¼ teaspoon salt
A small saucepan   Melt the fats slowly; do not let them get
¼ pound butter (½ cup)   too hot. Stir them thoroughly into the corn
¼ pound lard (½ cup)   mixture and lastly add the baking powder.
¼ teaspoon baking   You will have a very loose paste.
    powder   Put about 1½ tablespoons of the *tamal* mix-
The fresh corn leaves   ture onto each leaf; if the leaf does not cover
Soaked corn husks, if   the mixture with a substantial overlap, then
    necessary   use a corn husk as well. Fold the husks in the
usual way (page 90) and place the *tamales*
horizontally into the steamer. Steam, as for
A steamer   ordinary *tamales* (page 90), for 3 hours.

I have obviously had to modify the original recipe by adding the grits to
make up for the lack of starch content in the corn here and by cooking
them horizontally, instead of vertically, in the steamer. (Unless you have
had a great deal of practice in folding the leaves over the paste, if the
husks are standing vertically in the steamer the paste will slip down to the
bottom of the husks, and you will have some bizarre-looking *tamales*.)

The traditional way of reheating these *tamales* through is to remove the
husks and keep turning them in a little melted butter on a griddle or in a
heavy frying pan.

TAMALES DE ELOTE FRESCO DE SAL
[*Savory fresh corn tamales*]

Grind the corn as in the recipe for Tamales Dulces de Elote Fresco above and add ¾ teaspoon salt and ½ teaspoon sugar. Fill with a large spoonful of plain tomato sauce (page 302), a strip of peeled *chile poblano* (in Jalisco the biting black-green *chile chilaca* would be used) and a slice of creamy white cheese, such as Muenster.

UCHEPOS FINGIDOS [*Mock uchepos*]

About 2 dozen uchepos

When the corn is new in August, everyone in Morelia is busy making *uchepos*. They are sold on the street corners and in the marketplaces and the smaller, typical restaurants.

There it is very simple. They just grind the corn, add a little salt, and fill the fresh corn husks with the mixture, which is then steamed just like ordinary *tamales*. But in this country the corn does not have the same starch content, so I have to fake them—and this is where the *fingidos* comes in. I would in most cases rather leave out a recipe than make drastic changes, but I just had to include the lovely dish Carne de Puerco con Uchepos (page 179), and I only hope my friends from Michoacán will forgive me.

6 or 7 fresh ears of corn, or enough to yield 4 cups kernels

Cut through each corn cob at the thickest part, just above the base. Unwrap the leaves very carefully, trying to keep them whole, and trim off the points. Rinse the leaves and set them aside to drain.

Cut the kernels from the cobs as near to the core as possible. You should have 4 cups of kernels.

A blender
½ cup water

Put the kernels into the blender with the water and grind them until they are very smooth. It will be much easier to do in two lots. You will have to keep stopping the

(*continued*)

blender and releasing the blades; but **do not add more water.** Set aside.

1⅓ cups Quaker Quick
  Grits (8 ounces)
¼ pound lard (½ cup)
½ cup chicken broth
¼ teaspoon granulated
  sugar
¼ teaspoon salt
¼ teaspoon baking
  powder
The corn puree

Following the instructions on pages 89–92, make a *tamal* dough with these ingredients.

Stir the corn puree in gradually. The mixture will be quite loose.

The fresh corn leaves
Soaked corn husks, if
  necessary

Put about 1½ tablespoons of the *tamal* mixture into each fresh corn leaf; if the leaf does not cover the *tamal* dough securely, then use a corn husk as well. Fold in the usual way (page 90) and place the *uchepos* horizontally into the steamer. Steam, as for ordinary *tamales* (page 90) for 3 hours.

A steamer

Another way to serve these is with Salsa de Tomate Verde Cocida (page 299), in which small pieces of a creamy cheese has been melted—Muenster is suitable. In Michoacán they would use the local *asadero* cheese, which is wonderfully creamy and melts easily. Or it is equally correct to eat them with sour cream and rock salt.

With any *uchepos* left over you can always make a savory *pastel* or *budín* on the same principle as the Budín Azteca (page 81). Let the *uchepos* get cold and cut them into halves lengthwise. Put a layer in the bottom of a casserole, then a layer of filling, and so on, topping off with some tomato sauce and strips of cheese. Rajas con Jitomate (page 261), with cheese and sour cream, makes an excellent filling. But there are no hard and fast rules, so you can please yourself.

TAMALES ESTILO VERACRUZANO [*Veracruz tamales*]

20 tamales

The *tamales* most typical of Veracruz are flavored with the banana leaf in which they are cooked, and also, more often than not, with the rather strongly anise-flavored leaf called *hoja santa* (*Piper sanctum*). (I put in a piece of avocado leaf, which was suggested to me as a mild substitute. It does give a delicious flavor.) The banana leaf does not absorb the fat like the corn husk, therefore less fat is needed. The dough itself is made of tortilla *masa* and not of specially prepared corn as it is in the center of Mexico; the result is a cooked dough that is damper, more finely textured, and a darker color than the basic *tamal* dough recipe given here.

In Veracruz they are quite often filled with fish. I have tried one filled with snook cooked in a green sauce and then wrapped in the large *hoja santa* leaf; it was extraordinarily delicious.

Have ready:

20 pieces of banana leaves
   approximately 9 × 7 inches
A steamer lined with banana leaves

THE FILLING

A saucepan
1 pound pork shoulder
¼ onion
1 clove garlic, peeled
½ teaspoon salt
Water to cover

Cut the pork into small cubes—it should have some fat on it—and put it with the onion, garlic, and salt into the pan. Cover with water and bring to a boil. Lower the flame and simmer the pork for about 35 minutes. Allow the pork to cool off in the broth, then strain the meat, reserving the broth, and set it aside.

A comal or griddle
3 chiles anchos

Heat the comal and toast the chilies lightly, turning them from time to time so they do not burn. While they are soft and pliable, remove the seeds and veins.

A bowl
Hot water to cover

Cover the chilies with hot water and let them soak for about 15 minutes, then remove with a slotted spoon and put into the blender jar.

(continued)

A blender
¼ small onion
1 clove garlic, peeled
1 medium tomato, broiled
    (*page 44*)
½ teaspoon salt
⅓ cup reserved pork broth

Add the remaining ingredients and blend to a smooth sauce.

A frying pan
1½ tablespoons lard

Melt the lard, and when it is hot but not smoking, cook the chili sauce for about 5 minutes, stirring it all the time so that it does not stick.

The cooked pork
½ cup reserved pork broth

Add the pork and broth to the sauce and let the mixture cook for about 5 minutes over a medium flame until it is all well seasoned and the liquid has reduced a little. Set aside.

THE DOUGH

An electric mixer
¼ pound lard (½ cup) at
    room temperature

Beat the lard for 5 minutes.

A bowl
2 cups masa harina
1¼ cups cold water
1 teaspoon salt
¾ cup reserved lukewarm
    pork broth

Meanwhile, mix the *masa* to a dough with the cold water and salt.

Beat the broth and dough alternately into the lard. Continue beating for about 5 minutes more. (Don't try and float a piece of the dough; it will be a much softer and damper consistency than that for ordinary *tamales.*)

The banana leaf pieces
The dough

Pass the leaves quickly over a bare flame to make them a little more flexible. Spread 1 large tablespoon of the dough over an area about 4 × 3 inches and ⅛ to ¼ inch thick. Put

The meat
The sauce
3 avocado leaves, broken
    into pieces
The steamer

two cubes of the meat and a little of the sauce into the center of the dough, then add a small piece of avocado leaf. Fold the edges of the banana leaf over until they completely cover the dough and filling. Stack the *tamales,* one on top of the other, in the steamer. Cover them with more leaves and then cover the top of the steamer with a thick cloth or piece of toweling. Steam, in the normal way (page 90), for 1 hour.

These *tamales* freeze extremely well. To reheat put them—frozen and covered with foil—into a 350° oven for about 40 minutes.

MUK-BIL POLLO [*Chicken and pork tamale pie*]

6 servings

This is a Yucatecan *tamal* pie, filled with a highly seasoned mixture of chicken and pork and cooked in a banana leaf. It is the Mayan *tamal* pie offered to the dead on All Saints' Day, traditionally accompanied by a cup of hot chocolate. *Muk-bil* literally means "to put in the ground" or to cook in a *pib.*

John L. Stevens, in *Incidents of Travel in Yucatán,* describes the feast of *todos los santos* in the middle of the nineteenth century in Yucatán:

. . . and besides the usual ceremonies of the Catholic Church throughout the world, there is one peculiar to Yucatán, derived from the customs of the Indians and called Mukpipoyo. On this day every Indian, according to his means, purchases and burns a certain number of consecrated candles, in honor of his deceased relatives, and in memory of each member of his family who has died within the year. Besides this, they bake in the earth a pie consisting of a paste of Indian corn, stuffed with pork and fowls, and seasoned with chili, and during the day every good Yucateco eats nothing but this. In the interior, where the Indians are less civilised, they religiously place a portion of this composition out of doors, under a tree, or in some retired place, for their deceased friends to eat, and they say that the portion thus set apart is always eaten, which induces the belief that the dead may be enticed back by appealing to the same appetites which govern them when living; but this sometimes accounts for by malicious and skeptical persons, who say that in every neighbourhood there are other Indians, poorer than those who can afford to regale their deceased relatives, and these consider it no sin, on a matter of this kind, to step between the living and the dead.

We have reason to remember this fete from one untoward circumstance. A friendly neighbour, who, besides visiting us frequently with his wife and daughter, was in the habit of sending us fruit and dulces more than we could eat, this day, on top of a large undisposed-of present, sent us a huge piece of mukbipoyo. It was as hard as an oak-plank, and as thick as six of them; and having already overtasked ourselves to reduce the pile on the tables, when this came, in a fit of desperation we took it out into the courtyard and buried it. There it would have remained until this day but for a malicious dog which accompanied them on their next visit; he passed into the courtyard, rooted it up, and, while we were pointing to the empty platters as our acknowledgment of their kindness, this villainous dog sneaked through the sala and out at the front door with the pie in his mouth, apparently grown bigger since it was buried.

The dish is still cooked in the villages in *pibs* and comes out with a golden, crisp top and a faintly smoky flavor. Very often the chicken will just be jointed, but it makes it a great deal easier to serve if the bones are removed.

As you can imagine, it is a very solid dish, and needs perhaps just a green salad with it.

THE FAT FOR THE DOUGH

A small frying pan
½ pound pork fat, cut into small cubes
1 teaspoon water in which the achiote *(see below) was soaked*

Heat the fat over a medium flame, or in the oven, until the lard renders out of it. Turn the pieces from time to time so that they do not burn but become evenly crisp and brown. Add the *achiote* water to give the fat a little color, then set both melted lard and crisp fat bits aside.

THE FILLING

A large saucepan
A 3-pound chicken
½ pound pork shoulder
4 cloves garlic, toasted
      (page 43)
¼ teaspoon oregano,
      toasted (page 43)
1½ teaspoons salt
Water to barely cover

Cut the chicken into serving pieces and the pork into 1-inch squares. Put them into the pan with the other ingredients and barely cover with water. Bring to a boil, lower the flame, and simmer until the meat is just tender—the chicken should take about 35 minutes; the pork a little longer.

Strain the meat, reserving the broth. Remove the bones from the chicken. Set the meat aside.

A small saucepan
1½ cups reserved meat
      broth
1½ tablespoons masa
      harina

Stir the *masa harina* gradually into the broth. Bring to a boil, lower the flame, and stir the mixture until it thickens a little. Set the thickened broth aside.

A blender
¼ teaspoon peppercorns
⅛ teaspoon cumin seeds
¼ teaspoon oregano,
      toasted (page 43)
1 tablespoon mild white
      vinegar
¼ teaspoon salt
1 tablespoon softened
      achiote (page 12),
      soaking liquid
      reserved
2 cloves garlic, peeled

Grind all the seasonings together to a smooth sauce and set aside.

A frying pan
3 tablespoons rendered
      pork fat
⅓ medium onion, finely
      chopped

Melt the pork fat and fry the chopped onion, chili, green pepper, and *epazote*, without browning, until they are soft.

(continued)

1 **chile habanero,**
    or cayenne, *whole*
½ medium green pepper,
    finely chopped
1 large sprig epazote
The ground seasonings

Add the ground seasonings and continue cooking the mixture for about 3 minutes.

1 large tomato, skinned,
    seeded, and chopped
    (page 43) or
¾ cup canned tomatoes
The cooked meats

Add the tomato and the cooked meats to the ingredients in the pan and continue cooking the mixture for 10 minutes over a medium flame. Set aside.

PREPARING THE PAN

A metal baking pan about
    8 × 8 × 2 inches
4 lengths of string, each
    measuring about 30
    inches (see note
    below)
Some large pieces of
    banana leaves

Lay 2 pieces of the string parallel across the length of the dish and the other 2 pieces across the width—there will be a large overlap for tying.

Quickly pass the leaves over a flame to make them more pliable, and line the dish with them, smooth, shiny side up (see note), so that they overlap the pan by about 5 inches all the way around. Set the pan aside while the dough is prepared.

Preheat the oven to 350°.

A mixing bowl
3½ cups masa harina
2 teaspoons salt
¼ teaspoon hot paprika
2 cups boiling water
The melted fat and fat
    pieces

Mix the dry ingredients together and add the boiling water, mixing it in well with a wooden spoon.

When the dough is cool enough to handle, work in the melted lard with the little bits of crisp fat. Knead the dough well.

THE PIE

The prepared pan
The dough

The filling
The thickened broth
A piece of banana leaf
approximately 11 ×
11 inches
The remaining dough

Press about two-thirds of the dough into the prepared pan to form a crust about ¼ inch thick on the bottom and sides of the pan.

Put the filling into the lined pan and pour the thickened broth over it.

With the smooth, shiny side of the leaf upward, press out the remaining dough onto it about ¼ inch thick. This will be the cover for the pie.

Carefully turn the leaf upside down so that the dough completely covers the pan, with enough of an overlap to seal it together with the dough around the sides of the pan.

Fold the leaves over the top of the pie and tie them down firmly with the string.

Bake the *muk-bil pollo* for 1½ hours and serve it immediately (see note below).

In Yucatán they do not use strings to tie up the pie. They use the hard central vein of the banana leaf and make the rest by tying together ¼-inch strips torn off a banana leaf, with the grain. It is a lot of work but it looks nicer, and I always do it.

If you look at the banana leaf you will see that it has a shiny, smooth side, and a less shiny ridged underside. Always put the *tamal* dough onto the shiny side.

If you can time it so that you serve it hot, straight out of the oven, it is well worthwhile. However, if you have to reheat it, then put it into the oven in a water bath to keep the dough soft. It freezes quite well cooked. Put it frozen into a 350° oven in a water bath to reheat.

Appetizers (*Antojitos*)

Without doubt the Mexicans are the most persistent noshers in the world; who wouldn't be, with such an endless variety of things to nibble on along the streets and in the marketplaces? A whole book could be devoted to that alone. Even if you think you are not hungry you will be enticed, by the smell, the artistry with which the food is displayed, or just because it is something new to try, for Mexican cooks are among the most creative anywhere. Next time you wander around the streets of any Mexican city or small town, pause a little at the *taquería* on the corner and see if your mouth doesn't start to water as the floppy, hot tortillas are crammed with shredded meat or *carnitas* and doused in a robust green tomato sauce from an enormous black *molcajete*, or as the *quesadillas* are patted out and stuffed with squash flowers and browned on a comal. Any hour of the day and well into the night there will always be groups of people standing and eating with great concentration—for this is no time to talk.

I often think of what is perhaps my favorite of all *taquerías*, one I was introduced to only last summer in the Bajío. The whole town knows that promptly at five in the afternoon the pig that Pasquelitos has killed and cooked will be coming out of the oven, and long before that the line starts to form. Everything goes by the board so people can get there on time, for even a 120-pound porker doesn't last forever, especially when the flesh is so succulent. The tortillas are straight off the comal and the *guacamole* is simple and delicious, made of the little black avocados of the region that have that subtle flavor of anise and hazelnuts.

In Ensenada it is the pismo clam that is the favorite of the sidewalk carts; in the La Paz market the *tacos* are made of shredded fish, and in Morelia they are made of brains sprinkled with chopped coriander. As you wander around the markets of central Mexico you will be offered completely pre-Hispanic food, small fish wrapped in corn husks and cooked over charcoal, or *tlacoyos*, oval pieces of rather thick dough filled with a paste of beans; at the back of the Oaxaca market you can snack on toasted grasshoppers and the perennial favorite everywhere, ears of corn hot from the steamer or roasted to a dark brown over charcoal. And with all the marvelous *antojitos* that exist in Yucatán, I can't help but raise my eyebrows every time I see a little cart, proudly displaying a sign "hot dogs," being pushed around the cathedral plaza. If you are looking for something less substantial there are always peanut and pumpkin seeds, still warm and their shells blackened slightly from the recent toasting, and in Chihuahua the tiniest acorns I have ever seen, slightly sweet and at the same time bitter.

At practically any street corner a poor woman may come along with her charcoal brazier and a large metal cooking sheet with a shallow circular well in the center for the fat and wide, sloping sides to hold the cooked filling or the newly fried *enchiladas*. I shall never forget the streets around the Puebla market at dusk on a Saturday evening. Everybody seemed to be scurrying around with braziers, charcoal, or baskets of food, and the smoke drifting out of every other doorway brought with it the pungent fragrance of *ocote*—the thin strips of resinous pine—used to fire the charcoal.

As I travel alone around the country, I have plenty of time in the evenings to wander around the streets, and one thing that never ceases to fascinate me is the ingenuity of the cooking arrangements on the small carts that are set up on street corners. An oil lamp will be slung from the awning overhead, somewhere a gas tank will be wired to a small stove; a large wooden chopping block and a cleaver are a must, as are little dishes of *chiles en escabeche*, shredded lettuce, sliced tomatoes, various fiery sauces, and piles of chopped onion—something for everybody's taste. If the carts' owners don't cook on the spot, there will be an arrangement like an ice-cream stand, and the *barbacoa* and tortillas will come steaming from their deep wells.

To combat the midday heat, stands covered with decorative green leaves will be selling skinned mangoes, cut like flowers and stuck onto thin sticks like lollipops, as well as another recent innovation: small paper cones, held in racks, and brimming over with mixed fruits—watermelon, melon, pine-apple, and cucumber—and everything sprinkled with salt and powdered *chile pequín* as it is served. And later on in the year, sliced *jícama,* cucumbers opened up lengthwise like flowers, and hot yams will appear.

My maid said to me one day when I lived in Mexico, "Of course you got sick this afternoon. You ate an avocado at lunchtime and then you lost your temper." Antonio Mayo Sánchez in his book *Cocina Mexicana* writes a delightful introduction to his chapter on *antojitos,* reminding me of this incident and the folklore that has grown around the strong links between food and the emotions: "Never eat chocolate, eggs, or avocados, if you are in a bad humor; eat sugar for shock and stress." In this same vein, blood-curdling spectacles such as bullfights and boxing call for lusty foods like *carnitas, barbacoa, cecina enchilada* with strong, *picante* sauces—chicken and fish would never do. And everyone knows that if the bulls are bad or the boxers weak, then sales will be down. The cinema, on the other hand, as Sr. Sanchez reminds us, is a product of Anglo-Saxon sangfroid and calls for nothing more hearty than popcorn, Cokes, and commercial candies.

Food vendors will push their little barrows for miles to post themselves outside some big institution or government office, hospital, school, or prison to offer sustenance to the constant flow of people coming and going. Whenever a crowd gathers to watch the police or firemen at work, out of nowhere appears a little man pushing his cart of goodies to sustain the excited onlookers. And so Sr. Sanchez once more reminds me both of the scenes that I took for granted during my years in Mexico and the brilliant cartoons of Abel Quezada in *Excelsior,* whose devastatingly witty pen comments on the foibles of his fellow countrymen. He concludes: "Any of the dozens of varieties make ideal snacks to appease the appetite while waiting for dinner or to bolster the stomach against the effect of cocktails when entertaining guests, or simply to justify their very name *antojito*—a little whim."

In addition to the recipes below, some of the recipes in the seafood section (page 218) are meant to be served as appetizers.

CARNE COCIDA EN LIMÓN   [*Meat marinated in lime juice*]

4 servings

Not so very long ago, the *pulquerías* of Mexico City were renowned for their little cups of fiery shrimp broth and spicy *botanas* (*botana* literally means "a plug or stopple," is used colloquially for "snack"), provided free of charge to encourage a greater thirst.

Possibly nowhere else in the republic could the *botanas* of Tuxtla Gutiérrez be rivaled. Unfortunately only men are allowed in the *cantinas,* and over a glass or two of beer they can sample perhaps as many as seven or eight: fried fish roe, crisp *chicharrón* in a fresh sauce, crispy pork ribs and chitterlings, fried beans and fresh white cheeses, little cups of a *picante* broth of dried shrimps or fresh water snails (*shote*), to name a few. *Carne cocida en limón* is a very unusual and refreshing one on a hot day.

A glass or china bowl
½ cup lime juice
½ pound ground sirloin,
    absolutely free of fat
1 small tomato, finely
    chopped
2 tablespoons finely
    chopped onion
3 or 4 chiles serranos with
    seeds, finely chopped
¼ teaspoon salt, or to taste

Mix the lime juice well into the ground meat and set it aside to "cook" in the refrigerator for at least 4 hours.

Mix in the rest of the ingredients and set the meat aside to season for at least 2 hours more.

Serve with crisp tortillas, either toasted or fried.

BOTANAS DE CAMARÓN SECO [*Dried shrimp snacks*]

About 24 botanas

Another *botana* from Tuxtla Gutiérrez.

A blender
¼ pound flour
1 cup cold water
¼ heaped teaspoon salt

Blend the flour, water, and salt together for 2 minutes and leave the batter to stand for at least 2 hours.

A bowl
¾ cup dried shrimps
Hot water to cover

Cover the shrimps with hot water and leave them to soak for 20 minutes—no longer.

A bowl and beater
1 egg white
½ medium onion, finely chopped
5 chiles serranos with seeds, finely chopped

Beat the egg white stiff and fold it into the batter.

Drain the shrimps and add them, with the chopped onion and chilies, to the batter.

A frying pan
Peanut or safflower oil (½-inch deep)
Paper toweling

Heat the oil and drop tablespoons of the mixture into it, a few at a time. Fry the *botanas* until they are golden brown, turning them over once. Drain them on the paper toweling and serve immediately.

CARNITAS [*Little pieces of browned pork*]

6 servings

Certainly throughout the central part of Mexico, *carnitas*—literally "little meats"—are the very favorite snack. They can be crisp or juicy, with a little bone or without, and sometimes mixed with the soft rind and little bits of fat all chopped up together. Whatever you choose, douse it well with a fresh sauce—Salsa Mexicana Cruda (page 297), Salsa de Tomate

Verde Cruda (page 297), or Guacamole (see below)—and wrap it in a hot, floppy tortilla—the simplest and most delicious *taco*.

A flameproof dish
3 pounds pork shoulder,
    skin and bone
    removed (see note
    below)
Cold water to barely cover
2 teaspoons salt, or to taste

Cut the meat, with the fat, into strips about 2 × ¾ inches. Barely cover the meat with water, add the salt, and bring it to a boil, uncovered.

Lower the flame and let the meat continue cooking briskly until all the liquid has evaporated—by this time it should be cooked through but not falling apart.

Lower the flame a little and continue cooking the meat until all the fat has rendered out of it. Keep turning the meat until it is lightly browned all over—about 1 hour and 10 minutes.

There is no need for an expensive cut. Shoulder, butt, or country-style spareribs are all suitable.

The meat will get more evenly cooked if the dish is rather large and shallow. Do not add too much water at the beginning or the meat will fall apart at the frying stage. If the meat is still fairly hard when the water has evaporated, then add a little more water and continue cooking. Choose pork that has a fair amount of fat or you will have to add some lard for it to brown properly.

GUACAMOLE [*Avocado dip*]

About 1¾ to 2 cups

The word *guacamole* comes from the Nahuatl words *ahuacatl* (avocado) and *molli* (a mixture, or concoction). In Mexico it is often eaten at the beginning of the meal with warm tortillas—and that is how one can really savor it—or with *tacos* and sour cream, rice, or *chicharrón*.

(*continued*)

A molcajete *or mortar and pestle*

¼ *small onion, finely chopped*

1 *or* 2 chiles serranos

2 *sprigs fresh coriander*

¼ *teaspoon salt, or to taste*

1 *very large or* 2 *medium avocados*

Grind the onion, chilies, coriander, and salt together to a smooth paste.

1 *large tomato* (½ *pound*)

¼ *small onion, finely chopped*

2 *sprigs fresh coriander, finely chopped*

Cut the avocado in half. Remove the seed and scoop out the flesh. Mash the flesh roughly with the chili paste in the *molcajete*.

Skin, seed and chop the tomato (page 43) and add it, with the chopped onion and coriander, to the *guacamole*. Mix well and serve immediately.

This is such a beautiful concoction, pale green flecked with the red of the tomato pieces and the darker green of the coriander, and a delight aesthetically if served in a *molcajete*, where it rightfully belongs. It is so delicate it is best eaten the moment it is made. There are many suggestions about keeping it—leaving the pit in, adding a little lime juice, not adding the salt until last, putting it into an airtight container. They all help a little, but in no time at all that delicate green has aged.

There are many variations—making it with *tomates verdes*, or leaving out the tomato altogether, mashing the avocado with just a little chili and salt and a suspicion of lime juice. Practically anything goes, but within certain limits, which does not include the unnecessary additions that I see in most pedestrian cookbooks.

SALPICÓN DE JAIBA [*Shredded crabmeat and chopped vegetables*]

Enough to fill 12 small tortillas

One of my favorite regional restaurants was until recently in the Hotel Inglaterra in Tampico, and it was the owner, Fidel Loredo, who is a truly creative and enthusiastic cook, who introduced this *salpicón* to me.

A *frying pan*	Heat the oil and cook the onion gently, without browning, until it is soft.
¼ *cup peanut or safflower oil*	
⅓ *medium onion, finely chopped*	
½ *cup celery, finely chopped*	Add the celery, chilies, and crabmeat and fry until they just begin to brown slightly.
5 **chiles serranos** *with seeds, finely chopped*	
1 *cup cooked, shredded crabmeat*	
3 *tablespoons finely chopped fresh coriander*	Lastly, add the coriander and salt and cook for 1 minute more.
Salt to taste	

Serve with hot tortillas.

This is also a simple and delightful filling for Tacos (page 116). The delicate meat of the hard-shell crabs should be used, and 5 large ones should yield 1 good cup of meat. I always choose female crabs so that the eggs and the crab fat can be used to enhance the flavor even more. (To prepare live crabs, see Jaibas en Chilpachole, page 152. Use the eggs and fat but not the gills.)

SOPES

Just watch a Mexican peasant, cook, or anyone who loves to prepare food handle a piece of tortilla dough. In a trice it will have been patted and coaxed into any one of a hundred shapes or sizes, and filled, garnished, or mixed with any leftovers from the previous meal. One of these is the *sope—* or *garnacha* or *picada*, depending on where you are in Mexico and what the topping consists of—which can be served as an appetizer or first course.

The instructions below are based on the tortilla recipe on page 62.

After you prepare the tortilla dough, take a small piece and roll it into a ball of roughly about 1¼ inches; flatten it in the tortilla press until it is rather thicker than the usual tortilla and about 3½ inches across. Cook lightly on one side on the comal, turn it over, and as you cook the second side pinch up the edges of the cooked side to form a small ridge, or "retaining wall" for the sauce and filling. Flip it back onto the first side and press down the center of the *sope* to cook the dough a little more. If it appears to be too thick and doughy in the center, then take off a layer of the dough. Put a small amount of melted lard into the center of the *sope* and let it warm through and sizzle for a few seconds. Then fill with one or more of the fillings below. (The shells can be kept hot in a cloth or plastic bag and then, at the last moment, heated through on the comal with the fat and the filling added.)

FILLINGS FOR SOPES

A layer of Frijoles Refritos (page 282), some Papas con Chorizos (page 124) with *chipotle en vinagre,* chopped onion and crumbled white cheese

Frijoles Refritos (page 282), *chorizo,* Salsa de Tomate Verde Cruda (page 297), chopped onion, and crumbled white cheese

Salsa de Tomate Verde Cruda (page 297), chopped onion, crumbled white cheese, and/or sour cream

Salsa de Chile Cascabel (page 303), chopped onion, crumbled white cheese, and/or sour cream

Frijoles Refritos (page 282), shredded meat, a little Salsa Ranchera (page 299), shredded lettuce, radish slices, and crumbled white cheese

Shredded chicken or pork with Salsa de Tomate Verde Cruda (page 297), chopped onion, and crumbled white cheese

TACOS

The most common and popular *antojito* of all is the everyday *taco.* You just take a warm tortilla, put some cooked and shredded meat across it, douse the meat with a sauce, and roll up the tortilla. In true Mexican style, while you tip one end of it toward your mouth you should curl the other up with your little finger so that none of the sauce is lost.

Not quite so common is the fried *taco*. You fill it as before and secure it with a toothpick. Then you fry it in hot lard—which gives a much better flavor to the tortilla than oil. As it becomes golden brown underneath, turn it over and fry the side that has the opening—it will then be easy to take the toothpick out without the *taco* opening up. It should not be too tightly closed, on the other hand, because just before it is eaten a spoonful or so of sauce, or *guacamole* and sour cream, will be put just inside and over the opening.

If you want to follow the general Mexican rule, which says *"no deben tronar"* (they mustn't thunder or explode) and which applies to most of the *antojitos, tacos* should not be fried crisp. Of course there are exceptions to this, as there are to all of these rules, for in parts of Jalisco and Sinaloa they make thin tortillas especially for crisp *tacos,* and in Yucatán the *cotzito* is a *taco,* tightly rolled around some shredded meat and fried crisp. In Chihuahua and Baja California they just double the tortilla over and fry it—but it is practically never fried crisp.

Fried *tacos* should be served immediately after they come out of the pan with some sauce, and sour cream if desired—the serving of 2 or 3 *tacos* per person can be garnished with some shredded lettuce, sliced tomato, onion rings, and/or radishes cut like flowers.

Some suggested fillings for *tacos* follow, but you can use your imagination and fill them with whatever you happen to have on hand.

FILLINGS FOR ORDINARY TACOS

Carnitas (page 112) and Salsa de Tomate Verde Cruda (page 297)
Shredded chicken or pork, well seasoned with Salsa Cruda Mexicana (page 297)
Cooked and shredded lamb with Salsa Borracha (page 306)
Birria (page 185) with finely chopped onion
Cochinita Pibil (page 169) and Salsa (page 171)
Queso Relleno (page 133) and Salsa Picante a la Yucateca (page 306)
Salpicón de Jaiba (page 114)
Picadillo for Chiles Rellenos (page 263) and in fact any meat left over that has been cooked in a *mole* or *pipián*—or anything you like.

FILLINGS FOR FRIED TACOS

Cooked and shredded chicken or pork, well seasoned; serve with Chile Cascabel Sauce (page 303) or Guacamole (page 113) and sour cream

Papas con Chorizos (page 124); serve with Salsa de Tomate Verde Cruda (page 297)

Puerco en Salsa de Jitomate (see below); garnish with shredded lettuce, onion rings, sliced tomato, and radish flowers

Pork in Salsa de Tomate Verde Cruda (page 297); garnish with shredded lettuce, onion rings, sliced tomato, and radish flowers

Lamb, cooked and shredded and heated up in Salsa Borracha (page 306); serve with onion rings and lettuce

Pork, cooked and shredded and heated up in Salsa de Chile Pasilla (page 304); serve with sour cream and chopped onion

Birria (page 185); serve with onion rings, shredded lettuce, sliced tomatoes, and radish flowers

PUERCO EN SALSA DE JITOMATE [*Pork in tomato sauce*]

Enough for 12 to 15 small tacos

A blender

2 medium tomatoes (¾ pound), broiled (page 44)

1 clove garlic, peeled

¼ teaspoon salt

Blend the tomatoes with the garlic and salt until almost smooth. Set aside.

A small frying pan

2 tablespoons peanut or safflower oil

¼ medium onion, sliced

The tomato puree

2 fresh chiles jalapeños with seeds, finely sliced

Heat the lard and cook the onion, without browning, until it is soft. Add the tomato puree and the sliced chilies and let the mixture cook over a medium flame for about 5 minutes.

1⅓ cups boiled and
*   shredded pork (about*
*   1 pound) (page 42)*

Add the meat and continue cooking the mixture for 8 to 10 minutes, or until it is all well seasoned and the sauce fairly dry.

Fresh *chiles jalapeños* seem to be more and more in evidence in the markets, and they give the sauce a very special flavor. If you substitute the long thin *chiles cayennes* or the smaller *serranos,* use about 6, removing quite a lot of the seeds.

CHALUPAS [*Tortilla "boats"*]

In Mexico the word *chalupa* means "small canoe," and the *antojito* of that name is boat-shaped and pinched up at the edges. You can make them by rolling a 1½-inch ball of tortilla dough (page 62) into a narrow cylinder about 5 inches long and ½ inch wide slantwise into the tortilla press. Cook as you would for Sopes (page 115) and garnish with shredded pork or chicken, Salsa de Tomate Verde Cruda (page 297), finely chopped onion, and some crumbled white cheese.

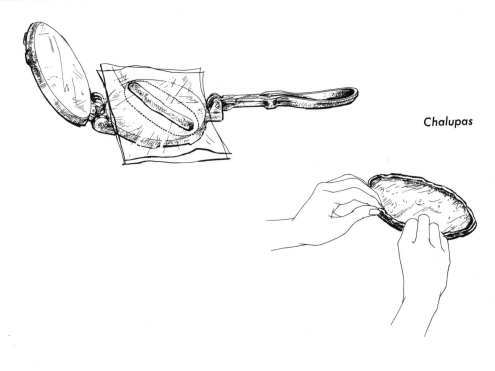

Chalupas

TOSTADAS [*Fried and garnished tortillas*]

For *tostadas* make some thin tortillas (page 62) about 5 inches across, fry them crisp in lard or oil, and garnish them with the following: a layer of Frijoles Refritos (page 282), a few small pieces of *chile jalapeño en escabeche*, or *chile chipotle en vinagre* or *adobado*, some poached and shredded chicken breast, shredded lettuce, a slice of tomato, grated cheese, sliced radish, and sometimes a dollop of sour cream. There are no hard and fast rules, and it depends very much on how high you can stack it and eat it without a major disaster.

QUESADILLAS [*Filled tortilla "turnovers"*]

Quesadillas are small filled "turnovers" of tortilla dough; they can be either toasted on a comal or fried in lard.

For 12 *quesadillas,* make a dough with 1½ cups *masa harina* and just under 1 cup cold water. Roll the dough into 12 balls, each about 1½ inches in diameter. Press one of the balls out to a rather thick tortilla about 4¼ to 4½ inches across. To fill them, use one of the fillings on page 122 and follow one of the methods below.

1. After pressing the tortilla out, remove the top polyethylene bag, place a tablespoonful of the filling on one half of the tortilla—away from the edge. Lift the bottom bag up, press the other half of the tortilla over the filling, and press the edges together well.

2. Put the tortilla onto your hand and fill it and seal it—it helps to grease your hands lightly.

If you wish to prepare the *quesadillas* ahead of time, make them and fill them but keep them covered with a damp cloth or in a polyethylene bag so that the dough does not dry out.

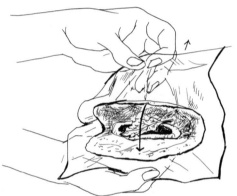

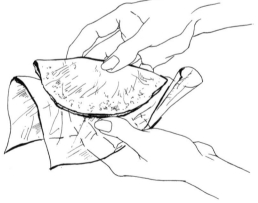

COOKING QUESADILLAS ON THE COMAL OR GRIDDLE

This is the style preferred by those who love the rustic flavor and texture of ground maize. Grease the comal very lightly and cook the *quesadillas* on both sides and then cook the broad, curved part. It should be well cooked on the outside, with some dark brown patches on the dough. The comal should be over a medium flame so that the *quesadillas* do not get burned on the outside while staying raw inside. Serve immediately; they become leathery if left to stand around or kept warm.

FRYING QUESADILLAS

If you can bear to use lard, do so, for the flavor is so much better than oil. It should be just less than ½ inch deep. Heat it well and fry the *quesadillas* until a deep golden brown on both sides. (Like the *tacos* in central Mexico, *quesadillas* are never crisp throughout when they are fried; I think this rather doughy texture takes some getting used to.) Serve immediately. If you really have to reheat them, immerse them in very hot fat for a minute or so.

FILLINGS FOR QUESADILLAS

The ordinary, everyday filling is simple and very delicious. The Mexicans use some strips of the white stringy *queso de Oaxaca,* a strip of roasted and peeled *chile poblano,* salt, and some fresh *epazote* leaves. The canned peeled, green chilies can substitute for the *poblanos,* and I suggest Muenster cheese, which melts easily and is creamy. If you have no fresh *epazote,* then soak a dried leaf or two—or just leave it out, but you will miss its *muy mexicano* taste. Other fillings:

Sesos para Quesadillas (page 125).

Papas con Chorizos (page 124).

Flor de Calabaza para Quesadillas (page 124).

Huitlacoche para Quesadillas (page 123).

HUITLACOCHE PARA QUESADILLAS
[Corn fungus filling for quesadillas]

Enough for 12 quesadillas

I quite imagine that huitlacoche, the corn fungus, may have been the ambrosia of the Aztec gods. I never find it is quite enough to eat *quesadillas* filled with them, so every summer that I am in Mexico I go to the Bola Roja in Puebla to eat a large plateful of the fungus served with strips of creamy white cheese and lots of hot tortillas.

The word is derived from the Nahuatl words *huitlatl,* meaning "excrement," or "excrescence," and *cochtli* or *cochin,* of uncertain etymology, although, according to Sahagún, it may be connected in some way to the verb *coch,* which means "to sleep"—(T. Sullivan).

About 1 pound
   huitlacoche
A frying pan
3 to 4 tablespoons peanut
   or safflower oil
¼ medium onion, finely
   chopped
1 clove garlic, peeled and
   finely chopped
2 small **chiles poblanos,**
   roasted, peeled, and
   cut into strips (page
   45), or 2 canned,
   peeled green chilies
The **huitlacoche**
1 large sprig **epazote**
¼ teaspoon salt, or to taste

Cut the fungus from the corn cobs and chop it roughly. Set it aside.

Heat the oil and cook the onion and garlic, without browning, until they are soft. Add the chili strips, *huitlacoche, epazote,* and salt and cook over a medium flame until the mixture is soft and the liquid from the fungus has evaporated—about 15 minutes.

FLOR DE CALABAZA PARA QUESADILLAS
[*Pumpkin blossom filling for quesadillas*]

Enough for 12 quesadillas

2 bunches pumpkin or
    squash flowers—
    about 28 or 45
    respectively
A frying pan
3 tablespoons peanut or
    safflower oil
1 clove garlic, peeled and
    finely chopped
1 clove garlic, finely
    chopped
1 small chile poblano,
    roasted, peeled, and
    cut into strips
    (page 45), or 1
    canned, peeled green
    chili, or 2 fresh chiles
    serranos
¼ teaspoon salt, or to taste

Cut the stems off the flowers and strip off the stringy green sepals. Chop the flowers roughly and set them aside.

Heat the oil and cook the onion and garlic gently, without browning, until they are soft. Add the rest of the ingredients and cook them, uncovered, over a medium flame until they are tender and the juice from the flowers has evaporated—about 15 minutes.

The filling must not be watery or it will make the dough soggy.

PAPAS CON CHORIZOS [*Potato and chorizo filling for quesadillas*]

Enough for 12 quesadillas

½ pound red bliss or
    other waxy new
    potatoes, cooked
A small frying pan
3 chorizos

Skin the potatoes and cut them into small cubes. Set aside.

Remove the skin from the *chorizos*, crumble them, and let them cook slowly over a low flame, stirring them from time to time.

The potatoes
2 *canned* chiles chipotles
    en vinagre *or*
    adobades *with their*
    seeds, chopped

It should take about 10 minutes before they
are cooked through and the fat has rendered
out—do not let them become hard and overcooked.

Add the potatoes and chilies and let the
mixture cook over a medium flame, stirring
it from time to time until the potato has
browned just a little. Set the mixture aside to
cool off a little before using.

SESOS PARA QUESADILLAS [*Brain filling for quesadillas*]

Enough for 12 quesadillas

A bowl
¾ *pound calves' brains*
Cold water to cover

Cover the brains with cold water and leave
them to soak for at least 4 hours. Change the
water frequently.

Remove the skin and wash the brains carefully in warm water to remove all traces of
blood.

A saucepan
Hot water to cover
1 *teaspoon salt*
2 *tablespoons mild white*
    vinegar

Bring the water to a boil, lower the flame,
add the salt, vinegar, and brains—the water
should cover the brains completely—and let
them poach for 15 minutes but **do not let the
water boil on any account.** It should just
shudder. Let the brains cool off in the liquid.

A colander

Remove the brains from the liquid and
drain them for a few moments. Chop fine.

A small frying pan
3 *tablespoons peanut or*
    safflower oil
1 *tablespoon finely*
    chopped onion
1 *clove garlic, peeled and*
    finely chopped

Heat the oil and cook the onion and garlic
over a medium flame, without browning, until
they are soft.

(continued)

1 large tomato (about ½ pound), skinned, seeded and chopped (page 43)	Add the tomato and let it cook over a medium flame for about 5 minutes.
The cooked brains 1 or 2 chiles serranos with seeds, finely chopped Salt to taste A large tablespoon chopped epazote	Add the brains, chilies, and salt and continue cooking until the brains are well seasoned and the mixture almost dry—about 8 minutes. Stir in the epazote and set the mixture aside to cool a little before using.

PANUCHOS [Small fried, filled tortillas]

12 panuchos

Before we even went to Yucatán for the first time, the Círculo del Sureste was one of our favorite eating places in Mexico City, and we would often drop in just before the evening rush hour to eat *panuchos*. We always resolved to try something else, but the sight of those piles of carefully shredded spicy pork—*cochinita pibil*—and the chicken in *escabeche oriental* on the counter in the tile-lined entrance was too much. It was *panuchos* again.

The crunchiness of the acidy onion, the delicately spiced meat, and the bean-paste-filled tortilla make it, I think, the supreme *antojito* of all.

Have ready:

½ recipe tortilla dough (page 62)
12 tablespoons Frijoles Colados y Refritos a la Yucateca (page 284)
2 hard-boiled eggs, sliced into 6 pieces each

1½ cups shredded Cochinita Pibil (page 169) or Pollo en Escabeche Oriental (page 209)
Cebollas Encurtidas (page 307)

The tortilla dough	Divide the tortilla dough into 12 pieces and make 12 small tortillas so that they puff up on the comal (page 65). When they are cool

enough to handle, make a "pocket" in each one by lifting up the thin layer of dough that has puffed up. To do this, insert the blade of a small pointed knife—taking care not to pierce the underskin of the tortilla—from ¼ to ½ inch from the edge of the tortilla and make a slit, following the edge, for about one-quarter of the way around it.

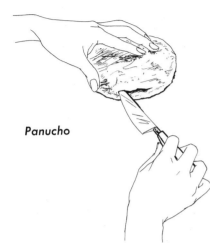

Panucho

The frijoles colados
The tortillas
The slices of hard-boiled
egg
A large frying pan
About ¼ pound lard
  (½ cup)
Paper toweling
The shredded meat
The cebollas encurditas

Spread one tablespoon of the bean paste inside the "pocket" of the tortilla and top it with a slice of egg. Press the lifted skin back down onto the tortilla and set aside.

Melt the lard, and when it is very hot but not smoking, fry each *panucho* until it is *slightly* crisp around the edge. Drain on the toweling.

Cover the *panuchos* with some shredded meat and garnish with the pickled onion rings.

If the *cochinita pibil* is used, sprinkle the shredded meat with some of the savory, orange-colored fat at the bottom of the dish.

You can prepare *panuchos* ahead of time all ready to fry, keeping them covered so that they do not dry out around the edges too much; but the frying itself has to be done at the very last moment, and they should be eaten straight out of the pan.

GARNACHAS YUCATECAS [*Filled masa tartlets from Yucatán*]

12 garnachas

Garnachas are "tartlets" of fried *masa* filled with black bean paste and ground beef, covered with tomato sauce, and sprinkled with cheese. They are excellent for an appetizer or first course.

The enormous Maya women, looking so splendid in their white *huipils* colorfully embroidered around the neck and hem, chuckled over my first *garnachas*. The temperature was up near the hundred mark and the humidity was frightful, so no wonder the dough kept sticking to my hands and the shapes of the first ones were a little bizarre.

Have ready:

1 cup Picadillo Sencillo para
    Garnachas (*page 129*), *warmed*
1 cup Frijoles Colados y Refritos a la
    Yucateca (*page 284*), *warmed*

½ cup Salsa de Jitomate Yucateca
    (*page 303*), *warmed*
3 tablespoons Parmesan cheese, *finely
    grated*

2 *cups* masa harina
1¼ *cups cold water*
¼ *teaspoon salt*

Mix the *masa harina*, water, and salt together to a soft dough. Roll the dough into 12 balls, each roughly 1¾ inches in diameter.

Press the ball of dough onto a floured surface and make a well in it with both thumbs together. Press out the sides of the well and mold the dough into a small basket shape about 3 inches across and ¾ inch deep. The dough should be about ¼ inch thick.

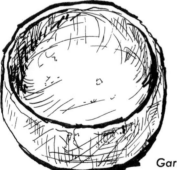

Garnacha

A small frying pan
Melted lard or oil (about
    ¾ inch deep)
Paper toweling

Heat the fat until it smokes and fry the *garnachas*, hollow side down first, until they are a pale gold and just a little crisp on the outside. Drain the *garnachas* on the paper toweling and keep them warm.

The frijoles colados	Fill one half of each *garnacha* with a table-
The picadillo	spoon of the bean paste, and the other half
The tomato sauce	with a scant tablespoon of the *picadillo*.
The Parmesan cheese	Cover the top of the filling with a large tea-
	spoon of the tomato sauce and sprinkle it
	with the cheese.

Garnachas should be served as soon as possible after frying or they will become leathery. They can be prepared up to the point of frying some hours ahead, but they should be kept covered so that the *masa* does not dry out. The white cheese of Yucatán, used there for *garnachas,* is dry and salty. A good substitute is Parmesan, or better still the less expensive Sardo—the Parmesan-type cheese from the Argentine.

The Yucatecan cooks usually put some wheat flour into the *masa* to make it puff up in the fat; however, this is not really necessary with dough made of *masa harina,* which has a different consistency and will puff up sufficiently without it.

The *picadillo*, bean paste, and sauce will freeze perfectly well, so you could always keep some on hand and whip up some *garnachas* at the drop of a hat—Mexican pizza.

PICADILLO SENCILLO PARA GARNACHAS
[*Ground meat filling for garnachas*]

A frying pan	Melt the lard and fry the garlic and onion,
1 tablespoon lard	without browning, until they are soft.
1 clove garlic, peeled and finely chopped	
½ medium onion, finely chopped	
2 medium tomatoes (about ¾ pound), skinned, seeded, and finely chopped (page 43) or 1 cup canned tomatoes	Add the tomato and fry for a minute or so more.

(*continued*)

1 pound ground beef
½ teaspoon salt, or to taste
Freshly ground pepper to
    taste

Add the ground meat and seasoning and cook over a medium flame until it is tender.

ENCHILADAS DEL SANCTUARIO

12 enchiladas

Those lovely clear evenings in San Luis Potosí bring everyone out to amble up the long Paseo lined with fragrant trees toward the *sanctuario* (cathedral). From far off you can see the blinking specks of light from the candles set up just below the cathedral steps, where, for a few *centavos*, you can eat *enchiladas del sanctuario*.

Despite their name, these are a type of *quesadilla*. The ones I have eaten in San Luis have been filled with a delicious white cream cheese and topped with a sprinkling of finely grated dry and salty cheese.

A frying pan
1 chile ancho
1 tablespoon lard
A blender
2 peppercorns
¼ teaspoon salt
A small bowl
The ground chili
⅔ cup water
1 cup masa harina
A tortilla press
The dough

Slit the chili open and remove the veins and seeds. Heat the lard and sauté the chili lightly on both sides, then remove with a slotted spoon and transfer to the blender jar. Blend with the peppercorns and salt until smooth.

Mix the ground chili and the water into the *masa harina*, and knead the dough well. Set it aside—do not refrigerate—to season for 1 hour.

Take pieces of the dough and roll them into balls about 1¼ inch in diameter. Press the balls out as you would for Quesadillas (page 120), slightly thick tortillas 4 inches in diameter.

Heat the griddle over a medium flame. Place the pieces of dough on the griddle.

An ungreased griddle or
    comal
¼ pound farmer cheese,
    crumbled

Immediately put 1 scant tablespoon of the cheese on one half of the dough, but away

Salt to taste

A frying pan
Melted lard or oil
(¼ inch deep)
Paper toweling
6 tablespoons finely grated
Romano or Parmesan
cheese
6 tablespoons finely
chopped onion

from the edge. Fold as for Quesadillas (page 120).

Cook the dough well on both sides. It will take about 3 to 4 minutes.

Heat the fat until it smokes and drop the hot *enchiladas* into it. Fry them lightly on both sides—they should not be very crisp. Drain them on the paper toweling and serve immediately, sprinkled with the cheese and onion.

Like the other members of the *quesadilla* family, these really have to be cooked and eaten right away; if you try and keep them warm the dough becomes leathery. But if you really must prepare some in advance, cook them on the comal and keep them covered first in a cloth, then in foil, until you are ready to fry them.

BURRITOS

Tortillas de harina de trigo filled and rolled up are called *burritos,* and can be filled with the following:

Chilorio (page 132)
Mochomos (page 133)
Machacado de Huevo (page 244)
Pinto or pink beans fried to a loose paste with pieces of Muenster cheese added at the last moment so that it just starts to melt
Pinto or pink beans fried to a loose paste with cooked, crumbled *chorizo*

Burritos can also be fried crisp, just like a fried taco, at which point they become *chivichangas.*

All of these should be served with Salsa de Jitomate del Norte (page 301).

CHILORIO [*Shredded pork filling for burritos*]

Enough to fill 12 tortillas

2 pounds pork shoulder,
   without bone but with
   some fat
A flameproof dish

A molcajete or mortar and
   pestle or 2 forks
A bowl
5 chiles anchos
Hot water to cover
A blender
The chilies
4 cloves garlic, peeled
⅛ teaspoon cumin seeds
¼ teaspoon oregano
6 peppercorns
⅓ cup vinegar (make up
   to ½ cup of liquid by
   adding water)
Lard as necessary
The shredded pork
The chili sauce

Cut the meat into 1-inch squares and cook as for Carnitas (page 112). When the water has evaporated and the fat has rendered out of the meat but the meat has not browned—about 45 minutes—remove the meat from the dish and pound it in the *molcajete* until it is in shreds, or shred it finely with two forks.

Meanwhile, prepare the sauce. Slit the chilies open, remove the seeds and veins, and cover them with hot water. Leave to soak for 15 minutes, then remove with a slotted spoon and transfer to the blender jar and blend until smooth with the rest of the ingredients.

The sauce should be thick, more like a paste. You will have to keep stopping the blender to release the blades.

There should be about ¼ cup of fat in the dish in which the meat was cooked; if not, make up to that amount with lard. Add the meat and mix the chili sauce well into it. Cook the mixture over a low flame for 15 to 20 minutes, or until the meat is well seasoned and the mixture rather dry, scraping the bottom of the dish so the sauce does not stick.

As I mention elsewhere, the Culiacán market is where you see mounds and mounds of *chilorio* already prepared. It is a marvelous filling for *tacos* as well as *burritos*. You can make a lot of it at one time; it will keep for a very long time in the refrigerator, or you can freeze it.

MOCHOMOS [*A crisp shredded beef filling for burritos*]

Enough to fill 12 tortillas

Mochomos are prepared as a filling for *burritos* all over the northwest of Mexico, and this is a version from Sinaloa, a favorite supper dish with a mug of *atole*.

A saucepan
2 pounds chuck steak cut into 1-inch squares
½ onion
2 cloves garlic, peeled
2 teaspoons salt
A colander
2 forks or a molcajete *or mortar and pestle*

Put the ingredients together into the pan, cover with water, and bring to a boil. Lower the flame and let the meat simmer, covered, until it is tender—about 55 minutes. Leave the meat to cool off in the broth, then strain and shred it finely with two forks, or better still pound it a little in the *molcajete*.

A frying pan
¼ cup lard
½ medium onion, finely chopped
The shredded meat

Heat the lard and cook the onion gently, without browning, until it is soft. Add the shredded meat and fry it until it is crisp and browned.

There should be enough salt in the cooking water to give the meat plenty of flavor.

BOLA DE QUESO RELLENO [*Stuffed cheese*]

8 servings

This is a round Dutch cheese stuffed with a meat filling, steamed until slightly runny, and served with tomato sauce and thickened broth or gravy poured over it. It makes a very impressive and delicious first course that can be served in *tacos*.

Dutch cheeses are available at a very reasonable price in the free ports of Chetumal and Cozumel in the neighboring territory of Quintana Roo. Although this dish is a relative late-comer to the Yucatecan cuisine, it is now firmly entrenched. Curaçao has its version too, stuffed with shrimps. Prince Bernhard is reported to have said on one of his visits to Mexico that he couldn't think why the Dutch hadn't thought of it first.

There is a round cheese made in Chiapas that is also stuffed and served in a tomato sauce. But the *bola de Chiapas* is a strong, salty cheese that drys out and hardens in a very short time; it has a thick skin made of toughened curds. The cheese is cut in half and then hollowed out until only the skin remains. It is filled with a *picadillo* of pork, peas, carrots, green beans, and raisins. The two halves are put together, and the join sealed in hot fat. It is then heated through in a sauce of tomatoes and *rajas* of chili.

One day ahead (if necessary):

A 4-pound Edam cheese	Pare off the red skin. Cut a ½-inch-thick slice off the top of the cheese; this will make the "lid." Hollow out the inside of the cheese until the shell is about ½ inch thick. If the cheese is very hard, leave it to soak overnight (see note below). Reserve the scooped-out cheese for another use.

On serving day:

MEAT FOR THE STUFFING

A saucepan	Cut the meats into ½-inch cubes, and add it
½ pound pork	with the rest of the ingredients to the pan.
½ pound beef	Bring to a boil, lower the flame, and cook
3½ cups water	until the meat is tender—about 30 to 35
½ teaspoon salt	minutes. Let the meat cool off in the broth.
3 cloves garlic, toasted	
(page 43)	
¼ teaspoon oregano,	
toasted (page 43)	
A colander	Strain the meat, reserving the broth. Chop
	the meat fine.

THE TOMATO BASE (FOR THE STUFFING AND THE TOMATO SAUCE)

A small frying pan
2 tablespoons lard or oil
½ medium bell pepper, finely chopped
½ medium onion, finely chopped
1 heaped tablespoon capers

Heat the lard and fry the pepper, onion, and capers slowly, without browning, until they are soft.

1¼ pounds tomatoes, peeled, seeded, and chopped (page 43)
15 small green olives, pitted, roughly chopped
1 heaped tablespoon raisins
½ teaspoon salt

Mash the tomatoes and add them, with the rest of the ingredients, to the pan. Cook over a medium flame for about 8 minutes.

Divide the mixture in two, half for the stuffing and half for the sauce.

THE STUFFING

A molcajete or mortar and pestle
10 peppercorns
2 whole allspice
2 whole cloves
¼-stick cinnamon
½ teaspoon salt, or to taste
3 cloves garlic, peeled
½ tablespoon mild white vinegar

Crush the spices together with the garlic and vinegar.

A frying pan
The chopped meats
The seasoning
Half the tomato mixture

Put the meats, seasoning, and the tomato mixture into the pan and mix them well together.

(continued)

4 hard-boiled eggs

Separate the whites and the yolks, being careful to keep the yolks whole. Set the yolks aside. Chop the whites fine and add them to the ingredients in the pan.

Cook the mixture over a medium flame for about 10 minutes—it should be almost dry.

The hollowed cheese
The whole egg yolks

Put half of the stuffing into the cheese; set the whole yolks into it and cover with the remaining stuffing.

The cheese "lid"
A little peanut or safflower oil
Cheesecloth
A small plate
A steamer

Replace the top slice of the cheese.

Smear the outside of the cheese well with oil and wrap it tightly in the cloth, tying it on top. Place the cheese on a small plate in the steamer. Cover the steamer with a tightly fitting lid and cook the cheese until it is soft (see note below).

THE GRAVY

A small saucepan
2 cups reserved meat broth
2 tablespoons all-purpose flour
A pinch of saffron
1 chile güero, or any available fresh green chili, toasted (page 43)

Meanwhile, prepare the gravy. Heat the broth. Add a little of it to the flour and stir to a smooth paste. Stir the rest of the broth into the paste until it is smooth. Return to the pan and cook over gentle heat until the gravy thickens slightly, stirring constantly. Add the saffron and chili, set aside, and keep warm.

THE TOMATO SAUCE

A small saucepan
The remaining tomato mixture
½ cup reserved juice from the tomato can
Salt as necessary

Heat the tomato mixture and juice together and add salt as necessary.

To serve, unwrap the cheese, remove the "lid," and pour the hot tomato sauce and the gravy over it. Serve with plenty of hot tortillas and Salsa Picante a la Yucateca (page 306). Each person will make his own *tacos.*

It is very difficult to give exact cooking time, as it will vary tremendously depending upon the age of the cheese and such considerations as, for instance, the conditions under which it has been stored. Always hollow out the cheese the day before using. If it is dry and rather hard, then leave it to soak overnight in cold water. If the cheese is new and soft, do not soak it but leave it out of the refrigerator overnight and until you finally cook it. The cheese will sag when it is cooked through, but the trick is to have the inside and outside cheese melted evenly without letting it lose its shape and go completely flat. Both warming the stuffing before you put it into the cheese and cooking it over a medium flame will help. The time can vary from 15 to 35 minutes. After the first 10 minutes, feel the cheese to see how soft it is.

One of the cooks I was speaking to in Campeche likes to wrap the cheese in a banana leaf first, and this not only gives it a very nice flavor but forms an attractive base for it in the serving dish. In Yucatán it is very often cooked submerged in the meat broth, but it then becomes rather messy to untie and serve. They also serve it in wedges almost swimming in sauce, as a first course, as well as in *tacos,* which I think is the more practical way of serving it here.

FRIJOLES PUERCOS [*Rich well-fried beans*]

6 servings

This is a Jalisco version of *frijoles refritos* that is served as an appetizer with drinks. A *queso ranchero*—a strong, dry, rather salty cheese—is used there. Possibly a Romano would be the nearest thing, if not an Argentinian Sardo would be a perfectly acceptable substitute.

Have ready:

A warm serving dish
½ pound pinto or pink beans, cooked
   as for Frijoles de Olla (page 281)
   (3½ to 4 cups with broth)

2 tablespoons finely grated Sardo
   cheese
Toasted tortillas or Totopos (page
   139)

(*continued*)

A large frying pan
1 Spanish chorizo *(about*
3 ounces)
6 strips bacon
3 tablespoons lard or
bacon fat
The cooked beans

Skin and crumble the *chorizo,* and chop the bacon. Cook over a slow flame, covered, until most of the fat has rendered out. Be careful not to let them burn.

Add the lard to the pan and let it melt. Add the beans and broth and cook them over a high flame, mashing them as you would for Frijoles Refritos (page 282). If they start to dry out and stick to the pan, add a little more fat.

20 small, pitted green
olives, chopped
2 chiles jalapeños en
escabeche, seeded
and chopped
The serving dish
The remaining chopped
olives and chilies
The finely grated cheese
The toasted tortillas or
totopos

When the beans have been mashed to a coarse puree and are almost dry, ready to roll (see Frijoles Refritos, page 282), add about two-thirds of the olives and chilies.

Roll the beans, then turn onto the serving dish and garnish with the remaining olives and chilies.

Sprinkle the roll with the cheese and serve with the toasted tortillas or *totopos.*

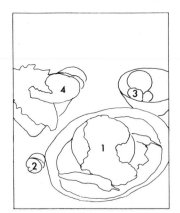

AN ANTOJITO FROM YUCATÁN—STUFFED CHEESE
1 bola de queso relleno, ready to serve; **2** the bitter lime
(lima agria) of Yucatán; **3** *chiles habaneros* in a *molcajete;*
4 tortillas in a *chiquihuite*

TOTOPOS or TOSTADITAS [*Crisp tortilla pieces*]

6 dry tortillas

Cut each tortilla into 6 triangular-shaped pieces.

A frying pan
Melted lard (¼ inch
deep)
The tortilla pieces
Paper toweling

Heat the lard, and when it is smoking, fry the tortilla pieces, stirring them from time to time until they are an even, deep gold and quite crisp. Drain them on paper toweling.

These can be used for Guacamole (page 113) or other dips, and to garnish Frijoles Refritos (page 282).

SALSA DE ALBANILES [*Bricklayers' sauce*]

Salsa de Tomate Verde
Cruda (page 297)
1 small avocado, thinly
sliced
Thin strips of cream,
farmer, or mild Ched-
dar cheese

Put the sauce into a shallow bowl and garnish the top liberally with the avocado and cheese. Serve as an appetizer with hot tortillas.

SOME MEXICAN TORTILLA DISHES AND THEIR INGREDIENTS
1 a serving of *enchiladas;* **2** *flores de calabaza* (pumpkin flowers); **3** *epazote;* **4** Mexican *chorizos;* **5** a potato; **6** *queso de Oaxaca* (cheese from Oaxaca); **7** *huitlacoche* (corn fungus); **8** *chile poblano;* **9** toasted *quesadillas;* **10** *sopes;* **11** fried *quesadillas*

Soups (*Sopas*)

Canned soups have been appearing on the shelves of Mexican supermarkets for some time now, but I cannot think that trade is overwhelming. Even the youngest maid, newly arrived from her *tierra,* is able to produce a simple but delicious soup—she usually stipulates that the kitchen be equipped with a *liquadora* (blender). But wherever you are in Mexico, and no matter how hot or humid the climate, soup appears on the menu. In my wanderings up and down the country, when in doubt I usually ask for a *caldo de pollo,* always a safe bet. There will usually be a lot of shredded chicken in it, a little rice, perhaps a slice or two of avocado, a sprig of fresh coriander—and always wedges of lime on the side. As you travel it is well worthwhile looking for the regional specialties: the *caldillos* of Nuevo León and Chihuahua; the *caldo de queso* of Sonora; the *chilpachole* and *caldo largo* of Veracruz and the Gulf Coast; the *sopa de lima* of Yucatán; and the *sopa Tarasca* of Michoacán. The variety is endless.

Some of the lesser-known soups are outstanding in their own right. In Tampico there is a thick shrimp soup called *huatape*—or *guatape*—either red or white, thickened with *masa* and the ground leaves of the chili plant, *santa hoja* (*Piper sanctum*), or *epazote,* and if one of them is not available you can add the leaves of the *tomate verde* plant.

When I was last in Oaxaca I was trying in vain to find a good *sopa de guías*—*guías* are the tender new shoots and tendrils of the zucchini squash plant. A countrywoman selling flowers nearby overheard my inquiries and told me to return at lunchtime. The soup she had cooked was just ready on the small charcoal stove at the back of her flower stand. The new shoots cut from the plant still had the flowers on the stem, giving birth to half-formed and very tender little squash. They had been cut into short lengths and cooked with fresh corn cobs cut into rounds, a few more tender squash, and some herbs often used in Oaxaca, *chipilin (Protalaria maypurensis)* and *piojo (Porophyllum punctatum)*. It was unbelievably sweet and fragrant, and I left the fiery sauce, with which it is traditionally pepped up, to the others. The next day that soup did turn up on the menu of a small and fairly good commercial restaurant, but it came nowhere near my market soup.

In the north I suppose the counterpart of that soup would be the *pozole de milpa* of Sonora. The *milpa* is the cornfield or plot. If you have ever looked at one late on in the rainy season when the corn stalks are tall and solid, you will see around the edges, and twining themselves in and out, green beans, peas, and squash, with wild purslane wandering along the ground. The soup is enriched with pork and—being in the great wheat country—ten handfuls of whole wheat grain are thrown in. All these go into the pot with the first corn to ripen.

Two of the most delicious soups I know anywhere—one, a deep golden yellow, of squash blossoms, and the other, inky black from the fungus on the corn (*huitlacoche*)—seem to be served only in and around Mexico City.

CALDO DE POLLO [*Chicken broth*]

14 cups of strong broth

Several of the soup recipes given here call for a base of good chicken broth. You could use canned broth, but I personally find them wishy-washy; and the omnipresent cubes for broth are too strong in something other than chicken flavor. It is well worthwhile making your own.

For a good broth, avoid using strongly flavored herbs or root vegetables, and too much carrot. If you have to use an ordinary chicken, buy extra backs and giblets to strengthen the flavor. In Mexico, with the help of my

Jewish neighbor, the ladies in the poultry market, and maids I learned how to make a very creditable chicken broth. But you can't be squeamish about it. Everything goes into the pot. The feet are singed and peeled; the beak is cut from the head, and the neck feathers plucked. The intestines are slit open and washed well; the unlaid eggs are removed intact to add to the soup. I shall never forget the look on a young friend's face when he went into my kitchen to help himself to more broth and fished out the head. Now all my soup is suspect, and he still pales at the mention of chicken broth.

A large saucepan
A large boiling fowl
The giblets
1 carrot
1 small onion
2 cloves garlic, peeled
10 peppercorns
2 teaspoons salt
A few celery leaves

Cut the fowl into pieces. Clean and slice the vegetables. Cover all the ingredients with cold water and bring them to a boil. Lower the flame and simmer for about 3½ hours.

Let the ingredients cool off in the broth, then strain the broth and set it aside to get completely cold. Skim the fat carefully from the top and store the broth ready for use.

For a light soup course with a Mexican touch, serve a bowl of broth with a few sliced and sautéed mushrooms on top and a good sprig of *epazote* thrown in at the last moment just to flavor it. Of course, wild mushrooms would be much better, and that brings back thoughts of a memorable soup in the house of a well-known Mexican gastronome: the tiny wild mushrooms called *clavitos* (little nails) had been added to an excellent broth with *epazote*: supremely simple but excellent. Or you could add some slices of avocado, a sprig of fresh coriander, and a *chile chipotle*.

SOPA DE TORTILLA [*Tortilla soup*]

6 servings

This is probably one of the most popular soups in central Mexico—simple but delicious.

Have ready:

12 small stale tortillas, cut into strips
6 cups Caldo de Pollo (*page 141*)
3 chiles pasilla, *fried and crumbled* (*see note below*)
6 tablespoons grated Cheddar cheese

A large frying pan *Melted lard* (¼ *inch* *deep*) *The tortilla strips* *Paper toweling*	Heat the lard and fry the tortilla strips until they are well browned but not too crisp. Drain them on paper toweling. Pour off all but 2 tablespoons of the lard.

A blender
2 medium tomatoes
  (¾ *pound*), *broiled*
  (*page 44*)
⅓ *medium onion, roughly*
  chopped
1 clove garlic, peeled
	Blend the tomatoes, onion, and garlic to a smooth sauce, then cook in the lard for about 8 minutes, until the sauce is well seasoned and has reduced somewhat.

A saucepan *The chicken broth* *The fried tortilla strips*	Add the sauce to the broth in the pan and bring to a boil. Add the tortilla strips to the broth and cook them for about 3 minutes.
2 large sprigs epazote	Just before serving, add the *epazote*. Cook for 1 minute more.
The fried, crumbled chiles pasilla *The grated cheese*	Serve each portion garnished with pieces of crumbled chili and grated cheese.

The chilies should be fried in lard until they are crisp; let them cool off a little before attempting to crumble them.

In Mexico, *queso Chihuahua* would be used for this soup.

SOPA DE LIMA [*Lime soup*]

6 servings

This is considered to be *the* soup of Yucatán, and on the hottest day—and that seems to be the year round—you will be served a bowl of sizzling lime soup. Sizzling because of the hot, crisp tortilla pieces that are dropped in at the last moment, and lime because of the unique flavor given it by the rind and juice of the bitter lime—*Citrus limetta*. This lime must be used in other regions, but I have not come across it. It is small, roundish, and pale green when ripe and looks as though it has had its nipple pushed in along the way. Its flavor cannot be compared to that of any other citrus fruit—although there is something of the same astringent quality of the bitter orange, but it is stronger and more fragrant.

As a substitute for the bitter lime, use a piece of Seville orange and lime—or lime and a little grapefruit peel.

Have ready:

12 stale tortillas, cut into strips
6 soup bowls
4 small bowls
¾ cup finely chopped onion
⅓ cup finely chopped chile serrano,
    with seeds

Freshly ground pepper
⅓ cup unpeeled, finely chopped bitter
    lime

A saucepan
4 chicken gizzards
6 chicken livers
    (8 ounces)
10 cloves garlic, toasted
    (page 43)
¼ teaspoon oregano,
    toasted (page 43)
6 peppercorns
1 teaspoon salt
8 cups water
2 chicken breasts

Cover all the ingredients with water and simmer them for about 15 minutes.

Add the chicken breasts and continue cooking for another 15 minutes, or until the meats are tender.

A strainer

Strain the broth and set it aside. Shred the breasts, chop the livers, remove the gristle from the gizzards, and chop them. Set the meats aside.

A small frying pan
1½ tablespoons lard
⅓ cup onion, finely chopped
¼ cup green pepper, finely chopped

Heat the lard and gently fry the onion and pepper until they are soft, but not browned.

1 large tomato (about ½ pound), skinned seeded, and mashed (page 43)
The broth
Salt, as necessary
The meats
½ bitter lime

Add the tomato to the mixture in the pan. Let the mixture cook for about 5 minutes over a medium flame, then add to the broth and let it simmer for about 5 minutes.

Add salt as necessary, then add the chopped and shredded meats and heat them through.

Squeeze a little of the juice into the broth. Drop the squeezed lime half into the broth for a few seconds only, then remove. Keep the broth warm, and do not put it into the soup bowls until you are draining the fried tortilla strips.

A frying pan
Lard for frying
The tortilla strips
Paper toweling
The soup bowls

Heat the lard until it is smoking and fry the tortilla strips until they are crisp. Drain them on the toweling, and while they are still very hot drop some of them into the broth in each soup bowl.

4 small bowls
The chopped onion
The chopped chile serrano
The freshly ground pepper
The chopped bitter lime

Put each of the last ingredients into a small bowl so that each person can help himself.

CALDO DE QUESO [*Cheese broth*]

6 servings

The *epazote* and cheese give this simple peasant soup from Sonora a delicious touch. When I first tried it in Hermosillo, the pieces of potato were quite large and the cheese was cut from a huge homemade cheese from a nearby ranch—it was crumbly, slightly acidy, and tasted of pure cream. It melted immediately in the hot broth.

¾ pound red bliss or
  waxy new potatoes
A saucepan
5 cups beef broth or
  bouillon
2 large tomatoes (1
  pound)

Peel the potatoes and cut them into 1-inch squares. Bring the broth to a boil, add the potatoes, and let them cook over a medium flame for 10 minutes. They should be *just* cooked.

Cut a thin slice off the top of each tomato and grate the flesh on the coarse side of a grater. In a very short time you will have the skin of the tomato left flat in your hand. Don't forget to grate the flesh from the top slices.

A small frying pan
2 tablespoons peanut or
  safflower oil
½ medium onion, sliced
1 small clove garlic, peeled
  and finely chopped
The tomato pulp

Heat the oil and gently fry the onion and garlic, without browning, until they are soft.

Add the tomato pulp and cook the sauce over a brisk flame for 10 minutes, by which time it will have thickened somewhat and be well seasoned. Add the tomato sauce to the broth and potatoes.

1 large canned, peeled
  green chili
1 large sprig epazote,
  fresh or dried
Salt as necessary
6 thin strips mild Cheddar
  cheese or crumbled
  Boursault

Remove the seeds from the chili and cut it into strips. Add the chili strips and the *epazote* to the broth and let it cook over a medium flame for 5 minutes. Add salt as necessary. Just before serving, add the cheese. Serve the soup as the cheese melts.

SOPA DE AGUACATE

6 servings

A lovely pale green soup, very good served either hot or cold. However, much will depend on the quality of the avocados; the watery tasteless ones that we only too often get on the eastern seaboard will not produce a good soup.

Have ready:

Small tortilla squares, fried crisp as for Totopos (page 139)

2 large avocados, or enough to yield 2 cups pulp	Cut the avocados into halves. Remove the seeds and scoop out the flesh.
A saucepan	Heat the broth, transfer it to the blender
6 cups well-seasoned Caldo de Pollo (page 141)	jar, add the avocado pulp, and blend to a smooth puree.
The avocado pulp	
	Return the soup to the pan and just heat it through gently. **Do not let it boil.**
The fried tortilla squares	Serve the soup immediately, garnished with the tortilla squares.

CALDO TLALPEÑO [*Vegetable broth from Tlalpan*]

6 servings

Nobody can tell me exactly how this broth came to be named for a community on the outskirts of Mexico City—Tlalpan. It used to be, and still is for that matter, a favorite place for a Sunday outing to eat *barbacoa* or *carnitas.* This simple peasant broth was probably first served at the stands along the highway, and dispensed with the barbecued meats, or perhaps in the *pulquerías,* where many a new *antojito* or broth has been born.

There are many versions of this broth, some of them with chick-peas, like this one, or rice. The *chile chipotle* gives an interesting smoky flavor to the broth. If you are unable to get the dried ones, then use canned—but only add them at the last moment, since they are usually canned in *adobo* sauce or pickled.

Have ready:

6 soup bowls
1 cup chicken, cooked and shredded
1 small avocado, peeled and cut into
    strips

6 lime wedges

½ pound green beans
¼ pound carrots (2
    medium carrots)
1 small tomato (about 4
    ounces)
A saucepan
6 cups Caldo de Pollo
    (page 141)
½ cup cooked chick-peas
A large sprig epazote
2 chiles chipotles, *dried
    or canned*
The soup bowls
The shredded chicken
The chili strips
The avocado strips
The lime wedges

Trim the beans and cut them into halves. Scrape the carrots and cut them into rounds about ¼ inch thick. Skin, seed, and roughly chop the tomato (page 43).

Heat the broth, and when it comes to a boil add the vegetables and cook for about 20 minutes, or until they are tender.

Add the chick-peas, *epazote*, and chilies and cook the broth for about 5 minutes more. Remove the chilies from broth and tear into strips.

Add to each bowl a little of the shredded chicken, some chili strips, and some avocado strips. Serve the lime wedges on the side.

SOPA DE FLOR DE CALABAZA [*Pumpkin blossom soup*]

6 servings

A saucepan
40 large pumpkin flowers
  (about 1 pound; 3
  bunches in Mexico)
4 cups well-seasoned
  Caldo de Pollo
  (page 141)
A blender

Remove the stems from the flowers, strip off the sepals, chop the flowers, and put them into the saucepan. Cover with the broth and cook them until tender, about 15 minutes.

Transfer to the blender and blend until smooth. Then return to the pan.

A blender
2 medium
  tomatoes (12 ounces),
  broiled (page 141)
½ small onion, chopped
A small frying pan
3 tablespoons butter
The tomato puree
The flower broth
A sprig of epazote

Blend the tomatoes together with the onion to a smooth puree.

Melt the butter and cook the tomato puree over a high flame for 5 minutes, stirring. Add it to the broth in the saucepan and cook the mixture over a medium flame for about 10 minutes. At the last moment, add a sprig of *epazote* to flavor the soup.

SOPA DE FLOR DE CALABAZA (CREAM VERSION)

To make a cream version of this soup, omit the tomatoes. Sauté the flowers and onion together with the butter. Cover the pan and let the flowers cook until tender. Add 2 cups of chicken broth and blend to a puree. Add 1½ cups of milk and cook for a few minutes. Last of all, add ¾ cup cream. Some cooks thicken with egg yolks or flour, but this soup doesn't really need any thickening; the flowers have plenty of substance when blended.

SOPA TARASCA [*Tarascan bean and tomato soup*]

6 servings

This is a thick, hearty soup, marvelous in cold weather. It is almost a meal in itself. One of the outstanding cooks in Morelia, Sra. Beatriz Dávalos, introduced it to me. It is named for the Tarascan Indians who live in the highlands of Michoacán.

Have ready:

6 soup bowls
Small cubes of Muenster cheese
3 chiles pasilla, fried and crumbled
Tortilla strips fried crisp as for
    Totopos (page 139)
Thick Sour Cream (page 20)

A blender
½ pound cooked pink or
    pinto beans (about
    3½ to 4 cups with
    broth)

Blend the beans, together with their broth, to a smooth puree. Set aside.

A blender
2 medium tomatoes
    (about ¾ pound),
    broiled (page 43),
    or 1¼ cups canned
    tomatoes
1 clove garlic, peeled
¼ onion, roughly chopped

Blend the tomatoes, garlic, and onion together to a smooth sauce.

A heavy saucepan
3 tablespoons lard or pork
    drippings
The tomato mixture
The bean puree
2 to 2½ cups chicken or
    pork broth
Salt as necessary

Melt the fat and cook the tomato mixture over a high flame for about 5 minutes, then stir the bean puree into the tomato mixture gradually and let it cook over a medium flame for about 8 minutes, stirring it all the time.

Add the broth and let the soup cook for another 10 minutes over a low flame. Add salt as necessary.

The soup bowls
The cheese

Put a few pieces of the cheese into each bowl. Pour the hot soup over them and

The soup
*The fried, crumbled
     chilies*
The tortilla strips
The sour cream

garnish with the chilies, some tortilla strips, and a dollop of sour cream.

This soup will thicken considerably as it stands and will have to be diluted with broth or water. It freezes well. To be authentic you really need a cheese in it that will "thread" as it melts—a typical Mexican requirement. And the sour cream should be very cold.

SOPA DE APATZINGÁN [*Apatzingán melon and potato soup*]

6 servings

Some of the finest cantaloupe melons come from the country around Apatzingán in the low *tierra caliente* of Michoacán, and here is a very unusual soup made from them. It is sweet and creamy, with a lovely, delicate, deep-yellow color and a strong melon flavor, which is accentuated by the cooking.

Have ready:

6 soup bowls

A blender
*1 pound potatoes, cooked,
     peeled, and diced*
*1 pound cantaloupe flesh
     (about ½ large
     melon), diced*
1 cup milk
A saucepan
¼ cup butter
The melon puree
1 cup milk
*¼ teaspoon salt, or to
     taste*

Thin Sour Cream (page 20)

Blend the potato and melon together with the milk to a smooth puree.

Melt the butter and cook the puree for a few moments. Add the milk, the salt and pepper and continue cooking the mixture for about 5 minutes over a low flame.

(*continued*)

Freshly ground pepper to taste	
A beater and bowl	Beat the egg yolks together well until they
4 egg yolks	are creamy and stir them gradually into the soup. Remove the saucepan from the flame as soon as they have been added.
The soup bowls	After serving the soup, add a little sour
The sour cream	cream to each bowl.

This soup is also good iced.

JAIBAS EN CHILPACHOLE [*Crabs in a picante tomato broth*]

6 servings

This is one of the really distinguished soups of Mexico. It is a specialty of Veracruz, and that is where I learned to cook it—under the sharp eye of Sra. María Cano Carlín, one of the many meticulous and enthusiastic cooks at the Brisas del Mar Restaurant in Boca del Río. There are many versions of the soup cooked with *chiles anchos* or *chipotles*, but this version calls for the *chile gordo* of Veracruz (actually the fresh *chile jalapeño*, which can sometimes be obtained in New York and elsewhere). You can substitute *chiles serranos*. I have substituted olive oil for the original lard, and I think it is an improvement. The soup should be rather *picante* and have a strong flavor of *epazote*.

A large saucepan	If you dare, scrub the crabs well in cold
6 live female crabs	water, and then drop them into the boiling
1½ quarts boiling, salted water	water. Let them cook for no more than 3 minutes.
A strainer and some fine cheesecloth	Remove the crabs and let them cool. Reserve the broth.
	When the crabs are cool enough to handle, first remove the heart-shaped piece of the shell on the front. Then pry off the back shell.

A *mortar and pestle or*
molcajete

A *strainer and some fine*
cheesecloth

Aluminum foil
3 *medium tomatoes, about*
1 pound
½ *large onion, thickly*
sliced
6 *cloves garlic, peeled*
2 chiles jalapeños
A *blender*
½ *cup reserved crab*
broth
A *deep saucepan or flame-*
proof pot that can be
used for serving the
soup
3 *tablespoons olive oil*
5 *cups reserved crab broth*
The tomato sauce
Salt as necessary
The paste of eggs and gills

The crabs
6 *sprigs* epazote, *fresh if*
possible

Scrape the fat and little orange eggs from the shell and the crab itself. Remove the small spongy gills, rinsing them well if they are gritty, and grind them to a paste with the eggs and fat. Cut each crab in two and crack the claws.

Return the shells and debris to the broth and let them simmer for about 5 minutes. Strain the broth through the cheesecloth. Set aside.

Preheat the oven to 400°.

Wrap the onion slices, garlic, tomatoes, and chilies, keeping the tomatoes separate, in foil and roast them until they are cooked through —about 20 minutes—then blend together with the crab broth to an almost smooth puree.

Heat the oil and cook the puree for about 10 minutes over a high flame, stirring it from time to time.

Add the broth to the tomato sauce and let it simmer for about 5 minutes. Add salt as necessary.

Add the paste to thicken the soup and let it simmer for a few minutes longer.

A minute or so before serving, add the crabs, including the claws, and *epazote.* Warm just a bit, to let the crabs heat through and the *epazote* flavor the soup.

SOPA DE ELOTE [*Fresh corn soup*]

6 servings

This is a rather unusual and delightful soup. The flavor and color will undoubtedly be much better if you can get the real *chiles poblanos.* Canned chilies can be substituted, but they must be of the very best quality. A strong, acrid canning solution can ruin the flavor of the chilies and thus the soup.

Have ready:

6 soup bowls
3 tablespoons chile poblano or canned, peeled green chilies, diced

6 tablespoons crumbled cream cheese or Boursault
6 small tortillas, cut into small squares and fried crisp as for Totopos (page 139)

A blender
4 cups corn (1½ pounds frozen corn or kernels from 5 ears)
1 cup water
A food mill

Blend the corn together with the water at high speed until you have a smooth puree.

Put the puree through the medium disk of the food mill.

A saucepan
¼ cup butter
The corn puree

Melt the butter but do not let it get too hot. Add the corn puree and let it cook over a medium flame for about 5 minutes, stirring it all the time.

3½ cups milk
½ teaspoon salt, or to taste

Add the milk and the salt to the mixture and bring it to a boil. Lower the flame and let the soup simmer for about 15 minutes, stirring it from time to time so that it does not stick to the pan. By this time it will have thickened slightly.

The soup bowls
The diced chili
The cream cheese
The fried tortilla squares

Put about ½ tablespoon diced chili and 1 tablespoon of crumbled cheese into each bowl. Pour the hot soup over them and garnish with the crisp tortilla squares.

Unless you can get very fresh corn it is best to use frozen. Measure it frozen and then let it defrost. Do not on any account use canned corn, which has been precooked.

When I first cooked this for a class, Grayson Hall, the actress, said, "This is such a comforting soup." It is a delicate pale yellow and has a subtle flavor, complemented but not overpowered by the chili. I always prefer to make this kind of soup a day ahead to improve the flavor. If you do this you will need to thin it down a little with from ½ to 1 cup milk. You could also serve it in a most un-Mexican way, chilled and sprinkled with chopped dill or chives.

The soup freezes quite well.

SOPA DE ELOTE DE GRANO [*Fresh corn kernel soup*]

6 servings

Have ready:

6 soup bowls
6 tablespoons crumbled farmer or
    cream cheese
6 tablespoons Thick Sour Cream (page
    20)

Some strips of chile poblano, *roasted
    and peeled* (*page 45*), *or canned,
    peeled green chili*

8 small chiles poblanos,
    roasted and peeled,
    or 2 4-ounce cans
    peeled green chilies
    (about 10)
A blender
½ cup Caldo de Pollo
    (page 141)
A saucepan
¼ cup butter
6 cups Caldo de Pollo
    (page 141)

Remove the seeds and veins from the chilies, and if they are very *picante* leave them to soak in salted water from 30 minutes to 1 hour.

Blend the chilies, together with the broth, to a puree, then melt the butter and cook the puree for about 3 minutes over a high flame.

Add the broth and corn to the chili puree and cook over a gentle heat until the corn is

(*continued*)

About 2 cups corn (1 10-ounce package frozen corn or kernels from 2 large ears)

tender—from 10 to 20 minutes, depending on the corn. Add salt to taste.

Salt to taste

The soup bowls
The crumbled cheese
The sour cream
The chili strips

Put a tablespoon of cheese into each bowl. Pour the hot soup over it and garnish with a dollop of sour cream and a few strips of chili.

SOPA DE ELOTE Y RAJAS [*Fresh corn and chili soup*]

6 servings

I make no excuses for including recipes for three corn soups. After all, corn is *the* staple of Mexico, and I think each soup is outstanding in its own right. This recipe was given to me by Sra. Cantù, a very young and talented cook in Monterrey who talked about Mexican food with great relish.

This soup will curdle easily if you don't take care—it won't look as nice, but the rich flavor will still be there.

A blender
1 large tomato (about 8 ounces), broiled (page 44)
¼ onion, chopped

Blend the tomato and onion to a puree and set it aside.

A large saucepan
3 tablespoons butter
3 small chiles poblanos or 5 canned, peeled green chilies

Melt the butter. Clean the chilies, remove the seeds and veins, and cut them into narrow strips. Fry them gently for about 3 minutes—they should not brown.

The tomato puree

Add the tomato puree to the chili strips and cook the mixture for about 5 minutes over a medium flame until the sauce has reduced somewhat. Set it aside to cool.

A blender

Blend the corn, together with the milk, at

*About 3 cups corn (1½ 10-
    ounce packages
    frozen corn or kernels
    from 4 ears)*
3 cups milk
A food mill

high speed to a very smooth puree. This will
probably have to be done in two stages.

Put the corn mixture through the medium
disk of a food mill and add it very gradually
to the **cooled** tomato puree, stirring all the
time.

¾ cup whole corn kernels
½ teaspoon salt, or to taste

Add the kernels and salt and cook the
soup over a very low flame—it should just
simmer—for about 25 minutes.

6 soup bowls
*Cream or farmer cheese
    or Boursault,
    crumbled*

Add a little cheese to each bowl before
pouring the hot soup into it.

Hearty Soup-Stews (*Pucheros*)

A truly Mexican *cena* would be a few *antojitos* and a bowl of soup. But what soup! More like a stew, with plenty of meat and sustenance, sometimes *picante* but always comforting—whether against the cool evenings in the altitudes of the central plateau or the ravages of the night before.

PREPARATION OF WHOLE HOMINY FOR SOUPS

In the parts of Mexico where the *maíz para pozole* is used (whole, large white corn kernels), you can buy it prepared, ready for cooking. If, however, you have to start from scratch, this is how you do it:

Two days ahead, put 1 pound whole corn kernels into an earthenware pot and cover it with water; leave it to soak overnight. The following day, change the water and bring the corn to a boil. Dilute about one large teaspoon of unslaked lime in a little cold water and add it, through a strainer, to the corn. Boil the corn for 10 minutes. Cover it and let it soak for 30 minutes. Wash the corn well in several waters, rubbing it between your hands so that the thin transparent sheaths on each kernel are removed. Remove the "eye" at the base of the sheath from each kernel so that it will "open like a flower," as the Mexican expression goes. Rinse well again and it is ready to cook.

MENUDO ESTILO NORTEÑO [*Tripe soup*]

7 or 8 servings

A hearty tripe soup as it is prepared in the north of Mexico, this is especially recommended as a cure for a hangover. It is always made for New Year's morning.

A large saucepan (see note below)

1 calf's foot (about 1 to 1½ pounds)

2 pounds honeycomb tripe

1 large onion

3 cloves garlic, peeled

6 peppercorns

2 teaspoons salt, or to taste

4 quarts water

Have the butcher cut the calf's foot into four pieces. Cut the tripe into small squares. Put them into the pan with the rest of the ingredients. Cover with water and bring to a boil. Lower the flame and simmer uncovered for about 2 hours, or until the tripe and foot are just tender but not too soft.

A comal or griddle

3 large chiles anchos

A spice grinder

Meanwhile, toast the chilies well (page 43). Slit them open and remove the seeds and veins. Grind them dry to a fine powder. Add it to the saucepan as the meat is cooking.

1 large chile poblano, roasted and peeled (page 44) or 2 canned, peeled green chilies

The calf's foot

Remove the seeds and veins from the *chile poblano*, cut it into strips, and add to the meat while it is cooking.

Remove the pieces of calf's foot from the pan, and when they are cool enough to handle strip off the fleshy parts. Chop them roughly and return them to the pan.

1½ cups canned hominy (1 pound), drained (see note below)

Salt as necessary

1 scant teaspoon oregano

Add the hominy and continue cooking the *menudo* slowly, still uncovered, for another 2 hours.

Add salt as necessary. Sprinkle with oregano and serve (see note below).

This amount is sufficient for 7 or 8 people. It should be served in large,

(continued)

deep bowls, with hot tortillas and small dishes of chopped *chiles serranos*, finely chopped onion, and wedges of lime for each person to help himself, along with Salsa de Tomate Verde Cruda (page 297) to be eaten with the tortillas.

Menudo is traditionally cooked in an earthenware pot: a very large bean pot would be suitable.

Of course, if you can obtain and prepare the real hominy (page 158) and cook it with the meats right from the beginning the flavor will be far superior.

This soup should be *picante*—after all, it is to shake you up after the night before. If it is not, then toast and grind some of the chili seeds and add them to the *menudo*.

MOLE DE OLLA [*Mole cooked in a pot*]

6 servings

This is a substantial peasant soup, wonderfully savory and a great favorite in Mexico. It is slightly *picante* and has a predominating flavor of *epazote*.

3 *pounds pork neck bones or 3 pounds boiling beef (brisket or a shoulder cut), with bone*

2 *quarts water*

2 *teaspoons salt, or to taste*

A *comal or griddle*

4 chiles anchos

4 chiles pasilla

A *blender*

1 *cup tomates verdes, drained*

½ *medium onion*

2 *cloves garlic, peeled*

A *pinch of cumin seeds*

Have the butcher cut the meat and bones into serving pieces. Cover them with the water, add the salt and bring to a boil. Lower the flame and simmer the meat, uncovered, until it is tender—about 50 minutes for the pork and 1 hour and 10 minutes for the beef.

Meanwhile prepare the chilies. Heat the comal and toast the chilies well, turning them frequently so that they do not burn. When they are cool enough to handle, remove the seeds and veins—do not soak them—and put them into the blender. Blend the chilies with the rest of the ingredients until smooth.

A small frying pan
3 tablespoons peanut or
safflower oil
½ pound zucchini squash
(2 medium)
¼ pound green beans
1 large ear of corn
1 small chayote (½ pound)
3 small potatoes (½
pound)

3 sprigs epazote
Salt as necessary

Heat the oil and fry the sauce for about 5 minutes. Add it to the meat in the pan.

Clean and trim the squash and cut them into halves, then into fours lengthwise. Trim the beans and cut them into halves. Cut the corn into 6 pieces. Cut the *chayote* open and remove the core, then cut into ¼-inch wedges. Skin the potatoes and cut them into cubes.

When the meat is tender, add the vegetables and cook the *mole* slowly, uncovered, for about 30 minutes, or until the vegetables are cooked. Add the *epazote* about 5 minutes before the *mole* is ready, and add salt as necessary.

Serve in large, deep soup bowls, with hot tortillas, wedges of lime, and finely chopped onion on the side.

Traditionally two acid, green prickly pears called *xoconostles* are cut up and boiled with the meat. Though there is really no substitute, the acidity of the lime juice will help. The *epazote* growing wild here is not as strong as the Mexican plant; you will, therefore, need to use 3 large sprigs. Do not soak the chilies before blending them, or they will lose the flavor and piquancy needed in this sort of dish. Some Mexicans prefer to have the vegetables cooked separately and then added to the *mole;* otherwise, they say, it is too sweet. If you like a more pungent chili flavor, then use all *chiles pasillas,* or *chiles guajillos,* and do not use the *anchos.*

GALLINA PINTA [*Oxtail, pork, and bean soup*]

6 to 8 servings

This is a thick peasant soup-stew of oxtail, pork, whole hominy, and beans from Sonora; no one seems to know how it got its name, which means, literally, "speckled hen."

(continued)

A large saucepan
1 oxtail (about 1½ to 2
*   pounds)*
½ onion, roughly sliced
2 cloves garlic, peeled
2 teaspoons salt
½ cup pinto beans
6 peppercorns
2 quarts water
1 pound country-style pork
*   spareribs, cut into*
*   small pieces*
1½ cups prepared whole
*   hominy (page 158)*
*   or 1 1-pound can,*
*   drained*
Salt as necessary

Have the butcher cut the oxtail into small pieces and trim off most, but not all, of the fat. Put it into the pan with the onion, garlic, salt, pinto beans, and peppercorns. Cover with the water and bring to a boil. Lower the flame and simmer for 1 hour.

Add the spareribs and hominy and continue cooking over a low flame, uncovered, for another 1 to 1½ hours, until the meat is very tender and the beans soft. Add salt as necessary.

Gallina pinta is served in deep bowls, with Tortillas de Harina de Trigo (page 66) and Salsa de Jitomate del Norte (page 301) on the side for each one to help himself.

POZOLE DE JALISCO [*Pork and hominy soup*]

12 to 14 servings

This is a superb and unique recipe of the Marín family of Jalisco. The earthy character and flavor of the broth, corn, and meats with the crunchiness of the raw vegetables and the fieriness of the sauce combine to give an incomparable sensation of flavors and textures.

Two days ahead:

1 pound whole hominy or
*   large white dried corn*
*   kernels*

Put the corn to soak as indicated on page 158.

One day ahead:

1½ *pounds pork, tender-*
loin or butt without
bone
½ *pig's head (not more*
than 3 pounds)
1 pound pork neck bones
Cold water to cover
2 *cups* **chiles serranos secos**
(about 3 ounces)
Cold water to cover

On serving day:

A very large pot, prefer-
ably earthenware, for
the pozole
The hominy
14 cups water
(No salt)
A saucepan
The pig's head
Water to cover
(No salt)

The corn
1½ *tablespoons salt*
The soaked meat and neck
bones

Clean and prepare the hominy for cooking.

Cut the pork into large serving pieces and put it, with the head and bones, in cold water to soak overnight. Change the water as often as is practical.

Cover the chilies with cold water and let them soak overnight.

Cover the hominy with the cold, unsalted water. Bring to a boil and cook, uncovered, over a brisk flame until it opens up like a flower—about 1 hour. **Do not stir the corn** during this time, but, if necesary, skim the surface of the water from time to time.

Cover the head with cold, unsalted water. Bring to a boil, then lower the flame and let it simmer, uncovered, until the flesh can be removed from the bone—but do not over-cook—about 1 hour. Set it aside to cool.

When the head is cool enough to handle, remove all the meat, skin, etc., and cut it into serving pieces. Cut the ear up (there should be a piece for everyone) and set the eye aside for the honored guest. Add the pieces of head, and the broth in which it was cooked, to the corn in its pot.

Add the salt. Place the meat on top of the corn and let the *pozole* cook, uncovered, over a gentle flame for about 4 hours. Throughout the cooking time skim the fat from the sur-

Boiling water as necessary

face. Keep some water boiling in a kettle at the side to add to the liquid in the pan. On no account should cold water be added. The liquid should be maintained at almost the same level from start to finish.

THE SALSA PICANTE

A blender

A fine sieve

The soaked chilies and the soaking liquid

Blend the chilies with the water in which they were soaking. Strain the sauce through a sieve. Do not add salt.

To serve:

Place the meat onto a serving dish so it can be divided up more easily and everyone can have the part that he likes best. Serve the *pozole* with the corn in large, deep bowls, with the following small side dishes to which everyone can help himself:

The salsa picante

Finely chopped onion

Sliced radishes

Finely shredded lettuce

Wedges of lime

Note: *Pozole de Jalisco* is not served with oregano, as it is in the neighboring state of Michoacán.

The chili used for the sauce in Jalisco is *chile de árbol*, a long, thin dried red chili; a suitable substitute is *serrano seco*.

The *pozole* should be cooked with plenty of salt; you may need to add more just before the end of the cooking time.

Only those who know the wonderful flavor and consistency of a soup made with the specially prepared corn will appreciate how hard it is for me to say: if you can't get the real corn, use canned. In that case, cook the head first, add the rest of the meat, and an hour later add the drained canned hominy.

Meats (*Carnes*)

A description of a rural dinner outside Jalapa: "A plentiful repast was served up in the Spanish style, in a house built of sticks. Of the greater portion of the dishes I could not learn the component parts; but one striking feature was a pig three months old roasted whole, and stuffed with walnuts, which I thought an excellent dish and well cooked."

—From *Six Months Residence and Travel in Mexico*, BY W. H. BULLOCK

Saturday mornings for me meant markets for all the years I lived in Mexico. I would start off early and go first to San Juan and then stop off at Juárez on my way home. By that time Sr. Raúl, the butcher, was preparing his *almuerzo;* you could smell it the moment you entered the market almost a block away, and he used to make everyone very hungry and very envious. He loved to cook, and this *almuerzo* of his was no ordinary "brunch." A little girl would come by, always at the same hour, with a large, thick tumbler full of milky coffee and a bag of the *panes dulces* that have a rounded top latticed with cinnamon sugar; an old crone would push some steaming, flabby tortillas across the counter and we would all peer curiously toward the little stove to see what he was cooking that day.

Quite often it would be a piece of *carne enchilada*—meat seasoned with a paste of *chiles guajillos*—or a pork chop *adobada* that he used to prepare for his clients. Once he was beating eggs and adding cooked and shredded flank steak. He dropped the mixture by spoonfuls into the hot fat and very soon the little *tortitas* were all puffed up and golden and ready for the tomato broth in which they were to be served.

He taught me how delicious veal kidneys could be; but his were not as large as those we are accustomed to. The whole kidney in its fatty sheath would be no more than about 2½ inches across, and each ripple about ¼ inch. He would slice them, fat and all, and fry them lightly. At his suggestion, I would buy these little kidneys and bake them, complete with their fatty casing until the outside was crisp and brown while the inside was still juicy and very tender.

Sr. Raúl also taught me how to cut the filet for *carne asada* and how to prepare the *adobo* for the pork chops. Since he didn't sell veal I would go to a nearby stand, where a group of cheerful and energetic young men would cut *scaloppine* to perfection and slice a whole calf's liver—pale reddish-brown and weighing no more than two pounds—into paper-thin slices. I can never eat liver anywhere else. So even if you couldn't get the best roast beef or lamb chops, there were so many other things.

The Mexicans are great pork eaters, especially the country people, who will often fatten up a couple of pigs in their back yard as an investment. Our maid Godileva always did, and no household scraps, potato peelings, or outside lettuce leaves escaped her eye; they were carried home along with the neighbors' stale bread and dried tortillas for the pigs. For many months after I had left Mexico I would hesitate on my way to the incinerator and wonder why there wasn't a pig around somewhere.

Whenever I am in Cuernavaca, I go to the large central market to buy pork. The meat is so soft that it seems to be dripping off the bone. It is cooked through in no time, and the flesh is unbelievably soft and succulent.

The butchers' shops in small villages and country towns are hung with yards and yards of thin meat—moist, drying, and dried *cecina*. I wanted to learn how to cut it, so one Sunday morning I went to the almost deserted market in Huauchinango, right on the border between Veracruz and Puebla. The two friendly butchers would take a rump of beef or pork, or a huge lump of ox lung, and with a long, thin knife cut a first fine layer, then turn the meat and cut the other way, backwards and forwards, turning it over and over until, in no time at all, the piece would be flattened out into one long continuous strip. With a flick of the wrist, they would throw on a fine layer of salt, squeeze plenty of lime juice on it and fold the meat up into a basket like a pile of laundry, where it was left to season overnight. The next day they would hang it up in an airy place to dry. I have tried to do it and have hung the results, scrawny bits of uneven pork, on a line across the window of my apartment on New York's West Side to dry in the spring sunshine. Despite its inexpert appearance it tasted very good broiled over charcoal and eaten with a green tomato or *chile cascabel* sauce. It will keep indefinitely in the refrigerator, getting drier and drier. You simply rinse it and oil it well before cooking.

The beef country is in the north of Mexico, and Chihuahua City has some of the most opulent steak houses in the whole of Mexico. They say the beef has an extra good flavor there because the animals feed on wild oregano. To the west, in Hermosillo, when you are served the biggest steaks of all in the large open-air restaurants, where they are cooked to order over wood fires, they go to the other extreme and have the flimsiest beef jerky— *carne machacada*—pounded to a fluff.

I have eaten *cabrito*—kid—in many places, but nowhere is it as good as in Monterrey. The kid must not be older than 30 days, for after that time it ceases to be milk fed, and as it starts to browse the flavor of the flesh becomes strong and goaty. Preferably it should be cooked, and eaten, out of doors, over a fire of *huisache* branches—but I would settle any day for the *cabrito* so carefully cooked in the Restaurante Principal in Monterrey. It is opened out flat and paled onto a stake, which is set at a 70-degree angle at the edge of the fire. It takes two hours to cook, and every half hour its position is changed. The cooking follows a strict pattern, and when there are at least ten *cabritos* being cooked at once you wonder how the cook remembers exactly which way each one should go next—but he does. The *riñonada,* the choicest part, is the lower part of the back, where the drippings from the fatty kidney sheath continually baste it. It is brown and crisp on the outside, but the flesh inside is as delicate and tender as the finest veal.

But there are other things that go along with the *cabrito:* a bowl of *frijoles rancheros* quite strongly seasoned with cumin; a sausage of the intestine stuffed with liver and kidney called *machitos* (not to be confused with the *machitos* served in the capital, which is something entirely different). And, most delicate of all, the steamed head of the little goat, the tongue of which is the delicacy of all time. Or you could have a stew of *cabrito* thickened with the blood—*fritada*—which I frankly don't like.

The meat stands in the Culiacán market are piled with brick-colored *chilorio*, a ready-made filling for *tacos* of shredded, crisp pork seasoned with ground chilies and spices, and cuts of beef called *gusano* for the local *asado sinaloense*. Curiously this is not roasted meat as the name implies, but boiled and then fried in cubes with potatoes, smothered in a tomato sauce and garnished with zucchini, carrots, onion rings, and lettuce. It is a very popular supper dish, especially in Mazatlán when the day has cooled off a little and you have eaten a light seafood lunch.

In Guadalajara the most touted meat is *birria,* and throughout the central plateau of Mexico the Sunday marketplaces are full of lamb and *pancita* barbecued in pits lined with maguey leaves. The *pancita* is lamb's stomach stuffed with chili-seasoned lamb's liver and kidney as well as the intestines of the lamb. In the smaller towns and villages you can nearly always be sure of getting *mixiote,* which is lamb seasoned with dried chilies and cooked in little packages covered with the membrane stripped from the outside of the maguey leaves. In Oaxaca, the *barbacoa* is of sheep or goat cooked on a bed of roughly crushed maize, which absorbs the juices and is wonderfully savory.

As you go further south to the Isthmus of Tehuantepec and Chiapas, the iguana comes into its own—and I shall always remember the armadillo that crawled across my foot in the Tuxtla Gutiérrez market as it was waiting with many others to be sold on the market floor. In the tall forests of Chiapas and Tabasco toward the Usumacinta River, the delicacies are spider monkey (now forbidden, I believe) and the paca—*tepezcuintle.*

If you go to the upper floor of the Mérida market, you will find every imaginable cut of cooked venison; they say it has been cooked in a *pib* in the ground. The flesh of the small deer that abounds in Yucatán is light in color and delicate in flavor, much more like veal than the gamy dark-red venison that we are more accustomed to. It is often served in a *pipián* made of very tiny pumpkin seeds that are toasted and ground, hull and seed together. Or it is shredded finely and mixed with minutely chopped radishes, onion, and coriander and moistened with Seville orange juice to make a *salpicón* for *tacos.*

Saturday seems to be the day for slaughtering cattle in Campeche, for *chocolomo* is the Saturday night special. It is made only with freshly killed beef and offal. It is one of those hearty soup-stews that are found all over Mexico, but with a difference: along with the meat, the brains, kidney, liver, and heart are cooked with toasted garlic and onion and flavored at the last moment with the bitter lime that gives its name to the typical lime soup of Yucatán.

One could go on forever. The variations are enormous and bear witness to the great creativity of Mexican cooks.

COCHINITA PIBIL [*Yucatecan barbecued pig*]

6 servings

Pib is the Mayan word for the traditional oven of Yucatán, a pit lined with stones, in which the famous *cochinita*—little pig, turkey, or the regional *tamal* pie—*muk-bil pollo*—is cooked.

A hole is dug in the ground about two feet deep and the bottom covered with large stones. A substantial wood fire is set alight on the stones, and when it has been burning for some time and they are very hot, the wood embers and some of the stones are taken out. The meat, wrapped in banana leaves, is set in a container onto the stones. It is first covered with a lot of wet sacking, and then the hot stones and embers are placed on top. The hole is filled in with earth and the meat left to cook for about three hours.

One day ahead:

3½ to 4½ pounds pork, preferably end of loin

Score the pork all over and set aside while you prepare the seasoning paste.

A blender
1 tablespoon softened achiote seeds (page 12)
¼ teaspoon cumin seeds

Crush the softened *achiote* a little before putting it into the blender. Add the rest of the ingredients and blend to as smooth a consistency as possible. Spread the paste over the meat.

(*continued*)

¼ teaspoon oregano
12 peppercorns
3 whole allspice
4 cloves garlic, peeled
⅛ teaspoon hot paprika
   (optional)
1 tablespoon salt
¼ cup Seville orange juice
   (page 27) or mild
   white vinegar

2 large pieces of banana
   leaf

Lightly sear the banana leaves over a bare flame to make them more flexible. Wrap the meat up in them and leave to season in the refrigerator for at least six hours or overnight.

On serving day:

Preheat the oven to 350°.

A Dutch oven, preferably
The wrapped meat
½ cup cold water

Place a rack at the bottom of the Dutch oven and set the wrapped meat on it. Add the water and cover the dish with a tightly fitting lid. Cook for 2½ hours. Turn the meat and baste it well with the juices at the bottom of the dish. Cook for a further 2½ hours, or until the meat is soft and falling off the bone.

A serving dish

Shred the meat roughly. Pour the fat and juices from the pan over it. Serve hot, with tortillas and Salsa para Cochinita Pibil (see below) so that each person can make his own *tacos* (put some shredded meat onto the tortilla, sprinkle it with the sauce, and roll the tortilla up).

SOME TYPICAL MEXICAN DISHES
1 *frutas cubiertas* (candied fruits); **2** *tamales;*
3 chocolate; **4** tortillas; **5** *papa-dzules,* a Yucatecan specialty; **6** *chiles rellenos en nogada* (stuffed chilies in walnut sauce); **7** *dulces Mexicanas* (sweetmeats)

SALSA PARA COCHINITA PIBIL

½ cup very finely chopped
   onion
3 chiles habaneros *or*
   chiles cayennes, *very*
   finely chopped
½ teaspoon salt
⅔ cup Seville orange juice
   (page 27)

Mix all the ingredients together. Serve in a separate dish.

The cuts from each end of the loin of pork are very good for this type of cooking. The meat is succulent and has just the right amount of fat. The center cut of loin tends to be too dry. Of course, if you have a huge oven or a *pib* in the garden you could cook a 20-pound pig—the ideal size. I have tried unsuccessfully to cook a very small suckling pig in this way, but the flesh and flavor are simply not right.

PUERCO EN MOLE VERDE [*Pork in green mole*]

6 servings

I have tried many variations of this dish all over Mexico but to my mind this is the most fragrant and satisfying one: it is a family recipe from Jalapa in the state of Veracruz. The original calls for the strong anise-flavored herb *hoja santa* (*Piper sanctum*) and some tender shoots of the *chayote* plant. If you have a garden and some zucchini squash growing, then use the young shoots that are very tender and sweet; if not, then use the substitutes suggested by the family in Mexico—a few young radish leaves and an avocado leaf.

(continued)

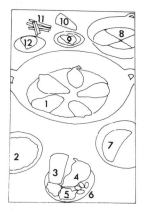

THREE OF MEXICO'S MOST POPULAR DISHES AND THEIR INGREDIENTS
1 *chiles rellenos* in tomato broth, ready to serve; **2** *relleno* (stuffing) for the chilies; **3** *acitrón* (candied cactus) for the stuffing; **4** *chile poblano,* cleaned and ready for stuffing; **5** raisins for the stuffing; **6** almonds for the stuffing; **7** batter-coated chili being fried; **8** the first stage in making *chongos,* the Mexican dessert of cooked milk curds; the milk is set and cut, ready for cooking, and the cinnamon and sugar have been added; **9** a portion of the finished *chongos;* **10** a cone of *piloncillo* (raw sugar); **11** cinnamon sticks; **12** a portion of *huevos reales,* a milk-curd dessert garnished with raisins and cinnamon

A large saucepan

4 pounds pork, preferably
    country-style spare-
    ribs

½ onion, roughly sliced

Have the meat cut up into serving pieces. Put them into the saucepan with the onion, garlic, peppercorns, and salt, cover with water, and bring to a boil. Lower the flame and simmer for 25 minutes.

2 cloves garlic, peeled

8 peppercorns

1 tablespoon salt

Water to cover

1 pound zucchini squash
    (3 medium)

1 pound chayote (1
    chayote)

½ pound green beans

Clean and trim the squash and cut them into quarters. Cut into the *chayote* and remove the core, then cut into wedges about ½ inch thick. Trim the beans and cut into halves. Add the vegetables to the meat in the pan and cook for a further 15 minutes, or until both meat and vegetables are just tender. **Do not overcook.** Drain the meat and vegetables and set them aside. Cool and skim the broth and set it aside.

½ pound frozen lima
    beans

A blender

3 cups tomates verdes,
    drained (see note be-
    low)

2 cloves garlic, peeled

6 chiles serranos

Cook the lima beans separately and set them aside.

Blend the *tomates verdes*, garlic, and chilies to a smooth sauce.

A frying pan

¼ cup lard

The sauce

2 cups reserved broth

Heat the lard and cook the sauce over a high flame until it has reduced and thickened a little—about 10 minutes.

Add the broth and continue cooking the sauce a few minutes more.

The cooked meat

The cooked vegetables

Add the meat and vegetables to the sauce and heat them through over a low flame while you prepare the greenstuff.

A blender
1 large sprig parsley
4 sprigs fresh coriander
3 large romaine lettuce
    leaves
A few radish leaves
1 avocado leaf, fresh or
    dried
A coarse sieve
Salt as necessary

Blend the leaves until smooth and strain them into the *mole* **at the last minute.** Bring the *mole* just to a boil, add salt as necessary, and serve immediately.

This *mole* is traditionally served with tortillas only.

Country-style spareribs—the shoulder or rib end of the loin cut horizontally between the bones—is ideal for this and for most Mexican dishes calling for pork.

Like any stew, this can be cooked ahead of time and heated through very slowly about 30 minutes before serving, but *add the greenstuff at the very last moment.* The stew does not freeze successfully.

CHULETAS DE PUERCO ADOBADAS
[*Pork chops seasoned with adobo*]

6 servings

Adobo, a paste made of ground chilies, spices, herbs, and vinegar, was originally used for pickling meat. In the recipe below the pork chops are marinated in it and then cooked very slowly. When I first tried this it was served with *Salsa de tomate verde cruda* and sour cream—a marvelous combination.

One day ahead:

A griddle or comal
4 large chiles anchos

A bowl
Hot water to cover

Toast the chilies lightly, turning them from time to time so that they do not burn. Slit them open and remove the seeds and veins.

Put the chilies into the bowl and cover them with hot water. Let them soak for about

A blender
The soaked chilies
⅛ teaspoon cumin seeds
⅛ teaspoon oregano
⅛ teaspoon thyme
1 tablespoon salt
2 cloves garlic, peeled
½ cup mild white vinegar
 or Seville orange juice
  (page 27)
6 thick shoulder pork
 chops
The paste

20 minutes, then remove with a slotted spoon and transfer to the blender jar. Add the rest of the ingredients and blend into a fairly smooth paste. Do not overblend.

Have the butcher pound the chops until flattened. Spread them with the paste on both sides and set aside to season, refrigerated, overnight.

On serving day, have ready:

1 medium onion, cut into thin rings   Sliced radishes
Shredded lettuce

A frying pan
Melted lard or pork fat
 (just enough to cover
 the bottom of the
 pan)
The pork chops
The sliced onion
The shredded lettuce
The sliced radishes

Heat the fat and fry the chops **very slowly** on both sides until they are well cooked—about 20 minutes, depending on the thickness of the meat. When they have cooked through, raise the flame and brown them quickly.

Serve the chops immediately, garnished with the sliced onion, and decorate the plate with the lettuce and radishes.

You can actually season the pork and keep it for several days in the refrigerator. The meat becomes drier, but the flavor improves daily.

Start with very little fat in the pan. You can always add more, but you do not want the meat to become saturated. Any of the savory chili-flavored fat left over can be saved and used when scrambling eggs.

PUERCO EN ADOBO [*Pork in adobo*]

6 to 8 servings

The *adobo* in this recipe is diluted with broth to make a sauce.

A large saucepan
3½ to 4 pounds pork, cut
  into 1½-inch cubes
1 pound pork neck bones
½ onion, sliced
2 cloves garlic, peeled
8 peppercorns
1 tablespoon salt, or to
  taste
Water barely to cover

Put the meat and the rest of the ingredients into the pan and barely cover with water. Bring the meat to a boil, then lower the flame and simmer it until it is tender—about 40 minutes. Let the meat cool in the broth.

A griddle or comal
6 chiles anchos
10 chiles pasilla
A bowl
Hot water to cover

Drain the meat, reserving the broth. Set them both aside. Discard the bones.

Toast the chilies lightly, turning them from time to time so that they do not burn.

A blender
The chilies
1 cup chili water
1-inch stick cinnamon
5 whole cloves
6 peppercorns
¼ teaspoon thyme
¼ teaspoon marjoram
¼ teaspoon cumin seeds
6 cloves garlic, peeled
2 tablespoons mild white
  vinegar

When the chilies are cool enough to handle, slit them open and remove the seeds and veins. Cover them with hot water and leave them to soak about 20 minutes.

Transfer the chilies to the blender with 1 cup of the water in which they were soaking. Add the rest of the ingredients and blend to a fairly smooth texture. Do not overblend.

(*continued*)

A flameproof serving dish	Melt the lard and fry the meat lightly. Remove and set aside.
10 tablespoons lard	
The meat	
The chili sauce	Add the chili sauce, bay leaves, and sugar to the dish and cook for about 15 minutes, stirring most of the time so that the sauce does not stick to the dish. Keep a lid handy, as it splatters rather fiercely.
2 bay leaves	
2 tablespoons granulated sugar	
	When the sauce becomes a very dark red and thickens so that it will barely slide off a wooden spoon, it is cooked.
3 cups reserved meat broth	Gradually stir in the broth and add salt as necessary. Add the meat and continue cooking the *adobo* over a low flame for another 10 minutes.
Salt as necessary	
The cooked meat	
1 large onion	Cut the onion into thin rings and sprinkle them over the *adobo* just before serving.

While in Mexico the *adobo* would be served with tortillas and nothing else, white rice (Arroz Blanco, page 290) goes very well with it.

This is how Godileva, our maid, used to cook it. We would take turns grinding the chilies on the *metate;* it was well worth the hard work because, as with *mole poblano*, there *is* a difference in texture and therefore flavor between this method and using the blender. Many Mexicans like their *adobos* and *moles* very sweet—it is entirely a matter of taste.

The sauce itself can be made 2 or 3 days ahead—in fact it improves in flavor—up to the point of adding the broth. The pork can then be cooked the day that you are going to use it. If there is any left over, the sauce freezes very well and makes a very good filling, mixed with shredded meat, for *tacos*.

You could use veal instead of pork for this recipe.

GUISO DE PUERCO [*Pork stew*]

6 servings

Rufina, the maid whose recipe this is and who was with us for some years, came from a very poor village in Oaxaca. She was young and impatient and didn't really like cooking—but she did like to eat—and everything she made for us was delicious. This dish, pork cooked in a sauce of tomatoes and pineapple—spiced and slightly sweetened—is very simple and refreshing and perfect for those who don't like *picante* food, since the chili is cooked whole, and while it lends a flavor to the sauce, it does not make it *picante*. The long, thin yellow-green *chile güero*, which has such a delicious flavor, was used in Mexico.

A saucepan
4 pounds of country-
    style spareribs
1 tablespoon salt
6 peppercorns
2 cloves garlic, peeled,
½ onion, sliced
Cold water to cover

Have the butcher cut the meat into 12 portions. Put the meat, together with the salt, peppercorns, garlic, and onion, into the pan, cover with cold water, and bring to a boil. Lower the flame and simmer the meat until it is just tender—about 35 minutes. Set aside to cool in the broth.

A fireproof serving dish
¼ cup lard
1 medium onion, thinly
    sliced
3 cloves garlic, peeled and
    sliced
A blender
2½ pounds tomatoes

Melt the lard and cook the onion and garlic, without browning, until they are soft.

Skin the tomatoes and remove the seeds (page 43). Chop the tomatoes roughly and put them, together with the juice strained from the seeds, into the blender. Blend them for a few seconds only. Add the tomato puree to the onions and garlic in the pan and cook over a high flame until it has reduced and thickened—about 15 minutes.

(continued)

1½ thick slices fresh
    pineapple
1 large ripe plantain
2 sprigs parsley
Scant ¼ teaspoon oregano
1 heaped tablespoon
    slivered almonds
2 tablespoons raisins
2 tablespoons granulated
    sugar
1 teaspoon salt
½-inch stick cinnamon
4 whole cloves
4 chiles serranos
    whole
10 green olives

Skin the pineapple and cut it into small wedges. Skin the plantain and cut it into thick rounds. Add them with the rest of the ingredients to the sauce and cook over a fairly high flame for 15 minutes. By that time the sauce will have thickened considerably and be very well seasoned.

The meat
1½ to 2 cups reserved meat
    broth, approximately
Salt as necessary

Strain the meat and add it with the broth to the sauce and cook for another 15 minutes over a low flame. Add salt as necessary. The sauce should be neither too watery nor too dry—you may need to add a little extra broth.

In Mexico this would be served, as are so many of the main meat dishes, just with tortillas, but white rice (Arroz Blanco, page 290) is very good if you wish to have something else instead. Don't overcook the meat in the first instance, since it has plenty of time to get more tender with the subsequent cooking in the sauce. It is best prepared the same day as you are going to eat it, but it could be made several hours ahead, just adding the meat and the broth at the last moment. This sauce does not freeze well.

This dish can also be made with chicken.

CARNE DE PUERCO CON UCHEPOS [*Pork with fresh corn tamales*]

6 servings

For years I had heard about *uchepos*, but never managed to be in Morelia just at the right time of year. Finally, about two summers ago, I made it. One of the great regional cooks, Beatriz Dávalos had them prepared especially for me at the Casino Charro and gave me the recipe. Since then, when anyone asks me what I consider to be the outstanding dishes of Mexico, *carne de puerco con uchepos* is high on my list. It has such a wonderful contrast of flavors and textures: the slightly crunchy fresh corn of the *tamales*, the soft pork in its broiled tomato sauce, and the biting, inky flavor of the chili strips against the sour cream and cheese; not to mention the colors—yellow, red, and white with a lattice of black-green.

A flameproof serving dish
4½ pounds country-
*   style spareribs*
Water to cover
2 teaspoons salt

Barely cover the meat with water, add the salt, and bring to a boil. Continue cooking the meat over a medium flame until all the water has evaporated and the meat is just tender—about 45 minutes. Let the fat render out of the meat and fry it until it is slightly browned (just like Carnitas, page 112). Remove the meat and all but about 4 tablespoons of the fat.

Meanwhile, prepare the tomato sauce.

A blender
3 pounds tomatoes, broiled
*   (page 44)*
4 chiles serranos, toasted
*   (page 43)*
2 large cloves garlic,
*   peeled*
1 teaspoon salt

Blend the tomatoes with the rest of the ingredients to a smooth sauce.

Add the tomato sauce to the fat in the dish and cook it over a high flame for about 8 minutes, until it has reduced and thickened a little.

(continued)

The meat

Lower the flame, add the meat, and heat through gently.

To serve:

18 *small Uchepos*
    Fingidos (*page 99*)
1 *cup Thick Sour Cream*
    (*page 20*)
½ *pound farmer cheese*
3 *large canned, peeled*
    green chilies with
    seeds

Serve each portion with 2 *uchepos,* meat and sauce, some sour cream, strips of farmer cheese, and finely shredded *picante* peeled chili.

This is one case where beans are served with the main course. Serve, on a separate plate, a small quantity of Frijoles Refritos (page 282), cooked without onion. (In Morelia a light-colored bean flecked with purple called *flor de mayo* would be used.)

I am afraid the canned, peeled green chilies are no real substitute for the biting piquancy of the *chilaca* (which when dried is the *chile pasilla*). If you are lucky enough to live where a great variety of Mexican products are readily available you may be able to find them—they are certainly in the Los Angeles markets. Roast them over an open flame as you would *chiles poblanos,* put them into a polyethylene bag to steam for about 10 minutes, then wash off the burned skin. Remove the seeds and veins—be careful of your hands, as the chilies burn quite fiercely—and tear the flesh into long thin strips.

The *uchepos* can be made several days ahead; and if there are any left over they freeze very well (see note on *tamales,* page 92). And the sauce and meat can be cooked several hours ahead. You may need to dilute the sauce a little with some water when you reheat it.

CARNE ASADA A LA TAMPIQUEÑA
[*Broiled meat in the Tampico manner*]

In the 1930s, José Loredo went from his native Tampico to Mexico City —where he now owns a number of successful restaurants—to start the Tampico Club. It was there that he invented *carne asada a la Tampiqueña,* which became immediately popular. It has now spread all over Mexico and is firmly established in the cuisine. It is very easy to prepare and usually makes a great hit.

For 1 serving:

2 strips of tender steak, 8 inches long, 2 inches wide, and between ¼ and ½ inch thick

2 Enchiladas Sencillas (page 78), with red or green tomato sauce and filled with farmer cheese

A small serving of Rajas de Chile Poblano (page 260)

A small serving of Guacamole (page 113)

A small serving of Frijoles Refritos (page 282)

—and, of course, plenty of hot tortillas.

To prepare the meat, open up a 4-inch slice of filet to make a flat strip. Cut through the slice, with the grain, to within ½ inch of the underside. With a very sharp knife open up each side, cutting the meat as if you were unrolling a jelly roll. Cut the strip into 2 2-inch-wide lengths. Flatten the meat a little with the side of a heavy cleaver.

Season the meat well on both sides with salt, pepper, and a little lime juice, and sear it quickly on both sides on a very hot, well-greased iron griddle or frying pan. Cook longer to taste and serve immediately surrounded by the *enchiladas, guacamole,* and the other accompaniments.

Since the price of filet is usually prohibitive—at least I think so for this type of dish—I use a piece of skirt steak, cut open horizontally, which is simply delicious. You may need to trim off the fat.

In San Luis Potosí I have eaten *carne asada a la Huasteca* which was almost the same, but it was served with a little ball of *asadero* cheese (page 16), Guacamole (page 113), and a small bowl of Frijoles de Olla (page 281).

BISTECES RANCHEROS [*Country steaks*]

6 servings

This dish is a typical example of the supremely simple but robust country cooking of Sonora. Nothing in it shrieks out loud, and the touches of flavor lent by the coriander and mild chilies are just right.

Preheat the oven to 350°.

6 shoulder or chuck steaks about ¼ inch thick (about 2 pounds) *1 large clove garlic, peeled* *Salt and pepper to taste*	Season the steaks on both sides with garlic, salt, and pepper and set aside for about 1 hour.
A large frying pan *¼ cup peanut or safflower oil* *The steaks* *An ovenproof serving dish*	Heat 2 tablespoons of the oil until it smokes. Quickly brown the steaks on both sides, adding more oil as necessary. Place them in one layer on the dish, set aside, and keep warm.
1 large onion, thinly sliced	Let the oil cool a little, then add the onion and cook it gently, without browning, until it is transparent.
4 large tomatoes (2 pounds) *A grater*	Cut a slice off the top of each tomato. Grate the flesh on a coarse grater until only the flattened skin is left in your hand. Don't forget to grate the flesh from the top slices.
The tomato pulp *4 whole sprigs fresh coriander* *1½ teaspoons salt, or to taste*	Add the tomato pulp, coriander, and salt to the onions in the pan and let the sauce cook fast over a fairly high flame for 5 minutes. Stir from time to time to prevent sticking.
1 pound red bliss or waxy new potatoes *The steaks* *The sauce*	Peel and slice the potatoes about ¼ inch thick. Place the slices on top of the steaks. Pour the sauce over the meat and potatoes.

3 canned, peeled green
chilies

Remove the seeds from the chilies and cut them into strips. Place the chili strips on top of the sauce, cover the dish, and bake for 35 minutes. Bake, uncovered, for another 55 minutes, by which time the sauce should be reduced and the potatoes just beginning to brown.

CARNE CLAVEATADA [Pot roast studded with almonds and bacon]

6 servings

This pot roast of beef from Oaxaca, studded with almonds and bacon and cooked with a sauce of *chiles anchos* and spices, is a very satisfying dish indeed.

Preheat the oven to 325°.

¼ pound bacon or ham
3 pounds brisket, trimmed
    of some of the fat
1½ tablespoons slivered
    almonds
A griddle or comal
3 large chiles anchos

A small bowl
Hot water
A blender
3 whole cloves
½-inch stick cinnamon
⅛ teaspoon thyme
⅛ teaspoon marjoram
⅛ teaspoon oregano
4 peppercorns
3 cloves garlic, peeled
2 teaspoons salt
1½ tablespoons vinegar
¾ cup water

Cut the bacon into small pieces. Gash the meat all over with a knife point and insert the almonds and bacon. Set it aside while the sauce is prepared.

Toast the chilies lightly, turning them from time to time so that they do not burn. Slit them open and remove the seeds and veins.

Put the chilies into the bowl and leave them to soak in the hot water for about 20 minutes, then transfer them with a slotted spoon to the blender jar. Add the rest of the ingredients and blend to a smooth puree.

(continued)

A flameproof casserole
3 tablespoons lard or
    bacon fat
The meat
The chili mixture

Melt the lard, and when it is very hot brown the meat well all over. Remove the meat and set it aside. Drain off the fat, leaving only 3 tablespoons in the pan.

Add the chili mixture to the pan and let it cook fast for about 5 minutes, stirring it all the time.

Return the meat to the pan and baste it with the sauce. Cover the casserole with a tightly fitting lid and cook the meat for 2 hours.

A saucepan
1½ pounds red bliss or
    new potatoes
Boiling water to cover
A colander

Put the potatoes, unskinned, into the pan, cover them with boiling water, and let boil fast for 5 minutes. Drain them and set them aside to cool.

When the potatoes are cool enough to handle, skin them.

Remove the casserole from the oven, turn the meat over, and baste it well with the sauce. Scrape the sauce from the sides and bottom of the pan and add a little water if it has thickened too much.

Put the potatoes into the sauce around the meat, replace the lid, and let the meat cook until it is very tender but not falling apart— test after about 1 hour and 10 minutes.

A warm serving dish

Slice the meat fairly thickly and place it on the dish with the potatoes around it. Pour the sauce over it.

This pot roast *could* be prepared a day ahead if necessary, but in that case the potato would have to be cooked separately and just warmed through in the sauce. A simple green salad would be a very good accompaniment to this dish.

BIRRIA [*Seasoned and baked meat*]

8 to 10 servings

The word *birria* means something deformed or grotesque, and it is used colloquially in the northwest to mean a mess or failure. This certainly looks a mess when it is cooked, but it is a very savory one.

It is a really rustic dish. Usually a whole goat or lamb, although in some places just the offal, is seasoned with a paste of ground spices and chilies and cooked in a pit barbecue. As you wander around Guadalajara at night, you can see that *tacos* of *birria* head the list of *antojitos* on the street-side stands and always appear prominently on the Sunday menus of the smaller regional restaurants.

One day ahead:

2 *lamb shanks*
A *veal breast*
A *lamb breast*
3 *pounds loin of pork, rib
    or shoulder end*
2 *tablespoons salt*
A *comal or griddle*
6 **chiles anchos**
3 **chiles guajillos**
10 **chiles cascabel**
A *bowl*
Hot water to cover
A *blender*
18 *peppercorns*
4 *whole cloves*
¼ *teaspoon oregano*
Scant ¼ *teaspoon cumin
    seeds*
¼ *cup vinegar*
2 *teaspoons salt*
6 *cloves garlic, peeled*
½ *small onion*

There will be approximately 6 to 7 pounds of meat. Slash the meats in several places down to the bone and rub the salt well into it. Meanwhile, prepare the chili paste.

Heat the comal and toast the chilies lightly, turning them from time to time so that they will not burn. Remove the veins and seeds.

Put the chilies to soak in hot water for about 20 minutes, then transfer with a slotted spoon to the blender jar, add the rest of the ingredients, and blend to a smooth sauce.

(continued)

Cover the meat thickly with the paste and set it aside to season for about 18 hours.

On serving day:

A large Dutch oven or casserole with a tightly fitting lid
1½ cups water
The meat
Flour and water paste

Preheat the oven to 350°.

Put the water into the bottom of the casserole and place the meat on a rack so that it is just above the water. Seal the lid with a paste of flour and water and cook for about 3½ to 4 hours, by which time the meat should be almost falling off the bones.

Strain off the juices from the bottom of the pan, cool, and skim off the fat. There should be about 2 cups of juices left—if not, make it up to 2 cups with water.

A blender
2 pounds tomatoes, broiled (page 44)
A saucepan
The sauce
The meat juice
1 cup onion, finely chopped
½ teaspoon oregano

Blend the tomatoes to a smooth sauce.

Put the sauce and the skimmed juices from the meat into a saucepan and bring to a boil.

Serve each portion of mixed meats in a deep bowl. Pour ½ cup sauce over the meat and sprinkle with the chopped onion and oregano. Eat with tortillas.

I have a friend in Guadalajara who always prepares this dish with mixed meats, but I have changed the recipe she gave me in two respects: (1) she uses all *chiles anchos,* which are boiled for 5 minutes, and (2) the meat is steamed. I find it much more delicious with the meat cooked in the oven and the chilies, with a few *cascabeles* and *guajillos* added, toasted and soaked in the usual way. It is customary in the northwestern states to boil chilies, but I think they lose a lot of their character.

Apart from the fact that it is unnecessary to buy expensive cuts, *birria* is a great opportunity to use the succulent and delicious parts of meat like lamb shanks and breasts, and veal breasts—you can also include some goat's meat, if you like. I know that these are very fatty cuts, but the fat cooks off and the broth is skimmed before it is used in the sauce.

ESTOFADO DE LENGUA [*Stewed tongue*]

6 servings

A large saucepan
A 5-pound fresh tongue
1 small onion
3 cloves garlic, peeled
2 tablespoons salt
8 peppercorns
Water to cover

A large frying pan
3 tablespoons lard
2 chiles anchos

A blender

*2 ounces almonds (a good
⅓ cup), unskinned*

1 small stale tortilla

*2 pounds tomatoes, un-
skinned*

A spice grinder or blender
*2 tablespoons sesame
seeds, toasted (page
43)*
⅛ teaspoon oregano
⅛ teaspoon thyme
⅛ teaspoon marjoram
½-inch stick cinnamon
2 teaspoons salt, or to taste
A frying pan

Put the tongue into the saucepan with the onion, garlic, salt, and peppercorns, cover with water, and bring to a boil. Lower the flame and simmer until the tongue is tender— about 3 hours. Let the tongue cool in the broth, and as soon as it is cool enough to handle remove and discard the skin. Return the tongue to the broth and keep it warm.

Slit the chilies open and remove the veins and seeds. Melt the lard and fry the chilies lightly on both sides. (Take care not to over- heat the lard, as the chilies burn very easily.) Using a slotted spoon, transfer the chilies to the blender jar.

In the same lard, fry the almonds until they are well browned. Crush them a little before adding them to the blender.

In the same lard, fry the tortilla crisp and crush it a little before adding it to the blender.

Chop the tomatoes finely and cook them in the same lard over a high flame for about 10 minutes. Add them to the blender jar.

Grind the toasted, cooled seeds and add to the blender.

Add the rest of the ingredients and blend until you have a very smooth sauce.

Melt the lard, add the sauce, and let it

(*continued*)

3 tablespoons lard or oil
The sauce

Tongue broth as necesary
Salt as necessary
A warmed serving dish
Salt as necessary
The sauce
½ cup green olives

cook over a low flame for about 10 minutes, stirring it from time to time. It should just lightly coat the back of a wooden spoon when cooked. If it is too thick, then add a little of the tongue broth. Add salt as necessary.

Slice the tongue thinly and sprinkle it with a little salt, if necessary. Arrange it on the serving dish, mask with some of the sauce and garnish with the olives. Serve the rest of the sauce separately.

This can be served with white rice (Arroz Blanco, page 290) or plain boiled potatoes. If necessary it could all be cooked a day ahead and left overnight in the broth; the flavor of tongue does not seem to suffer when it is warmed through. The sauce freezes well.

For those who like their food *picante, jalapeños en escabeche* could be served separately.

FIAMBRE POTOSINO [*Cold meats in a vinaigrette sauce*]

6 servings

Whenever Paul and I were making the drive north to Monterrey or Laredo, we would be sure to stop in San Luis Potosí for lunch at La Lonja, one of the really distinguished regional restaurants in Mexico. We would unfailingly order *fiambre*, which was refreshing and light after a long, hot drive.

Some years later, when I returned to San Luis to learn more about Potosino cooking, I met the owner/manager Don Miguel—a most distinguished and charming old man who with Arturo his maître d' took a great delight in introducing me to the local food. One unforgettable meal—and I know that this is irrelevant here, but the meal was so incredible I can't resist putting it in—was designed to show me the delicacies the desert can produce. It started with what I called desert hors d'oeuvre, for the dish had on it yucca flower buds cooked with egg; the delicate heart of a local palm with an excellent vinaigrette; pickled maguey flower buds, called *chochas*, and the round buds of the large cushion-shaped biznaga cactus, called *cabuches.* After that came a strip of flattened filet of beef, charcoal-broiled *a la huasteca* and served with a small dish of *garambullas*—the round, grapelike fruit of the organ cactus, juicy and sweet, with small, crunchy seeds inside. And for dessert there was a special *queso de tuna* made by an old man in a nearby village who makes it better than anyone else; nobody knows his secret. It is a thick brown paste of red prickly pears cooked with raw sugar and dried in the sun.

THE MEATS

A large saucepan
3 pig's feet, cut into halves
2 teaspoons salt
1 bay leaf
10 peppercorns
½ medium onion
2 cloves garlic, peeled
⅛ teaspoon thyme
⅛ teaspoon marjoram
Cold water to cover

Put the pig's feet into the saucepan with the rest of the ingredients and the cold water to cover. Bring the water to a boil, lower the flame, and simmer the feet until they are tender—about 1¾ hours—then leave them to cool off in the broth.

A saucepan
1 fresh calf's tongue—
    (about 1½ to 1¾
        pounds)
2 teaspoons salt
6 peppercorns
1 clove garlic, peeled
¼ onion
½ bay leaf
⅛ teaspoon thyme
⅛ teaspoon marjoram
Cold water to cover

Meanwhile, trim the tongue of all excess fat. Put it into the saucepan with the other ingredients, cover with cold water, and bring to a boil. Lower the flame and simmer until the tongue is tender—about 1 hour and 20 minutes. Leave the tongue in the broth to cool off a little. When it is cool enough to handle, skin it and put it back into the broth to get completely cold. Cut it into slices.

A saucepan
3 chicken breasts
¼ small onion
1 clove garlic, peeled

Put the chicken breasts into the pan with the rest of the ingredients, cover them with the broth and bring to a boil. Lower the flame and let the breasts simmer for about 20 min-

(continued)

Well-seasoned chicken
  broth to cover
A saucepan
4 large carrots
5 small red bliss or waxy
  potatoes (about ½
  pound)
Boiling water to cover
2 teaspoons salt

utes. Let them cool off in the broth, then remove the skin and slice them thinly.

Scrape the carrots and cut them into ¼-inch rounds. Scrape the potatoes and cut them into quarters. Cover the vegetables with boiling water, add the salt, and let cook for about 10 minutes. They should not be soft but *al dente*. Drain the carrots and set aside.

THE VINAIGRETTE

¾ cup olive oil
½ cup salad oil
½ cup best wine vinegar
¼ teaspoon granulated
  sugar
2 teaspoons prepared
  mustard
Salt and freshly ground
  pepper to taste
2 teaspoons juice from can
  of jalapeños en
  escabeche
1 clove garlic, peeled and
  crushed
1 teaspoon very finely
  chopped parsley

Mix the ingredients well together.

THE FIAMBRE POTOSINO

A large bowl
The cooked meats
The cooked carrots and
  potatoes
The vinaigrette
A large shallow serving
  dish

Put the meats and vegetables into the bowl and pour the vinaigrette over them. Mix all together well and let the *fiambre* stand for at least 2 hours to season. Stir it well from time to time.

Arrange the meats on the serving dish and pour the vinaigrette from the bowl over them.

Romaine lettuce leaves

6 or 8 radish flowers

Cebollas Encurtidas (page
    307)

12 olives

Pickled yellow chilies, or
    strips of seeded
    jalapeños en esca-
    beche

Put the lettuce leaves around the edge of the dish and garnish with the rest of the ingredients.

If you wish to serve anything else at all with the *fiambre* it will be just crisp rolls and butter. The dish has no Indian origins: tortillas are neither appropriate nor do they complement it in any way.

ALBÓNDIGAS DE JALISCO [*Meat balls*]

6 servings

Every region has its *albóndiga* recipe, but I think it really comes into its own in the northwest of Mexico—Sonora, Sinaloa, and further south in Jalisco. A delightful old lady in Guadalajara, with a great reputation as a cook, Sra. Rubio, gave me her family recipes and here they are—the recipe below and the one that follows on page 193. I think they are the best I have ever eaten. They are very soft, both because of the finely ground meat and the long, gentle cooking; then there is the texture given by the zucchini and the fresh flavor of the mint.

She also told me of a rather unusual regional dish that I had never heard of, called *pacholas*, which are nothing more than finely ground pork and beef mixed with a few cracker crumbs and seasoned with onion and garlic. Each *pachola* is rolled off the *metate*, a thin half-moon shape of ground meat that is quickly fried and served in a tomato sauce. What makes them relevant here is that sometimes two are stuck together and filled with an *albóndiga* mixture.

(*continued*)

A small bowl
1½ tablespoons long-
grain white rice
Boiling water to cover
¾ pound ground pork
¾ pound ground lean beef
2 small zucchini squash
(about 6 ounces)
A blender
2 eggs
¼ scant teaspoon oregano
3 sprigs fresh mint or 1
teaspoon powdered
dried mint
8 peppercorns
¾ teaspoon salt
¼ scant teaspoon cumin
seeds
⅓ onion, chopped
The rice

Cover the rice well with boiling water and leave it to soak for about 45 minutes.

Have the meat put twice through the finest blade of the meat grinder.

Trim the squash and chop them very finely. Add to the meat.

Blend the eggs with the rest of the ingredients until smooth and mix well into the meat.

A saucepan
2 medium tomatoes
(about ¾ pound)
Boiling water to cover
A blender

Drain the rice and add it to the mixture. Make 24 meat balls, each about 1½ inches in diameter.

Pour the boiling water over the tomato and cook it for about 5 minutes.

Skin the tomato and blend it until almost smooth.

A large flameproof dish
2 tablespoons peanut or
safflower oil
1 medium onion, thinly
sliced
The tomato puree

Heat the oil and cook the onion gently, without browning, until it is soft.

4 cups light meat or
chicken broth

Add the tomato puree, bring it to a boil, and let it cook fast for about 3 minutes.

Add the broth to the tomato sauce and bring it to a simmer. Add the meat balls, cover the pan, and let them simmer for 1¼ to 1½ hours. Serve in deep bowls with plenty of sauce.

You can cook these *albóndigas* ahead of time, the day before, or you can even freeze them.

You can always serve canned *chiles en escabeche* along with them, and if you wish to make a *picante* sauce for a change you can make the recipe that follows below; those *albóndigas* are cooked in a tomato and *chile chipotle* sauce.

ALBÓNDIGAS EN SALSA DE JITOMATE Y CHIPOTLE
[*Meat balls in tomato and chipotle sauce*]

6 *servings*

¾ *pound ground pork*
¾ *pound ground beef*
2 *small zucchini squash*
　　(*about 6 ounces*)
A blender
2 *eggs*
¼ *scant teaspoon oregano*
8 *peppercorns*
¾ *teaspoon salt*
¼ *scant teaspoon cumin*
　　seeds
⅓ *onion, chopped*
A saucepan
2 *pounds tomatoes*
Boiling water to cover
A blender
3 *to* 4 **chiles chipotles en**
　　adobo, *or to taste*
A large flameproof dish
3 *tablespoons oil*

Have the meat put twice through the finest blade of the grinder.

Trim the squash and chop them very finely. Add to the meat.

Blend the eggs together with the rest of the ingredients and mix well into the meat. Make 24 meat balls, about 1½ inches in diameter.

Cover the tomatoes with the boiling water and let them cook for about 5 minutes.

Skin the tomatoes and blend them with the chilies to a fairly smooth sauce.

Heat the oil, add the sauce, and when it comes to a boil, cook it over a high flame for

(*continued*)

The tomato sauce
¾ cup light meat or
    chicken broth
The meat balls

about 5 minutes.

Add the broth and bring to a simmer.

Add the meat balls and bring to a simmer once more. Cover the dish and continue cooking the meat balls over a low flame until they are done—about 50 minutes.

The squash will still be a little crisp.

CHORIZOS MEXICANOS [*Mexican sausages*]

About 21 to 24 chorizos

Probably most people are familiar with the Spanish *chorizos*, which are made with a high proportion of smoked pork. The Mexicans have their own version, made of unsmoked meat, which varies from region to region. Sometimes the meat is ground; the spices vary a little and in many places only *chiles anchos* are used. There are no hard and fast rules. *Chorizos* can be cooked and eaten freshly made, or they can be left to dry out thoroughly before using. The most important thing is to use a tender cut of pork—completely free from tendons and tough skin—or the meat will be hard from its rather brief cooking, and very indigestible. And be careful to use a good-quality, mild vinegar.

Three days ahead:

PREPARING THE MEAT

A large bowl
2 pounds pork tenderloin
½ pound pork fat
A comal or griddle
5 chiles anchos
2 chiles pasilla

Chop the meat roughly together with the fat.

Heat the comal and toast the chilies well, turning them from time to time so they do not burn. While they are still warm and flexible, slit them open and remove the seeds and veins. As they cool off they will become crisp.

A spice grinder
The chilies
½ teaspoon coriander
    seeds, toasted
3 whole cloves
½ teaspoon peppercorns
½ teaspoon oregano
⅛ teaspoon cumin seeds
4 cloves garlic, peeled and
    crushed
2 tablespoons sweet
    paprika
2½ teaspoons salt
⅔ cup mild white vinegar
2 ounces vodka

Grind the spices together with the chilies.

Mix the ground spices and chilies with the rest of the ingredients and rub them well into the meat with your hands.

Cover the mixture and set it aside in the refrigerator to season for 3 days, stirring it well each day. (Before filling the sausage casings, fry a little of the meat and taste to see if it has enough salt and seasoning.)

HAND-STUFFING THE CHORIZOS

Wash the casings to remove the salt in which they are packed and soak them in warm water for a few minutes.

Take a length of the casing and gradually ease it onto the tube of the funnel. (If you run water through the funnel into the casing, it inflates and is much easier to put on.) Tie a knot in the end of the casing. Take a handful of the meat in one hand, hold the funnel in the other and press the meat into the funnel; it will pass easily into the casing. Do not fill the casing too tightly, because you will need to tie the links when the casings are filled— they should be about 1 inch thick.

You then need some very fine string—I like to cut it first into small pieces —and tie the links at intervals of about 3 to 3½ inches. You should have from 21 to 24 links.

Coil the sausages on the table and prick them all over. Hang them in a cool, airy place for about 3 days to allow the moisture to drip out. Then store in a cool, airy place or the bottom of the refrigerator.

Hand-stuffing *chorizos*

To cook them, remove the skin, crumble them, and let them cook slowly over a low flame, stirring from time to time. It should take about 10 minutes until they are cooked through and the fat rendered out.

Hand-stuffing of sausages is much easier than it sounds. For about 80 cents you can buy a metal funnel designed especially for the job—I find the 3½-inch one with a ¾-inch tube opening is just right.

There still exist a few small pork butchers, especially in ethnic neighborhoods—Polish, Italian, Hungarian, etc.—who make their own sausages. They will sell you the casings and may even fill them for you, although the chilies and spices leave their evidence rather prominently in the machine.

Most butchers will order sausage casings for you.

If you want to hand-stuff the sausages and have the meat more finely ground, ask the butcher to grind the meat through the coarsest blade of the grinder. Then season and fill the casings following the recipe.

If you wish to have the meat more finely ground and use a meat-grinding and sausage-filling attachment on your mixer, follow the recipe up to the point of stuffing the sausage. Ease a length of sausage casing over the nozzle of the attachment and tie a firm knot in the end of the casing. Grind the meat with the coarsest blade of the grinder and fill the casings in one long length about 1 inch wide. Then roll and prick the filled casings as usual.

If you do not want to stuff the meat into casings at all, chop and season it according to the recipe and leave it to mature for about a week. Store it in containers in the freezer compartment of the refrigerator.

Poultry (*Aves*)

"I have heard it said that they were wont to cook for him the flesh of young boys, but as he had such a variety of dishes, made of so many things, we could not succeed in seeing if they were of human flesh or of other things, for they daily cooked fowls, turkeys, pheasants, native partridges, quail, tame and wild ducks, venison, wild boar, reed birds, pigeons, hares and rabbits, and many sorts of birds and other things which are bred in this country, and they are so numerous that I cannot finish naming them in a hurry . . ."

—FROM *The Discovery and Conquest of Mexico, 1517–1521,*
BY BERNAL DÍAZ DEL CASTILLO

A few weeks before Christmas a familiar sight in Mexico City is the traffic halted and horns blaring for blocks as a *campesino* drives his flock of turkeys across the Paseo de la Reforma. He sells them from door to door along the side streets, and from then until Christmas Eve you can hear the repetitive gobbling sounds of turkeys on the flat rooftops, where they are fattened up on household scraps. Even the roofs of the new and elegant high-rise apartments have their odd turkeys tethered amid the laundry cages and servants' quarters.

The wild turkey or *guajalote* is indigenous to Mexico and the New World. For centuries before the Spaniards arrived, the nobility ate roasted turkey, quail, and casseroles of turkey prepared with chilies, tomatoes and ground pumpkin seeds.

The turkey is still one of the most important foods in Yucatán, and every day there you can eat turkey *en escabeche oriental, en relleno blanco* prepared in the same way as the *queso relleno*—although the stuffing is far from white—and the *relleno negro,* ground meat mixed with a seasoning paste of burned, dried chilies and spices. In fact, I became so fascinated with the variety of ways turkey could be prepared that I counted in one modest regional Yucatecan cookbook twenty-nine typical recipes.

Further north toward Mexico City, they think more highly of the *gallina*—a good fat hen with a lot of flavor, without equal for making chicken broth. But times are changing, and "mass-produced" hens and rotisseries have now arrived in Mexico, and are flourishing.

MOLE POBLANO DE GUAJOLOTE [*Turkey in mole poblano*]

10 servings

The French were somewhat surprised one Christmas Day, during a broadcast from Mexico, to hear the correspondent say: "Today while you eat your turkey and chocolate *bûche de Noël* (chocolate log cake), just stop and think that what you are eating came originally from the New World: chocolate and turkeys both came from pre-Columbian Mexico. We, too, are eating them in Mexico today; the only difference is that we are eating them together."

No special festival is complete without *mole poblano de guajolote.* It is prepared with loving care, and even today, more often than not, it is the one dish that brings out the *metate:* chilies, spices, nuts, seeds, and tortillas are all ground on it. In the village fiestas each woman is given her allotted task: some to clean and toast the chilies, others to grind them; there are the turkeys to kill and prepare, the spices to measure, and the maize for the tamales to be soaked and cleaned meticulously.

It would be impossible to say just how many versions there are; every cook from the smallest hamlet to the grandest city home has her own special touch—a few more *mulatos* here, less *anchos,* or a touch of *chipotle* cooked with the turkey; some insist on onion, others won't tolerate it. Many cooks in Puebla itself insist on toasting the chilies, often *mulatos* only, over an open fire and grinding them dry. And so the arguments go on forever.

The word *mole* comes from the Nahuatl word *molli,* meaning "concoction." The majority of people respond, when *mole* is mentioned, with "Oh, yes, I know—that chocolate sauce. I wouldn't like it." Well, it *isn't* a chocolate sauce. One little piece of chocolate (and in Mexico we used to grind toasted cacao beans for the *mole*) goes into a large casserole full of rich dark-brown and russet chilies. And anyone I've ever served this to has been surprised and delighted, for in this, as in other Mexican sauces, the seasonings and spices are not used with such a heavy hand that they vie with each other for recognition, but rather build up to a harmonious whole.

There are many stories attached to its beginnings but they all agree that the *mole* was born in one of the convents in the city of Puebla de los Ángeles. The most repeated version, I suppose, is that Sor Andrea, sister superior of the Santa Rosa Convent, wished to honor the Archbishop for having a convent especially constructed for her order; trying to blend the ingredients of the New World with those of the old, she created *mole poblano.* Yet another story goes that the Viceroy, Don Juan de Palafox y Mendoza, was visiting Puebla. This time it was Fray Pascual who was preparing the banquet at the convent where he was going to eat. Turkeys were cooking in *cazuelas* on the fire; as Fray Pascual, scolding his assistants for their untidiness, gathered up all the spices they had been using, and putting them together onto a tray, a sudden gust of wind swept across the kitchen and they spilled over into the *cazuelas.* But, as one present-day Mexican philosopher says, "Whether it was prepared for archbishop or viceroy, by the nuns or the angels, the very thought of it makes your mouth water" (Alfredo Ramos Espinosa, *Semblanza Mexicana,* p. 216).

The day before:

8 chiles mulatos
5 chiles anchos
6 chiles pasilla
A large frying pan
¼ pound lard (*½ cup*)

A large bowl
Warm water to cover

Slit the chilies open with a knife and remove the seeds and veins, reserving at least 1 tablespoon of the seeds.

Heat the lard and quickly fry the chilies on both sides. Take care that they do not burn.

Put the chilies into the bowl, cover them with water, and leave them to stand overnight.

On serving day:

A 7- to 8-pound turkey

A Dutch oven
6 to 8 tablespoons lard

A saucepan
The turkey giblets
1 small carrot, sliced
1 medium onion, sliced
1 clove garlic, peeled
1 tablespoon salt
6 peppercorns
Water to cover
The pan juices from the
*   turkey*

A blender
The soaked chilies
1 cup water
A very large fireproof dish
¼ pound lard (½ cup)
The chili puree

A blender
½ cup tomates verdes,
*   drained*

A spice grinder
4 cloves
10 peppercorns

Preheat the oven to 325°.

Cut the turkey into serving pieces. Set the giblets aside.

Melt the lard and brown the turkey pieces well. Drain off the excess fat. Cover the pan and braise the turkey in the oven, without liquid, until it is tender—40 to 60 minutes, depending on toughness.

Put the giblets into the pan with the rest of the ingredients. Cover them with water and bring them to a boil. Lower the flame and simmer for 1¼ to 1½ hours. Strain the broth and set it aside.

When the turkey is cooked, pour off the juices in the pan and set them aside to cool, then skim off the fat and add them to the giblet broth. Set it aside.

Blend the chilies with the water until smooth—you may have to do them in two or three lots but try not to add more water.

Melt the lard, and when it is hot but not smoking, cook the chili puree over a medium flame for about 10 minutes, stirring it all the time. Keep a lid handy, as it will splatter about. Set it aside.

Put the *tomates verdes* into the blender jar.

Put the spices into the grinder and add the toasted, cooled seeds, reserving 4 tablespoons of the sesame seeds for later use. Grind the

(continued)

½-inch stick cinnamon
⅛ teaspoon coriander
    seeds and
⅛ teaspoon aniseed,
    toasted together
    (page 43)
1 tablespoon reserved chili
    seeds, toasted sep-
    arately (page 43)
7 tablespoons sesame
    seeds, toasted sep-
    arately (page 43)
3 cloves garlic, toasted
    (page 43)
A frying pan
6 tablespoons lard
2 tablespoons raisins
20 almonds, unskinned
A molcajete or mortar and
    pestle

2 ounces pumpkin seeds
    (just over ⅓ cup),
    hulled and unsalted

1 small stale tortilla

3 small rounds stale
    French bread

Turkey broth, if necessary

spices and seeds finely and transfer them to the blender jar.

Add the toasted garlic to the blender jar.

Melt the lard in the frying pan and fry the raisins briefly, just until they puff up, and transfer them with a slotted spoon to the blender jar. In the same pan fry the almonds, stirring them all the time, until they are well browned. Remove with a slotted spoon and crush them a little before adding them to the blender jar.

In the same pan fry the pumpkin seeds lightly, but have a lid handy, as they pop about explosively. Remove with a slotted spoon and add to the blender.

In the same pan fry the tortilla until very crisp. Remove with a slotted spoon and crush it a little before adding it to the blender.

In the same pan fry the bread until crisp, then remove with a slotted spoon and crush. Add it to the blender jar.

Blend all the ingredients together until they form a smooth paste. If it is absolutely necessary to add some liquid to blend it effectively, then add a little turkey broth.

The chili sauce

Add the blended mixture to the chile sauce and cook over a brisk flame for about 5 minutes, stirring the mixture constantly.

1 1½-ounce tablet of
Mexican chocolate

Break the chocolate into small pieces and add it to the mixture. Continue cooking the *mole* for about 10 minutes more, stirring it all the time so it does not stick.

4 to 5 cups turkey broth
Salt as necessary

Add the broth and continue cooking the *mole* for a minimum of 40 minutes. Add salt as necessary, then add the turkey pieces and heat them through.

The dish should be served with "Blind" Tamales (page 92), allowing 2 per serving, and each serving should be sprinkled with some of the reserved toasted sesame seeds.

When it is cooked the sauce should lightly coat the back of a wooden spoon. If it appears to be too thick then add a little more broth. If it is too thin, continue cooking the *mole* until it reduces a little more. You could easily prepare the *mole* several days ahead—in fact it improves in flavor—up to the point of adding the turkey broth. Then braise the turkey and cook the giblets on the day it is needed. Most cooks in Mexico today boil the turkey and then brown it in lard before adding it to the sauce. But it has a far better flavor and texture if cooked in the way I have given—very much as the old cookbooks indicate that it should be cooked. If you have any sauce left over, freeze it and use it to make delicious *enchiladas* at some later date.

The traditional way of grinding the ingredients on a stone *metate* is a long and laborious job, but it is very efficient. All the chilies and particles of seeds and spices get crushed and ground to a paste. The blender cannot do this without the addition of too much liquid. After cooking Mexican food for so many years, I feel strongly that one of the secrets of the unique flavor of a well-prepared sauce is frying the basic ingredients first over a high flame without very much liquid. And since most of these ingredients are briefly cooked alone before being combined, the instructions may seem rather laborious and repetitive. But because this technique best brings out all the flavors, it would be better not to take shortcuts.

PATO EN MOLE VERDE DE PEPITA
[Duck in a green mole of pumpkin seeds]

6 servings

It is recorded that at the time of the Spanish conquest Moctezuma and the other rulers were eating stews or chilies mixed with tomatoes and pumpkin seeds; long before that the Mayas to the south were cultivating pumpkins and using the seeds in their food. *Pato en mole verde de pepita* has a lovely, smooth, pale green sauce, thickened with pumpkin seeds and subtly flavored with herbs—a true classic of the cuisine of central Mexico.

Just to make it a little less confusing, generally speaking a *mole verde* is made with green tomatoes and herbs; a *pipián verde* is made with spices, ground pumpkin and/or sesame seeds, with even a few almonds or peanuts added, but no greenstuff. The *mole verde de pepita* has everything, as you will see.

Preheat the oven to 325°.

A saucepan
The duck giblets
1 small carrot, sliced
1 small onion, sliced
1 clove garlic, peeled
2 teaspoons salt
6 peppercorns
Water to cover

Put the giblets with the vegetables and seasoning into the pan, cover them with water, and bring to a boil. Lower the flame and simmer, covered, for about 1½ hours.

A flameproof casserole or
*   Dutch oven*
A 5- to 6-pound duck
Salt and pepper to taste

Heat the casserole well and brown the duck all over, pricking the skin to render out the fat from the layer underneath it. (Use the fork tines upwards, so as not to pierce the flesh and thus lose all the juices.) Drain off the excess fat from time to time and reserve.

Cover the casserole with a tightly fitting lid and braise the duck, without water, until it is tender—from 50 to 70 minutes, depending on how tender the duck is.

Set the duck aside to cool a little, then cut into serving pieces. Skim the fat from the

The giblet broth
A spice grinder
¾ cup hulled, unsalted
*   pumpkin seeds*
*   (about 3½ ounces),*
*   toasted (page 43)*
6 peppercorns
⅛ teaspoon cumin seeds
A bowl
1 cup duck broth

A blender
1 cup tomates verdes,
*   drained*
4 chiles serranos, *roughly*
*   chopped*
¼ medium onion, roughly
*   chopped*
2 small cloves garlic,
*   peeled*
3 sprigs epazote
3 sprigs fresh coriander
1 small bunch radish
*   leaves*
2 large lettuce leaves,
*   preferably romaine,*
*   torn into pieces*
A fireproof serving dish
2 tablespoons reserved
*   duck drippings*
The blended herbs
The pumpkin seed sauce

2 cups reserved duck
*   broth*

juices in the casserole and add them to the giblet broth. Set the broth aside.

Grind the toasted, cooled seeds, together with the peppercorns and cumin, as finely as you can.

Put the ground ingredients into a bowl and stir in the broth until you have a smooth sauce. Set it aside.

Blend the *tomates verdes* and the other ingredients to a smooth puree.

Heat the drippings, add the blended vegetables and herbs and cook the sauce over a brisk flame until it has reduced and is well seasoned—about 10 minutes. Stir it well from time to time.

Lower the flame and gradually stir in the pumpkin seed sauce. **Keep the flame very low, and on no account let the mixture boil.**

Gradually add the rest of the broth. Let the sauce heat through, still over a very low

(*continued*)

Salt as necessary
The pieces of duck

flame, stirring it or rather scraping the bottom of the dish with a large wooden spoon, for 20 minutes. Add salt as necessary.

Add the duck, let it heat through, and serve.

Take care not to use more than ¾ cup of the pumpkin seeds or the sauce will become too thick.

If you have the *mole* over too high a flame and it becomes grainy, simply pour it back into the blender and blend until smooth.

A chicken could be substituted for the duck.

The sauce should not be very *picante;* it should leave just a pleasant afterglow in your mouth.

In Mexico this would be served with just hot tortillas, but you could, of course, equally well serve a white rice (Arroz Blanco, page 290), or even red rice (Arroz a la Mexicana, page 288), with it.

POLLO EN PIPIÁN ROJO [*Chicken in red sesame seed sauce*]

6 servings

A large saucepan
A 3½- to 4-pound chicken
The chicken giblets
½ onion, sliced
2 cloves garlic, peeled
A sprig of parsley
A bay leaf
A little thyme
1 tablespoon salt, or to
taste
Water to cover
A strainer
A griddle or comal
6 **chiles anchos,** *approximately*

Put the chicken, giblets, and the rest of the ingredients into the pan, cover with water, and bring to a boil. Lower the flame and simmer the chicken until it is just tender—about 40 to 50 minutes. Let the chicken cool in the broth, then cut it into serving pieces and set aside. Strain the broth and reserve it.

Toast the chilies lightly. When they are cool enough to handle but still pliable, slit them open and remove the seeds and veins. Reserve the seeds.

A bowl

Hot water to cover

A spice grinder

*1 tablespoon chili seeds,
  or more to taste, well
  toasted (page 43)*

½-inch stick cinnamon

3 whole cloves

5 peppercorns

A small frying pan

¾ cup sesame seeds

A spice grinder

A fireproof serving dish

3 tablespoons lard

*The ground seeds and
  spices*

A blender

The soaked chilies

*½ cup reserved chicken
  broth*

1 clove garlic, peeled

The chili puree

The fried spice mixture

*3 cups of the reserved
  broth*

The cooked chicken

Salt to taste

A comal or griddle

*1 large avocado leaf, fresh
  or dried*

*A molcajete or mortar
  and pestle*

Cover the chilies with hot water and leave them to soak for 15 to 20 minutes.

Add the toasted, cooled seeds and the spices to the spice grinder and grind them finely. Set them aside.

Toast the sesame seeds well, until a deep gold color, in the ungreased pan and set them aside to cool off a little. Add the toasted, cooled seeds to the spice grinder and grind them very fine.

Melt the lard and fry the ground seeds and spices over a low flame for about 3 minutes, stirring them constantly.

Transfer the chilies with a slotted spoon to the blender jar. Add the broth and garlic and blend to a smooth puree.

Add the chili puree to the fried spice mixture in the dish and let it cook fast for about 5 minutes, stirring it constantly.

Add the remaining broth and let the sauce continue cooking over a low flame for about 20 minutes, or until it thickens and is well seasoned. Add the cooked chicken, salt to taste, and let the chicken heat through.

Toast the leaf briefly on a warm comal and then grind it finely. Add it to the sauce.

(continued)

This *pipián* is a deep-red, earthy-looking sauce. When it is cooked it should just lightly cover the back of a wooden spoon.

In Mexico this would be served with hot tortillas only, but plain white rice (Arroz Blanco, page 290) goes very well with it. It should not be very *picante,* but have just a pleasant afterglow from the chili seeds.

The sauce can be made several days ahead if you have some good chicken broth handy. The chicken can then be poached ready and heated through in the sauce when you are ready to serve. The sauce freezes extremely well.

POLLO PIBIL [*Chicken cooked in a banana leaf*]

1 serving

This dish consists of individual portions of chicken spread with the seasoning paste used for Cochinita Pibil (page 169) and cooked in a banana leaf.

About six hours ahead or the day before:

¼ *small chicken* *1 scant tablespoon season- ing paste (page 170)* *1 tablespoon water* *Salt to taste*	Prick the chicken all over with a fork. Dilute the seasoning paste with the water and set ¼ teaspoon aside. Rub the remainder, with the salt, well into the chicken.
A piece of banana leaf *The chicken*	Sear the leaf quickly over an open flame to make it more flexible, and wrap it around the chicken to make a small package. Set it aside to season, refrigerated, preferably overnight.
On serving day:	Preheat the oven to 350°.
A small frying pan *2 tablespoons lard* *4 thin slices onion* *4 thick slices tomato* *The reserved ¼ teaspoon seasoning paste*	Melt the lard and fry the onion, without browning, until it is soft. Add the tomato and the seasoning paste and fry it gently on both sides.

The wrapped chicken
The onion and tomato slices
An ovenproof serving dish

Unwrap the chicken. Put half the onion and tomato under the chicken and the other half on top. Wrap it up again in the leaf.

Place the "package" into the dish and cover it tightly. Cook for 20 minutes. Turn it over, baste with the juices, and cook for another 20 minutes, or until just tender. Do not overcook.

Turn the oven up to 450°.

Remove the cover, open up the leaf, and let the chicken brown on top.

Serve, still wrapped in the banana leaf.

This dish is very good served with plain white rice (Arroz Blanco, page 290).

POLLO EN ESCABECHE ORIENTAL
[*Chicken in an onion and chili souse*]

6 to 8 servings

Pheasant in souse is one of the classic dishes of Spain that has been adopted and adapted by some of the South American countries and Yucatán. It is a light and refreshing dish with a most interesting flavor.

The *curassow*—now rather rare—is the "pheasant" of Yucatán, and it was seasoned and cooked in a *pib* and served with lightly pickled onions and chilies.

Nowadays chickens or small turkeys are cooked in this way. The chicken used here is rubbed with a paste of ground spices and garlic, cooked, then broiled and served in a mild souse of onions and chilies.

If you are able to charcoal broil the chicken do so, for it makes all the difference to the flavor and simulates the smoky flavor of pib cooking. Some Yucatecan cooks prefer to use the purple onions, while others argue that they should be used in fish souses only.

(continued)

Have ready:

5 medium onions, sliced thin and prepared as for Cebollas Encurtidas (page 307) but left to soak in mild vinegar for 1 hour only.

A spice grinder
4 whole allspice
5 whole cloves
½ tablespoon pepper-
   corns
½ teaspoon oregano
   toasted (page 43)
½ teaspoon cumin seeds

Grind the spices together until they are almost a powder.

A molcajete *or mortar*
   and pestle
8 cloves garlic, peeled
2 teaspoons salt
1½ tablespoons mild
   white vinegar or
   Seville orange juice
The powdered spices

Crush the garlic and mix in the salt, vinegar, and powdered spices. The mixture should be like a rather thick paste.

A large chicken or small
   turkey (about 5
   pounds), cut into
   serving pieces
The paste

Using one-third only of the paste, coat each piece of the chicken very lightly. Set the pieces aside to season for at least 30 minutes.

A saucepan
The chicken
4 cloves garlic, toasted
   (page 43)
⅛ teaspoon oregano,
   toasted (page 43)
1 teaspoon salt
3 cups water, approxi-
   mately

Barely cover the chicken with the water, add the rest of the ingredients, and bring to a boil. Lower the flame and simmer the chicken until it is just tender—about 25 minutes; take care not to overcook it.

A rack

Drain the chicken and set it on a rack, reserving the broth and keeping it warm. As soon as the chicken is cool enough to handle,

The remaining paste

spread each piece lightly with the remaining paste.

A little melted lard or oil
A glazing brush
A broiler, preferably
     charcoal

Brush the chicken pieces with the lard and broil it until the skin is just crisp and a pale golden color.

The reserved chicken
     broth
The onions
6 chiles güeros, *toasted*
     (page 43)

Put the onions and chilies into the broth and bring it to a boil.

A warmed serving dish

Place the chicken pieces on the dish and pour the broth with the onions and chilies over them.

I think this is best served as it is in Yucatán with white rice (Arroz Blanco, page 290) and a salad of thinly sliced cucumbers and avocado; any left over can be shredded and used on Panuchos (page 126).

PECHUGAS DE POLLO CON RAJAS [*Chicken breasts with chilies*]

6 servings

This is a creamy casserole of chicken breasts and strips of chilies. It is only slightly *picante*.

6 small chicken breasts
Salt and freshly ground
     pepper

Remove the bones and skin from the breasts and cut each of them into 4 filets. Season them well with salt and pepper.

A frying pan
¼ cup butter
¼ cup peanut or safflower
     oil

Heat the butter and the oil together and sauté the chicken filets for a few moments on both sides until they are lightly browned. Set them aside.

1 large onion, thinly sliced

In the same fat, fry the onion gently, without browning, until it is soft. Peel and clean

(continued)

2¼ *pounds* **chiles poblanos**
　　(*or about 20 to 22*
　　canned, peeled green
　　chilies)
½ *teaspoon salt*

A blender
The reserved 3 poblanos
　　(*or 9 canned chilies*)
1 cup milk (*if the*
　　poblanos are used)
　　or ⅔ cup milk (*if the*
　　canned chilies are
　　used)
½ *teaspoon salt, or to*
　　taste
2 cups Thick Sour Cream
　　(*page 20*)

the *chiles poblanos* (page 44). Set aside 3 *poblanos* (or 9 canned chilies). Cut the rest into *rajas* (strips). Add the *rajas* to the onions in the pan, cover, and cook over a medium flame (8 minutes for *poblanos* and 5 for canned chilies).

Blend the reserved chilies until smooth with the milk and salt. Add the sour cream and blend for a few seconds longer.

Preheat the oven to 350°.

An ovenproof serving dish
　　at least 3 inches deep
　　and about 10 inches
　　in diameter
The chicken filets
The rajas
The sauce
¼ *pound cheddar cheese,*
　　grated

Arrange half of the chicken filets in the dish. Cover them with half of the *rajas* and half of the sauce. Repeat the layers.

Sprinkle the cheese over the top and bake until the chicken filets are done and the cheese melted—it is not necessary to brown it—about 30 minutes.

There will appear to be an enormous amount but most people will return for two helpings. Serve it with white rice cooked with corn kernels (page 291). You can prepare things well ahead of time: the breasts sautéed, the *rajas* cooked and the sauce blended, but do not put it all together until a few moments before it is to go into the oven.

The flesh of the fresh *chiles poblanos* is naturally harder than that of the canned chilies, so allow a little longer cooking time with the onion. Blended, they produce a thicker sauce than the canned chilies, so I have made allowances for their size and texture.

POLLO EN RELLENO DE PAN [*Chicken with fried bread crumbs*]

6 servings

I first ate chicken cooked this way in the home of María Luisa Martínez and her husband, who are two of the most knowledgeable people I know on Mexican regional food; María Luisa is one of the truly great creative cooks, and has given me hours of her time, year after year, talking to me about food and explaining the nuances that make Mexican food something very special. She and her husband were born and brought up in Michoacán, a state which for me has some of the best regional food in the republic. They tell me that they have never found this dish in any restaurants or the recipe in cookbooks: it is *muy casero* (real home cooking).

A large saucepan
A 4-pound chicken
½ small onion
1 clove garlic, peeled
2 teaspoons salt
5 peppercorns
Cold water to cover

Put the chicken into the pan with the rest of the ingredients, cover with cold water, and bring to a boil. Lower the flame and simmer for 20 minutes.

3 medium carrots (about
½ pound), scraped
and cut into small
cubes, not quite ½
inch
3 medium zucchini squash
(about ¾ pound),
cut into small cubes,
not quite ½ inch

Add the carrots and cook for 15 minutes more, add the squash and cook for a further 10 minutes. By this time the chicken and vegetables should be just cooked. They should not be too soft. Strain them and reserve the stock.

(continued)

A *blender*
1 *pound tomatoes, broiled*
    (*page 44*)
A *fireproof serving dish*
3 *tablespoons peanut or*
    safflower oil
½ *small onion, sliced*
1 *clove garlic, peeled and*
    sliced
The *tomato puree*
½ *cup reserved stock*

The **chicken**
The **cooked vegetables**
3 *tablespoons sultanas*
    (*white raisins*)
2 *tablespoons slivered al-*
    monds
1 **chorizo,** *crumbled and*
    fried
3 **chiles jalapeños en esca-**
    beche
2 *teaspoons juice from the*
    chili can

A *small frying pan*
⅓ *cup peanut oil*
1½ *cups dried and ground*
    bread crumbs (*see*
    note below)

Blend the tomatoes to a fairly smooth sauce.

Heat the oil and gently fry the onion and garlic, without browning, until they are soft.

Add the tomato puree and reserved stock, and let the sauce reduce over a medium flame for about 10 minutes.

Cut the chicken into serving pieces, and add it together with the rest of the ingredients to the sauce. Cook slowly for 10 minutes more, stirring the mixture from time to time so that it does not stick. The sauce by then should be almost dry.

Heat the oil, add bread crumbs, and fry them, stirring them all the time until they are an even gold color. Then sprinkle the bread-crumbs over the chicken and vegetables and **serve immediately.**

The very interesting texture of the crisp bread crumbs on the chicken and vegetables will be lost if the dish is left to stand after they have been added. If you want to prepare everything ahead of time you can do so quite easily by cooking it up to the point of reducing the sauce. About 15 minutes before serving, reheat and reduce the sauce—this will heat the chicken through sufficiently. Even the bread crumbs can be fried crisp and kept warm. The important point to watch is the type of bread you use. Try and find one with a tough texture like a sour dough or light rye—none of those packaged non-breads. The day before, cut the bread into thick slices and let it dry out well, or put it in the slowest of ovens but do not let it get brown. Grate it, but not too fine, or crush it with a rolling pin.

With the possible exception of a crisp, green salad, this dish is really best eaten alone—not even tortillas are necessary. The Spanish *chorizo* is a bit strong, since it is made almost entirely of smoked meats, but unless you make your own Chorizos Mexicanos (page 194) you will have no choice. If you have guests who do not like *picante* food, then do not add the chilies and juice, but serve them separately.

POLLO A LA UVA [Chicken cooked with grapes]

Very early on in the colonial period, vines were brought over from Spain and grafted onto an indigenous wild grape. They began to flourish on a small scale, especially in the missions from Oaxaca to Baja California. As they began to extend, the Spaniards feared that the wines produced would start to compete with Spanish wines brought over to the New World, and legislation was started in 1543 to discourage their cultivation. The final death blow came in 1771, when very heavy penalties were imposed for anyone found growing either vines or olives.

In recent years there has been a great boom in grape growing. Every year, since I first went to live in Mexico in 1957, while driving through Querétero, Guanajuato, and Aguascalientes, I have seen more and more vineyards. Quite recently I was taken to visit one just outside Dolores Hidalgo and was quite amazed by the quality, flavor, and variety of the grapes grown there, and the great care with which they were being cultivated.

Aguascalientes has always been one of the most important chili-growing areas, and now it is becoming an important grape-growing center—so this recipe seems particularly appropriate. It is certainly not a classic recipe, but in a few more years it will probably be considered one. One of the distinguished cooks of the area, Sra. Andrea, gave it to me just as she prepares it for local banquets. She decorates the edge of the dish with vine leaves and surrounds it with alternate black and white grapes glazed with a sugar syrup.

Preheat the oven to 350°.

A Dutch oven
2 chickens (about 3
pounds each)
2 tablespoons butter
2 tablespoons peanut or
safflower oil
Salt and freshly ground
pepper

Truss the chicken. Heat the butter and oil together and brown the chickens well all over. Season them and set them aside.

½ large onion, thinly
sliced
2 cloves garlic, peeled
2 stalks celery, chopped

In the same fat, fry the onion, garlic, and celery for about 5 minutes, without letting them brown.

2 pounds tomatoes, un-
skinned
¼ teaspoon thyme
¼ teaspoon marjoram
1 teaspoon salt, or to
taste

Chop the tomatoes roughly and add them, with the rest of the ingredients, to the vegetables in the pan.

The chickens

Place the chickens on their sides in the tomato mixture. Cover the pan and bake for about 20 minutes.

Turn the chickens over and continue baking them until they are tender—about 20 to 25 minutes. Remove them from the sauce and keep them warm.

A blender
The vegetables and pan
juices

Blend the vegetables and juices in the pan to a smooth puree. Return the puree to the pan and cook it over a medium flame until it has reduced and thickened—10 to 15 minutes.

⅔ cup dry white wine

1 pound white grapes,
    skinned and seeded
A warmed serving dish

Add the wine and continue cooking the sauce for about 5 minutes, stirring it from time to time.

Add the grapes and continue cooking the sauce over a brisk flame for 5 minutes more.

Place the chickens on the dish and pour the sauce over them.

Seafood (*Pescados*)

"The show of fish . . . for it was of such variety and beauty, as I have never before witnessed, nor even conceived. I was aware that the finny race presented more resplendent hues and varieties of forms, when fresh from the water, than birds and insects, but now I became convinced of this truth. Hundreds of various species glowing in all the colors of the prism; surpassing the lustre of precious gems and all the brilliant tints of the humming birds, covered the stones of the market place of Vera Cruz."

—FROM *Six Months Residence and Travel in Mexico,*
BY W. H. BULLOCK

There is an awful lot of coast to Mexico, but some day I am going to do the grand tour. I suppose I would inevitably end up in my favorite places eating my favorite seafood, but I also want to fill in the gaps and see the rest. I would start off, of course, in Ensenada and look for the pismo clams—they are called just plain *almeja* there. Last time I could only find them cut up into a cocktail—and if there is one thing that is death to seafood it's a cocktail and that simply awful catsup-base sauce. I had wanted to see the shell and I had wanted to see it opened in front of me. After a compromise meal of a rather tough turtle steak *ranchera*, I came out of the restaurant only to find the clams I had been looking for on a little street-side stand. The pismo has a large whitish shell with a pink, juicy muscle inside—as sweet and delicious a clam as you will find anywhere.

As I work my way down the west coast, I would have several meals of *totoaba,* a large basslike fish that abounds in the northern part of the gulf of California—wonderful eating. Then Guaymas for shrimps before heading to Mazatlán. The favorite midmorning snack from the street carts there is the fat, dark, ridged-shelled *pata de mula* (mule's foot). I would go to Mamucas for lunch before the crowd arrives to have a large bowl of *sopa marinera,* a wonderfully flavored and robust fish and shellfish soup, with lots and lots of *callos de hacha* to follow—they are the delicate, little pinna clams that could easily be taken for scallops.

Then a long hop to Zijuatanejo to eat those very large brownish clams at Los Gatos just across the bay. I was last there just before we left Mexico to move to New York. We were spending a few days fishing with friends. I remember we had just caught a large dorado—so beautiful in the water that it seemed a crime to pull it out and watch the lovely silvery-gold and blues fade. We pulled in to a sandy beach for a picnic and Goyo, the boatman, started a fire. In a crude frame of *huisache* branches, tied up well with strips of bark, he roasted half the dorado, cut off in one large fillet, after seasoning it with lime juice and rough salt. When the time came for him to turn it over, before our astonished eyes he walked out knee-deep into the sea and held the fish under the water for a couple of minutes. Then he returned to finish cooking it on the other side. There were hot tortillas; no more was necessary.

I remember eating oysters, just brought in from the sea; the smallest, sweetest shrimps, and broiled sierra by the water's edge on the Gulf of Tehuantepec after a long, hot ride from Oaxaca one August. Even the sea was hot to swim in, but the beer was very cold and the metallic freshness of the oysters and the lime juice with our food refreshed us.

From there I would continue almost due east to Palenque. I was there once to visit the Mayan ruins, continuing on to Bonampak and up the Usumacinta River, which divides Mexico from Guatemala, to Yaxchilán. Then our plane bumped down on what was no more than a few yards of loose stones, and we were met by a reception committee.

It was the village schoolmaster's birthday and our guide into the *selva,* a local rancher and hunter, had, with other friends, been helping him celebrate for quite some time that morning. So we were greeted warmly and driven off in the back of an old truck to share the ceremonial food. They were roasting a *peje-lagarto*—a prehistoric fish with thick tough scales, a species of gar—from the nearby river, over a wood fire. As the flesh was cooked, it was shredded, seasoned with some ground *achiote, epazote* leaves, and salt, and eaten in *tacos*.

By the next day I had persuaded the owner of a local restaurant to have a woman in the village, who was expert in preparing the native dishes, make us some *shote y momo*. *Shote* is the local Indian name of a fresh-water snail with an elongated shell about 1½ inches long. The snail is purged for a day or so in fresh water with *momo* leaves. *Momo* is the local name for a large heart-shaped leaf used a great deal in the cooking of Oaxaca, Vera-cruz, and Chiapas, where it is called *hoja santa* (*Piper sanctum*); it has a very strong flavor of anise and something more that defies description. The snails are then cooked and the broth seasoned with the ground leaves of *momo* (*Cnidoscolus chayamansa*) and thickened with a little tortilla dough. It was served in deep bowls, and on the side, to extract the snails, were large tough thorns about 2 inches long.

And from thence a brief stopover in Tabasco, where the large moro crabs are stuffed and then heated through in a pumpkin seed sauce, flavored and colored with achiote.

It would be worthwhile going back to the Bal Hai at Cozumel briefly to prevail upon Sra. Moguel to prepare the regional lobster soup—*sac kol* in Mayan, which translated literally means "white broth." The lobster should be just out of the sea, freshly killed and cleaned of the spines and inedible parts. The rest is cut up with the shell, and cooked, together with the head, in water seasoned in the typical Yucatecan way with toasted oregano, onion, and a roasted head of garlic. The broth is thickened with a little *masa* and colored with some ground *achiote*. While you're waiting for it, you have with your tequila the local appetizers—turtle egg sausage and the little, acidy berries of a bush that grows in the sandy soil in parts of southern Mexico—nance (*Byrsonima crassifolia*). The sausage is made by the local fishermen when they are out on their fishing and turtle-hunting expeditions. The turtle intestines are cleaned and stuffed with the eggs, and then the sausage is boiled so that the eggs are cooked. Sra. Moguel also makes a very good turtle stew—*ajiaco*—with spices, tomatoes, and white wine. But I prefer the more delicate river turtle as they prepare it in Tabasco, in a green sauce of various ground herbs and leaves of the chili plant.

I should never be forgiven by the Campechanos and Yucatecos if I didn't mention their favorite, *pan de cazón*. The *cazón* is a dogfish or small shark, the rather dry flesh of which is cooked and shredded and stuffed into an inflated tortilla with some bean paste—just like *panuchos*—and is then covered with a tomato sauce. The best cooks I talked to insisted that this was the correct version, and not the tortillas stacked in layers with the beans, fish, and sauce in between, as served in the restaurants.

Of all the fish in Mexico perhaps the greatest delicacy of them all is the *blanco de Pátzcuaro*—the famous white fish, a meal made upon which Calderón de la Barca said "would have rejoiced the heart of an epicure." You can, of course, eat it in the Mexico City restaurants, but it's much better to go to Lake Pátzcuaro itself in the lovely Michoacán countryside and eat it fried, fresh out of the water at El Gordo, the small restaurant at the *embarcadero*—the wharf for the little boats that ply to and fro across the lake. Or try the local *caldo michi*—a light vegetable broth, flavored with fresh coriander, and to which small white fish called *charales* are added at the very last moment so that the flesh is just tender but does not fall apart.

It is recorded that Moctezuma and his nobles ate shrimps. Sahagún describes a casserole of shrimps with tomatoes and ground squash seeds. Their seafood was brought up from the gulf to Tenochtitlán, the Aztec capital— where Mexico City stands today—by relays of runners in about twelve hours, or so it is said.

While fresh shrimp dishes are still not widespread today, dried shrimps are used throughout the country. From as near the coast as Escuinapa in Sonora, and Nayarit, come the famous *sopes de vigilia*. As their name implies, they are prepared on days when meat is forbidden and, of course, are especially popular during Lent. Dried shrimps are ground up and mixed with tortilla dough; rather thick little tortillas are made and cooked on the comal and then well pinched up around the edges to form *sopes* to hold the scrambled eggs, *nopales,* and potato that are piled onto them. They are then sprinkled with a tomato sauce and garnished with shredded lettuce and radish flowers.

Those who have eaten *cabrito* in the Correo Español in Mexico City will never forget the fiery little cups of dried shrimp soup that is served first; and there is the less harsh *caldo de camarón* (shrimp broth) served in the bars of Tuxtla Gutiérrez. And by far the most popular and esteemed dish served during Lent and at Christmas Eve dinner is *romeritos con tortas de camarón*, also called *revoltijo de romeritos*. The *tortas de camarón* are little fried cakes of dried shrimps mixed with stiffly beaten eggs, and the *romeritos* are little stringy greens with quite a pleasant flavor. These, with boiled potatoes, are heated through in a chili sauce.

Notes on Selecting and Preparing Fish

1. There are three things to look for when judging whether or not a fish is fresh. The eye should have a brilliant glaze over it, the gills should have a fresh reddish hue, and the flesh should be firm to the point that when you press it your fingers do not leave an impression.

2. When the recipe calls for a 3-pound red snapper, do not compromise and buy two smaller fish unless it is absolutely unavoidable. The flesh of the larger fish is much richer, and therefore much more tasty. Some markets seem to have a dearth of the larger snappers at times, but they can usually be found in the wholesale markets. To be sure, order one from your fish man a day or two before.

3. For recipes where the fish is cooked only half submerged in the sauce, I prefer to turn it just before half the cooking time has expired. (A Chinese cleaver may seem an amateurish thing to use in turning, but it's very effective.) If you don't turn it, the flesh on top may be perfectly cooked while the underneath is overcooked.

4. I generally suggest cooking a whole fish instead of fillets because the gelatinous quality of the head and bones gives a better flavor and consistency to the sauce. You can see it when the sauce gets cold: it jells. But apart from flavor, the dish looks so much more important, and generally more attractive. If you really can't stand the staring eye, then remove it and fill the socket with an olive.

5. When cooking a rather thick fish in a court bouillon, as in the recipe for Pescado Alcaparrado (page 227), measure the fish at its thickest part—usually behind the head—and allow 10 minutes per inch cooking time after the court bouillon covering the fish comes to the simmering point.

6. I have my own method for cooking shrimps that preserves all the flavor. Put the unshelled shrimps into a shallow oven dish lined with foil.

Sprinkle them with lime juice and salt. Seal them completely with the foil and bake them in a 350° oven for 25 minutes. Let them cool off, then remove the shells and veins. This method preserves all the flavor and juices.

7. When you are cooking a fish whole, test to see if it is done by cutting the flesh down to the backbone. It should come away from the bone easily, and be moist and opaque. If the flesh is very firm and rather dry it is overcooked.

HUACHINANGO A LA VERACRUZANA
[*Red snapper, Veracruz*]

6 first-course servings (see note below)

This is a very colorful dish from Veracruz—a large red snapper covered with a well-flavored tomato sauce. As I am always saying of Mexican dishes, there are many versions of this recipe. I have chosen what I think to be the best example and the most delicious of all those that I have tried. The more commercial way of serving *huachinango a la veracruzana* is to fry the filleted fish and serve it covered with the sauce, which has been cooked separately. In Veracruz some of my friends serve it as a casserole, with layers of the filleted fish and the sauce cooked together.

Preheat the oven to 325°.

An ovenproof serving dish
A 3-pound red snapper
1 teaspoon salt, or to taste
2 tablespoons lime juice
2 pounds fresh tomatoes

A large frying pan
¼ cup olive oil
1 medium onion (about 6 ounces), finely sliced
2 large cloves garlic, peeled and sliced

Have the fish cleaned, leaving the head and tail on. Prick the fish on both sides with a coarse-tined fork, rub in the salt and lime juice, and set it aside in the dish to season for about 2 hours.

Skin, seed, and chop the tomatoes roughly (page 43). Set them aside.

Heat the oil and fry the onion and garlic, without browning, until they are soft.

(continued)

The tomatoes
1 large bay leaf
¼ teaspoon oregano
12 pitted green olives, cut
into halves
2 tablespoons large capers
2 chiles jalapeños en esca-
beche, cut into strips
½ teaspoon salt, or to
taste

Add the tomatoes, with the rest of the in-gredients, to the pan and cook the sauce over a brisk flame until it is well seasoned and some of the juice has evaporated—about 10 minutes. Pour the sauce over the fish.

3 tablespoons olive oil

Sprinkle the oil over the sauce and bake the fish for about 20 minutes, uncovered, on one side. Turn the fish over and continue baking it until it is just tender—about 30 minutes. Baste the fish frequently with the sauce during the cooking time.

The sauce should be flavored by the chilies, but should not be too *picante*. If you are serving this dish as a main course, then Arroz Blanco (page 290) is a very good accompaniment. If it is to be served alone before the main course, then simply accompany it with hot tortillas. If you have any left over, it is even good cold; the sauce becomes gelatinous with the juice from the bones and head.

The recipe as given is intended as a first course for 6 people. If you serve it as a main course, then it would be better to have a 4- to 4½-pound fish and increase the sauce.

PESCADO EN CILANTRO [*Fish in coriander*]

6 first-course servings (see note below)

This dish seems to call for an excessive amount of coriander, but it cooks down to practically nothing and the flavor is not as strong as one would think—except, of course, for those who can't abide coriander. The chili, onion, and coriander flavors combined with the fiery juice from the can of chilies make for an extraordinarily interesting and fresh sauce. The friends in whose house I first tried it put shrimps in the sauce, which was extremely good. Nobody seems to know the origin of this dish, including the authors of the charming little book, *Herbs for Pot and Body*, whose recipe I have used.

A 3- to 3½-pound red
    snapper
An ovenproof dish just
    large enough to hold
    the fish (see note be-
    low)
1 scant teaspoon salt
Freshly ground pepper
1 medium onion (about
    6 ounces), finely
    sliced
⅓ cup lime juice

Have the fish cleaned, leaving the head and tail on.

Prick the fish well on both sides with a coarse-tined fork, and rub it with the salt and pepper. Place the fish onto the dish with half the onions underneath and the rest on top. Pour the lime juice over it and set it aside for about 2 hours, turning it over once during that time.

6 tablespoons olive oil
3 chiles jalapeños en esca-
    beche
3 tablespoons juice from
    the chili can
2 cups fresh coriander
    leaves, roughly
    chopped

Preheat the oven to 350°.

Cover the dish with foil and bake the fish for about 15 minutes on each side.

Add the rest of the ingredients and continue cooking the fish, covered, until it is just cooked, basting it from time to time with the juices in the dish—about 20 minutes.

If the dish is too large the sauce will dry up.

If you are serving this as a main course, then Arroz Blanco (page 290) is a very good accompaniment. If it is to be served alone before the main course, then hot tortillas alone should accompany it. This dish is also delicious cold, if there is any left over.

PESCADO RELLENO [*Stuffed fish*]

6 servings

The fish are small red snappers, one for each person, stuffed with a filling of shrimps, scallops, and crabmeat. This is a delicate and delicious recipe given to me by a distinguished old lady, Sra. Martínez from Veracruz. She has great patience, too; she has sat for hours talking with me about the regional food.

I prefer to serve this fish untypically—with boiled new potatoes, tossed in melted butter and freshly chopped parsley.

6 small red snappers (about ¾ pound apiece), one for each person

Have the fish cleaned, leaving the head and tail on. Have as much of the backbone removed as possible to form a good pocket for stuffing the fish without completely opening it up.

6 cloves garlic, peeled
Salt and pepper to taste
6 tablespoons lime juice

Crush the garlic and mix it to a paste with the salt, pepper, and lime juice.

Prick the fish all over on both sides with a coarse-tined fork and rub the paste well in—inside and out. Set the fish aside to season for at least 6 hours.

Preheat the oven to 350° and prepare the stuffing.

A frying pan
2 tablespoons butter
2 tablespoons olive oil
1 medium onion, finely chopped

Melt the butter with the oil and cook the onion, without browning, until it is soft.

1 pound tomatoes, peeled, seeded, and chopped (page 43) or 1¾ cups canned tomatoes

Add the tomatoes and cook them over a brisk flame until some of the juice has evaporated.

½ pound raw shrimps
(about 1 cup), peeled
and deveined
½ pound raw scallops
(about 1 cup)
2 tablespoons parsley,
finely chopped
Salt and pepper to taste
½ pound cooked crabmeat
(about 1 cup)
The fish
A coarse needle and
thread
An ovenproof serving
dish
6 tablespoons melted
butter
Foil to cover

Cut the shrimps into halves and the scallops into quarters. Add them, with the parsley and seasoning to the tomato mixture and let cook over a medium flame until the scallops and shrimps are **just** tender—about 10 minutes. Stir in the crabmeat.

Stuff each fish with about ½ cup of the filling and sew it up.

Put half of the butter into the dish, place the fish side by side, and sprinkle them with the remaining butter. Cover the dish with foil and bake until the fish is tender—about 20 to 25 minutes.

Everything can be done well ahead of time up to the point of stuffing the fish. That should be done at the last moment so that the stuffing does not get watery.

PESCADO ALCAPARRADO [*Fish in caper sauce*]

6 servings

One of the many excellent cooks I met in Tabasco gave me this unusual recipe. The fish is covered with a pale-green, creamy sauce.

An excellent fish for this dish is the *robalo*, a name you will often see on menus in Mexican restaurants. It is the *robalo blanco* or snook, a pikelike fish of the *Centropomus* family that has a rich, white flesh. With the red snapper, I suppose it is one of the most widely used fish in Mexico, particularly along the Gulf Coast, and apparently has been for a very long time. *Robalo* bones have been identified in kitchen hearths excavated at the Olmec site of San Lorenzo, dating back to 1200–1000 B.C.

(continued)

A saucepan
½ pound carrots, scraped
    and thinly sliced
½ pound turnips, peeled
    and thinly sliced
2 bay leaves
1 teaspoon salt, or to taste
⅓ medium onion, thinly
    sliced
12 peppercorns
2 tablespoons lime juice
4 cups water, or enough to
    just cover the fish

A fish poacher or deep
    ovenproof dish
A 3-pound striped bass or
    snook
The court bouillon

An ovenproof serving
    dish

A spice grinder or blender
3 ounces blanched al-
    monds
A blender
½ cup fresh bread
    crumbs, soaked
4 large lettuce leaves,
    torn into pieces
1 tablespoon capers
1 sprig parsley
2 cloves garlic, peeled
⅓ medium onion, sliced
1 cup court bouillon

Put all the ingredients in the saucepan and simmer the court bouillon for about 30 minutes. Strain and set it aside to cool; it must be completely cool before the fish is put into it.

Clean the fish, leaving the head and tail on. Place it in the dish and cover with the court bouillon. Bring the court bouillon to the boiling point, lower the flame, and let the fish simmer until it is just tender—about 30 minutes, depending on the thickness of the fish (see note page 222).

Carefully transfer the fish to the serving dish, and if you are using a striped bass, peel off the rather tough skin.

Strain and reserve the court bouillon.

Grind the almonds as finely as possible—this quantity should make ½ cup. Transfer them to the blender jar, and blend them with the rest of the ingredients to a smooth sauce.

A frying pan
½ cup olive oil
2 cloves garlic, peeled
The sauce
1 cup reserved fish
   bouillon
Salt as necessary

The heart of a romaine
   lettuce
1 tablespoon capers
12 olives
½ onion, sliced into thin
   rings
1 medium tomato, finely
   sliced

Heat the oil gently, add the cloves of garlic, and as soon as they start to brown remove them from the oil. Let the oil cool a little, then stir in the blended sauce.

Add the bouillon to the sauce, gradually stirring it in well. Simmer the sauce very gently for about 10 minutes. Add salt as necessary.

Pour the sauce over the fish and just heat it through in the oven.

Put the lettuce leaves around the dish and garnish with the remaining ingredients.

This is also very good served cold; the court bouillon gives the sauce a gelatinous quality and coats the fish well. The capers and almonds combined give it a very unusual flavor; but be careful not to overdo the capers when you are measuring them or their flavor will overpower that of the other ingredients.

PÁMPANO EN SALSA VERDE [*Pompano in green sauce*]

6 first-course servings

A taste for pompano is a very expensive one to cater to these days—at least in New York. But if you don't know this exceptionally delicious fish you should try it just once, or wait until the next time you go to Veracruz.

Drive a few miles south, or, for 2½ cents, take the shaky little bus that runs from the center every half hour to Boca del Río, and order *pámpano en hoja santa* in the Brisas del Mar Restaurant. The leaf (*Piper sanctum*) has a very strong and unusual flavor that goes particularly well with fish. And then on to Campeche for *pámpano en salsa verde,* pompano cooked in a refreshing sauce based on green—that is to say, unripe—tomatoes, the recipe for which follows.

2 pompano (each about
    1¼ pounds)

Have the fish cleaned, leaving the heads and tails on.

A molcajete or mortar and
    pestle
¼ teaspoon peppercorns
¼ teaspoon cumin seeds
½ teaspoon salt
Juice of 1 large lime

Grind the spices together dry and add the lime juice.

The fish
The seasoning
A large ovenproof dish

Prick the fish all over with a coarse-tined fork and rub the seasoning in well. Set aside, in the ovenproof dish, to season for at least an hour.

Preheat the oven to 300°.

A blender
2 cloves garlic
½ green pepper
1 chile serrano
3 sprigs fresh coriander
3 sprigs parsley
6 scallions
⅛ teaspoon oregano
1 tablespoon mild white
    vinegar
1 pound green (unripe)
    tomatoes
⅓ cup water
¼ teaspoon salt

Chop all the ingredients roughly and blend them to a smooth sauce.

6 tablespoons olive oil
The fish
The sauce

Put 2 tablespoons of the oil under the fish. Cover the fish with the rest of the oil and the sauce.

Cook the fish, covered, in the oven, for 20

minutes. Turn the fish carefully and cook for 15 to 20 minutes more, basting them, still covered, with the sauce from time to time.

This recipe has been used successfully with striped bass. A 4-pound bass is about right for this amount of sauce, and takes somewhere between 1 and 1½ hours to cook.

CEBICHE [*Raw fish marinated in lime juice*]

6 servings

One of the leading gastronomes of Mexico, Don Amando Farga, says that the word *cebiche* comes from the verb *cebar,* using its meaning "to saturate." It can probably be traced to the Oriental influence that crept into the western part of Mexico when the Spaniards opened up trade routes between the Philippines and the Pacific ports of the New World. The recipe varies considerably throughout the Latin American countries, and this one comes from the state of Guerrero.

A china or glass bowl
1 pound skinned fillets of mackerel or sierra
Juice of 6 or 7 large limes (1¼ to 1½ cups)

2 medium tomatoes (about 12 ounces)
3 or 4 canned chiles serranos en escabeche
¼ cup olive oil
½ teaspoon oregano
½ teaspoon salt, or to taste
Freshly ground pepper

Cut the fish into small cubes, about ½ inch, and cover them with the lime juice. Set the fish aside in the bottom of the refrigerator for at least five hours, or until the fish loses its transparent look and becomes opaque. Stir the pieces from time to time so that they get evenly "cooked" in the juice.

Skin, seed, and chop the tomatoes (page 43); chop the chilies with their seeds, and add them with the rest of the ingredients to the fish.

(continued)

Set the *cebiche* aside in the bottom of the refrigerator for at least 1 hour to season. (You should serve it chilled, but not so cold that the oil congeals.)

1 small avocado, sliced
1 small onion, sliced into
  rings
A little finely chopped
  coriander (optional)

Before serving, garnish each portion with slices of avocado and onion rings and sprinkle with a little chopped coriander, if desired.

Shrimps, scallops, crabmeat, and other seafood as well could be used instead of the mackerel. For 1 pound cleaned fish you will need to buy 2½ pounds Boston mackerel, or 2 pounds Spanish mackerel, or 1¼ pounds sierra. You can easily tell the difference because the Boston mackerel has a snake-like bluish marking on its back, while the Spanish mackerel has a lighter, silvery-gray skin faintly marked with yellow spots. The Boston, coming from colder waters, has a more oily flesh and thus a stronger fishy flavor. There is really no difference in flavor between the Spanish mackerel and the sierra, and the latter is much more easily skinned.

SIERRA EN ESCABECHE [*Soused sierra*]

6 first-course servings

The soused fish of Yucatán outshines that of any of the other regions; I shall stand by that and am quite willing to take on any enraged Veracruzano or Tampiqueño.

Either hot or cold, this makes a very refreshing first course, served with tortillas. It is another way of pickling fish, of course, and it will keep for a long time. However, I think it is best just a few hours after it has been made, so that the fish has had time to absorb the spicy souse, but has not been left long enough to become vinegary and hard.

I know of a Yucatecan cook who adds a few leaves of the guava, orange, and allspice trees to the *escabeche,* and it is wonderfully fragrant. The best

I could do was to add a few kumquat leaves that I had found in a green-grocer's.

A shallow overproof dish
1 cup water
¼ cup lime juice
1 teaspoon salt
6 1-inch-thick slices of
    sierra, kingfish, or
    striped bass (about 3
    pounds altogether)
	Pour the water, lime juice, and salt over the fish and set it aside for 1 hour, turning it once during that time.

A molcajete or mortar and
    pestle
½ teaspoon peppercorns
½ teaspoon coriander
    seeds
½ teaspoon cumin seeds
2 whole cloves
½-inch stick cinnamon
2 whole allspice
	Pulverize the spices.

2 cloves garlic, peeled
A saucepan
½ cup wine vinegar
½ cup water
½ teaspoon oregano,
    toasted (page 43)
2 small bay leaves
10 small cloves garlic,
    toasted (page 43)
    and peeled
2 teaspoons salt
½ teaspoon granulated
    sugar
	Crush the garlic and grind it to a paste with the spices. Put the spice-garlic paste into the saucepan with the rest of the ingredients and bring the mixture to a boil.

½ cup olive oil *¾ cup wine vinegar* *1¼ cups water*	Add the oil, the vinegar, and water and once again bring the mixture to a boil.

(*continued*)

A frying pan
The fish slices
½ cup peanut or safflower
    oil
The serving dish
6 chiles güeros, toasted
    (page 43)
2 large purple onions,
    thinly sliced and
    blanched as for Ce-
    bollas Encurtidas
    (page 307)

Dry the fish slices thoroughly. Heat the oil and fry them, about 3 minutes for striped bass or 5 minutes for the sierra, on each side. They should be barely cooked. Place them in the serving dish and pour the hot souse over them. Set the fish aside to season for at least 2 hours in the souse.

Serve hot or cold, garnished with the chilies and onions.

PESCADO EN TIKIN XIK [Fish in dried chili]

6 servings

This recipe for fish seasoned with an *achiote* paste and then charcoal broiled is from Campeche and Yucatán. The words *tikin xik* are Mayan and mean "dried chili," although little is actually used in the recipe.

A friend of mine was quite startled to be invited to brunch and see smoke pouring out of my apartment windows. The small hibachi I had set up inside was just large enough for one fish. This dish is excellent for a beach picnic too, as you can get it ready the day before. You can heat hot tortillas to accompany it over the fire.

One day ahead:

2 groupers or red snappers
    (about 2½ pounds
    each)

Do not have the scales removed from the fish. Have the heads and tails removed and the fish opened out flat in one piece. Remove the backbone.

A blender
1 tablespoon softened
   achiote seeds (page
   12)
¼ teaspoon peppercorns
1½ teaspoons salt, or to
   taste
¼ teaspoon oregano,
   toasted (page 43)
¼ teaspoon hot paprika
3 cloves garlic, peeled
¼ cup Seville orange
   juice (page 27) or
   mild white vinegar

On serving day:

A charcoal broiler, prefer-
   ably
A little olive oil

Blend all the ingredients together to a smooth paste. Spread the paste over the flesh of the fish and set it aside to season for several hours or overnight.

Brush the seasoned side of the fish with the oil and cook it, seasoned side down, over the charcoal or under the broiler for about 10 minutes.

Turn the fish over and cook it on the skin side for a slightly longer period or until the flesh is *just* cooked through—about 15 to 20 minutes, depending on the fish.

Serve the fish hot with fresh tortillas, so that everyone can make his own *tacos*, with small dishes of the following served separately:

Toasted oregano (page 43)
Chiles habaneros *or* **cayennes,** *chopped*
Sliced avocado

Cebollas Encurtidas (page 307)
Sliced tomato
Sliced Seville oranges

JAIBAS RELLENAS [*Stuffed crabs*]

6 first-course servings

This recipe is a great favorite in the gulf ports of Tampico and Veracruz, an excellent light first course that can be prepared well ahead of time, even the day before.

8 large female crabs, preferably alive
A saucepan
Boiling water to cover
2 tablespoons salt

Drop the crabs into the boiling, salted water and cover the saucepan. Bring them to a boil and cook them for about 3 minutes. Remove and drain.

When they are cool enough to handle, remove the heart-shaped breastplate and pry off the large back shell, keeping it intact.

Scrape out any fat and eggs that have remained in the shell, as well as those in the crab itself. Set them aside.

Scrub 6 of the shells well and set them aside. Remove the meat from the crabs and set it aside.

Preheat the oven to 350°.

A frying pan
¼ cup olive oil
1 clove garlic, peeled and finely chopped
½ medium onion, finely chopped

Heat the oil and fry the garlic and onion until they just begin to turn golden.

¾ pound tomatoes, peeled, seeded and mashed (page 43)
1½ tablespoons parsley, finely chopped
2 chiles serranos, finely chopped
1½ tablespoons capers

Add the tomatoes and the rest of the ingredients, except the crabmeat, and cook the mixture over a medium flame until it is almost dry—about 5 to 8 minutes. Stir in the crabmeat and remove from the heat.

½ teaspoon salt, or to
   taste
The crabmeat

The crab shells
The crabmeat mixture
6 tablespoons finely
   ground, toasted bread
   crumbs
3 tablespoons olive oil

Fill the crab shells with the crabmeat mixture, sprinkle with the bread crumbs and olive oil, and put the shells into the oven just long enough to heat them through.

Brown the filled shells quickly under the broiler and serve.

I don't recommend freezing the stuffed crabs because the filling becomes rather soggy. If *chiles serranos* are not available, the canned *serranos* or *jalapeños* can be substituted.

CAMARONES EN ESCABECHE ROJO
[*Shrimps pickled in red chili sauce*]

6 to 8 first-course servings

Some people don't take to this pungent, hard-hitting dish at first, but it grows on you. I have served cold shrimps cooked in this way with cocktails and they were wildly popular.

The sauce was originally evolved, of course, to preserve shrimps or fish before the days of refrigeration in the hot, damp climate of the gulf ports. Veracruz has its own variation, but it is *the* specialty of Tampico. The busy port is a twin town of Ciudad Madero, a large petroleum-refining center. There is constant activity; a lot of money changes hands, and the people live, laugh, and eat hard. In Tampico the shrimps are fried, added to the sauce as soon as it is made, and left to ripen in it. The first time I ate it there I wondered why the shrimps were rather tough and acidy. They had, of course, absorbed the vinegar. However, it is all a matter of taste. I have altered the recipe in that respect, but try it both ways and see what you think. Serve it as a first course—a little goes a long way.

(*continued*)

At least five days ahead:

A frying pan
5 chiles anchos
½ cup olive oil
A blender jar

¼ medium onion, roughly
    sliced
3 cloves garlic, peeled and
    roughly sliced
¼ teaspoon oregano
8 peppercorns
3 whole cloves

A small saucepan
1¼ cups mild white
    vinegar

The reserved oil
The chili puree
2 bay leaves
⅛ teaspoon oregano
½ teaspoon salt, or to
    taste

On serving day:

The sauce
Water as necessary
1 pound cooked shrimps
    (see note page 222),
    preferably small ones

Remove the seeds and veins from the chilies. Heat the oil and fry the chili pieces lightly on both sides. **Take care: they burn quickly.**

With a slotted spoon, transfer the chilies from the pan to the blender jar. Set aside.

In the same oil in which the chilies were fried, fry the rest of the ingredients for about a minute. With a slotted spoon transfer them to the blender jar. Reserve the oil.

Heat the vinegar and pour it over the ingredients in the blender jar. Set them aside to soak for about 20 minutes, then blend to a smooth, thick puree. No more liquid should be necessary, but if it is then add vinegar, **not water.**

Reheat the oil, but do not let it get so hot that it smokes, and add the puree, together with the bay leaves, oregano and salt. Once the mixture in the pan starts to bubble, lower the flame and continue to cook the sauce for about 15 minutes, stirring it from time to time so that it does not stick to the bottom of the pan. Put a lid over the pan, as the thick sauce will splatter about fiercely.

Leave the sauce in the refrigerator to ripen for at least 5 days before using it.

Dilute the sauce with a little water and add the shrimps for just long enough to heat them through.

Serve on a bed of Arroz Blanco (page 290), garnished with Cebollas Encurtidas (page 307).

This dish can also be served cold, garnished simply with onion rings, strips of *chiles jalapeños en escabeche,* capers, and green olives.

If the sauce has no water in it, it will keep indefinitely in the refrigerator; it will also freeze well, but let it ripen first.

It is most important to use the very best quality vinegar and olive oil—a white wine or Japanese rice vinegar, or you could use half that and half Vinegre de Piña (page 29).

CREPAS DE CAMARÓN CON SALSA DE CHILE PASILLA
[*Shrimp crêpes with chile pasilla sauce*]

6 first-course servings

This is one of the modern Mexican recipes—a really delightful one, from my old friend Maria Emilia Farias. It is a wonderfully rich first course, and should be followed by something very simple.

Have ready:

1½ pounds small, cooked shrimps (see note page 222)

12 thin crêpes, about 5½ inches in diameter, prepared according to any standard crêpe recipe

Preheat the oven to 350°.

A griddle or comal
6 chiles pasilla
A blender
1½ pounds tomatoes, broiled (page 44)

¼ medium onion

Heat the griddle and toast the chilies lightly, turning them from time to time so that they do not burn. Set aside to cool a little. When they are cool enough to handle, remove the seeds and veins being careful to remove them all or the sauce will be too *picante*. Without soaking the chilies, blend them, together with the tomatoes and onion, to a smooth sauce.

A frying pan
⅓ cup peanut or safflower oil

Heat the oil, but do not let it smoke. Add the sauce, sugar, and salt, and cook the mixture over a medium flame, stirring it from

The sauce
½ teaspoon granulated
sugar
1½ teaspoons salt

1½ cups Thick Sour
Cream (page 20)

An ovenproof serving dish
The cooked shrimps
The sauce
The crêpes

1¼ cups sharp Cheddar
cheese, grated
A little Thick Sour Cream
(page 20)

time to time so that it does not stick to the bottom of the pan. You will probably have to cover the pan with a lid, as the sauce splatters rather fiercely. After about 15 minutes the sauce will have thickened and seasoned. Set it aside to cool a little.

Stir the sour cream well into the sauce and let it continue to heat through for a minute or so. **Do not let it boil or it will curdle.**

Mix the shrimps into 1 cup of the sauce. Place a little of the mixture in each of the crêpes and roll them up loosely. Place the crêpes side by side on the serving dish and pour the remaining sauce over them.

Sprinkle the grated cheese over the sauce and put some dollops of sour cream around the edge of the dish.

Let the crêpes heat through in the oven and the cheese melt. Serve immediately.

The crêpes and sauce can always be made the day before—incidentally, the sauce freezes very well. They can be filled several hours ahead and the remaining sauce added just before they go into the oven. I have served this dish several times for cocktail parties, making very small crêpes that can be managed on a toothpick. They can also be made with a shredded chicken-breast filling.

If the sauce should curdle, don't try to make it come together with hot water or anything—it will taste just as good, although it will look a little more oily. Just cover the top with extra cheese.

Eggs (*Huevos*)

The hearty midmorning breakfast, *almuerzo*—"brunch," I suppose, would be a more appropriate name—is still very much an institution in Mexico City for those who can escape long enough from their jobs to enjoy it. It makes a wonderfully substantial cushion for the late *comida*. I, who have been brought up with British breakfasts and have continued in my belief over many years that they cannot be equaled, am just now beginning to find that bacon and eggs, tomatoes, mushrooms, and kippers all look pale beside a fresh slice of papaya, some Mexican eggs with lightly fried beans, *café con leche* and *pan dulce* or sweet *tamales*.

HUEVOS REVUELTOS A LA MEXICANA
[*Mexican scrambled eggs*]

1 serving

1 small tomato
2 chiles serranos
¼ small onion
A small frying pan
2½ tablespoons peanut or safflower oil

Chop together finely the unskinned tomato, the chilies with their seeds (see note below), and onion.

Heat the oil well and stir in the tomato-chili mixture.

(*continued*)

2 eggs
Salt to taste

Immediately break the eggs into the mixture, add the salt, and keep stirring the mixture until the eggs are set.

Serve immediately with hot tortillas.

This is the traditional and more rustic way of cooking *huevos revueltos.* You may find it easier, especially if you are cooking a large quantity, to beat the eggs together lightly with the salt before adding them to the tomato mixture. Another way is to fry the tomato mixture until it is well cooked before adding the eggs.

If you do not wish the eggs to be so *picante,* use the same amount of chilies but remove the seeds. You want to retain the crunchy texture that the chilies impart.

Nuevo León has its own version of scrambled eggs, called *migas*—the only difference being that pieces of crisp-fried tortillas are added to the mixture. For a change you might try substituting 3 tablespoons of Salsa de Tomate Verde Cruda (page 297) for the normal tomato-chili mixture. And then serve the eggs with a little sour cream or cream cheese.

HUEVOS REVUELTOS DE RANCHO
[*Farmhouse scrambled eggs*]

1 serving

These are eggs scrambled with *chile pasilla* sauce and served on fried tortillas.

Have ready:

2 small tortillas

2 tablespoons Salsa de Chile Pasilla
(page 304)

A small frying pan
2 tablespoons peanut or
*   safflower oil*
The tortillas
Paper toweling
A warmed plate

Heat the oil and fry the tortillas lightly on both sides. They should not get crisp. Drain them on the paper toweling and put them onto a warmed plate.

The 2 tablespoons chile
    pasilla *sauce*

In the same oil (add a little more if necessary), cook the sauce for a few seconds over a high flame.

A bowl and beater
2 eggs

Beat the eggs lightly and add them to the sauce in the pan. Stir the eggs until they are cooked.

A slice of cream cheese
1 tablespoon onion, finely
    chopped
1 tablespoon Thick Sour
    Cream (page 20)

Serve the eggs on top of the tortillas and garnish with the cheese, onion, and cream.

The sauce should be salty enough to season the eggs sufficiently—if not, add more salt.

HUEVOS REVUELTOS CON TOTOPOS
[*Eggs scrambled with tortilla crisps*]

1 serving

Have ready:

1½ small stale tortillas cut into strips   2 tablespoons *Salsa de Chile Pasilla*
                                   (*page 304*)

A small frying pan
¼ cup safflower or peanut
    oil
The tortilla strips

Heat the oil, and when it is smoking fry the tortillas until they are just crisp and a light golden brown.

Leaving the crisps in the pan, drain off all but about 1 tablespoon of the oil.

A bowl and beater
2 eggs
Salt to taste
The chile pasilla *sauce*
1 tablespoon onion, finely
    chopped
1 tablespoon crumbled
    cream cheese

Beat the eggs together with the salt and add them to the crisps in the pan. Stir the eggs over a medium flame until they are set.

Serve the eggs topped with the sauce, and sprinkled with the onion and cheese.

MACHACADO DE HUEVO [*Eggs scrambled with beef jerky*]

1 serving or enough filling for 6 burritos

I suppose, strictly speaking, this is not an egg dish, since the egg is used simply to bind the meat and other ingredients together. It is a typical break-fast and supper dish in the north, especially in Nuevo León and Chihuahua. It also provides the most popular filling for the wheat-flour tortillas, which then become *burritos*. Add some water and stew it for a while and you have a poor man's soup, *caldillo*.

Before the days of refrigeration, practically the only way of preserving beef in the arid cattle states of north and northwest Mexico was to make beef jerky. The meat is cut into thin slices, sprinkled with lime juice and salt, and then hung up in the sun to dry. It is then pounded into shreds and becomes *carne machada*—from the Spanish verb *machacar*, to pound.

The *machaca* of Sonora is slightly different. There the meat is pounded almost to a fluff, then cooked with potato, a little green chili (the Anaheim) and some grated tomato. I was intrigued to see that every cook I inter-viewed in Sonora and Sinaloa had, as part of her kitchen equipment, a large, black pebble, flat on one side and curved on the other to fit conveniently into the palm of the hand and be held firmly while pounding the meat (a clove of garlic is often pounded with it).

1 small tomato *¼ medium onion* 2 chiles serranos	Chop the unpeeled tomato, onion, and whole chilies finely.
A small frying pan *2 tablespoons peanut or* *safflower oil*	Heat the oil and fry the chopped ingredi-ents for about 5 minutes.

¾ cup shredded beef
  jerky (**carne macha-**
  cada) (*see note be-*
  low)
	Add the beef and fry the mixture for a few minutes more.

2 eggs	Break the eggs into the mixture and stir them until they are set.

The beef is quite salty so you will probably not need to add more salt. In the southwest there may be a really good beef jerky available—I know of one packaged product from Oregon, but it is not suitable for this recipe. I have tried to substitute the dried, potted beef always available in the supermarkets, but it is overwhelmingly salty. A very good substitute would be Mochomos (page 133), but cook the meat with some lime juice so that it gets that slightly acid flavor which is so good in the real beef jerky. It doesn't need any of those artificial flavorings, smoke and everything else, which are added to most commercial brands in the States. If you care to make your own, thinly slice a rump of beef, sprinkle it lightly with lime juice and salt, leave it to season overnight, then hang it out to dry in a cool, airy place.

HUEVOS REVUELTOS CON CHORIZO
[*Eggs scrambled with chorizo*]

1 serving

A small frying pan
4- to 5-inch chorizo

Heat the pan. Skin the *chorizo* and crumble it into the pan. Let it cook gently—if the flame is too high it will burn quickly—until the red fat has rendered out of the meat.

2 eggs

Break the eggs into the pan and stir until set.

This can be made with either the Spanish or Mexican *chorizo*.

HUEVOS REVUELTOS CON NOPALES
[*Eggs scrambled with nopal cactus pieces*]

1 serving

A frying pan
3 tablespoons peanut or
  safflower oil
1 tablespoon onion, finely
  chopped

Heat the oil and cook the onion, without browning, until it is transparent.

(continued)

½ cup canned cactus
    pieces, drained and
    rinsed
½ small tomato, chopped
1 chile serrano

Add the cactus pieces, tomato, and chili and fry the mixture for about 5 minutes, stirring from time to time.

2 eggs
Salt to taste

Beat the eggs lightly together with the salt and stir them into the mixture. Keep stirring until they are set.

Serve at once with hot tortillas.

Of course, if you are fortunate enough to have the fresh *nopales*, so much the better; just cook them as instructed on page 24.

HUEVOS RANCHEROS [*Country eggs*]

1 serving

These fried eggs are served on tortillas and covered with a *picante* tomato sauce.

Have ready:

½ cup Salsa Ranchera (page 299)
    warmed

An individual warmed serving dish

A small frying pan
2 tablespoons peanut or
    safflower oil
2 small tortillas
Paper toweling

Heat the oil and fry the tortillas lightly on both sides, as you would for *enchiladas*—they must not become crisp. Drain them on the toweling and place them on the warmed dish.

2 eggs

In the same oil, fry the eggs, then place them on the tortillas.

The sauce

Cover the eggs with the warmed sauce and serve immediately.

This makes an attractive breakfast or brunch dish served in a shallow *poêle* as I have often had it in a Mexican home: the tortilla is cut to fit the dish. The sauce is sprinkled with grated Cheddar cheese and the dish put briefly under the broiler until the cheese melts. For a change, you could garnish with strips of *chile poblano* or canned, peeled green chili and a little crumbled cream cheese. This can also be made with Salsa de Tomate Verde Cocida (page 299).

HUEVOS EN RABO DE MESTIZA
[*Eggs poached in a chili-tomato broth*]

6 servings

This makes a very substantial brunch dish. In San Luis Potosí it was served to me instead of soup before a *fiambre*. The traditional Potosina cook frowns on those who, for convenience, put hard-boiled eggs into the sauce. Incidentally, some of the best commercial dairy products are to be found in San Luis: the Carranco butter and cream cheese, and the Coronado *cajeta*. It was this very delicious creamy cheese that was used for *huevos en rabo de mestiza* when I last ate them in San Luis.

A large fireproof dish at least 3 inches deep
⅓ cup peanut or vegetable oil
1 large onion, thinly sliced
7 chiles poblanos, roasted and peeled, or 10 canned, peeled green chilies

A blender
2 pounds tomatoes broiled (page 44)

Heat the oil and cook the onion, without browning, until it is soft.

Remove the seeds from the chilies and cut them into strips. Add them to the onions in the pan and let them cook for about 3 minutes, stirring them so that they do not stick.

Blend the whole broiled tomatoes for a few seconds and add them to the onion-chili mixture. Do not overblend—the sauce should have some texture. Let them cook over a fairly high flame for about 10 minutes, or until the sauce is well seasoned and has reduced somewhat.

(*continued*)

3 cups water
1 teaspoon salt, or to taste
12 eggs
6 slices cream cheese

Add the water and salt and continue cooking for a minute or so more.

Crack the eggs, one by one, onto a saucer and carefully slide them into the hot broth. Arrange the slices of cheese on top.

Cover the dish with a lid or foil and let the eggs poach very gently until set, for about 6 to 8 minutes.

For each serving, put 2 eggs, some of the cheese, and plenty of the sauce and *rajas* in a shallow bowl. Sour cream can also be added.

The sauce can, of course, be made well ahead of time and even frozen ready for use.

HUEVOS MOTULEÑOS [*Eggs as they are prepared in Motul*]

1 serving

One might call these *huevos rancheros* with Yucatecan flourishes. A very substantial breakfast or brunch dish, much of it can be prepared ahead of time.

Huevos motuleños are named after a small town in Yucatán called Motul. Every morning in Mérida the cafés are crowded with the local businessmen, looking cool and clean in their *guayaberas* but carrying on heated discussions of the day's events over their *huevos motuleños* and great mugs of *café con leche*.

Have ready:

2 small tortillas
1 tablespoon chopped ham
1 tablespoon cooked peas

½ cup Salsa de Jitomate Yucateca
     (page 300), heated
½ tablespoon grated Parmesan cheese

A small frying pan
2 tablespoons lard or oil
The tortillas
Paper toweling
A warm serving plate

Heat the lard and fry the tortillas lightly on both sides. They should not be crisp. Drain them and set aside on the warm plate.

1 tortilla	Cover one tortilla with a thick layer of the
2 tablespoons Frijoles	bean paste.
Colados y Refritos a	
la Yucateca	
(see page 284),	
heated	
1 or 2 eggs	In the same fat, fry the egg and put it on
The second tortilla	top of the bean paste. Cover the egg with the
	second tortilla.
The chopped ham	Sprinkle the ham and peas over the tortilla.
The peas	Mask with the sauce, sprinkle it with cheese,
The sauce	and serve.
The grated cheese	

Once prepared, the eggs will hold in a warm oven for about 15 minutes without coming to much harm. Some cooks in Yucatán prefer to sauté some raw ham with a little onion and green peas as a garnish.

HIGADITOS [*A casserole of eggs with chicken and pork from Oaxaca*]

6 large servings

The literal translation of *higaditos* is "little livers." There is indeed a version of the recipe that calls for pork livers, but it is much drier, since no broth is added, and it is considered to be less festive. No local wedding would be complete without *higaditos;* and on market day I have seen huge *cazuelas* of it fast disappearing as market-goers in the small towns and villages near Oaxaca, many of whom have risen very early to walk down from their mountain hamlets, eat a late breakfast.

Most recipes stipulate pig's cheek and chicken as the main ingredients, and I have also seen one that specifies that at least half of the eggs be wild turkey eggs.

This would make a very good brunch dish for six very hungry people; it really is a little too heavy for breakfast.

(continued)

A saucepan
1 pound boneless pork,
    butt or tenderloin
1/4 onion
1 clove garlic, peeled
1/2 3-pound chicken,
    jointed
2 chicken gizzards
3 chicken livers
1/2 teaspoon salt
Water to cover

Cut the pork into small squares. Cover all the ingredients with water and bring them to a boil. Lower the flame, cover, and let them simmer for about 35 minutes, or until the meat is tender. The gizzards will need about 20 minutes longer.

A deep flameproof serving
    dish
2 tablespoons peanut or
    safflower oil
1 small onion, thinly sliced
3 cloves garlic, peeled and
    chopped
1 large tomato (1/2 pound)
1 cup tomatoes verdes (1/2
    pound)
1/8 teaspoon granulated
    sugar
2 cups reserved meat broth

Strain the meat. Shred the chicken and chop the pork and the giblets finely. Set them aside.

Cool the broth and skim off the fat. Put it aside.

Heat the oil and fry the onion and garlic, without browning, until they are soft.

Skin and chop the tomatoes finely, mash the tomates verdes. Add them to the onion-garlic mixture and let them cook for about 5 minutes over a high flame.

A spice grinder
1/8 teaspoon cumin seeds
4 peppercorns
2 whole cloves
A large pinch of saffron

Add the broth to the tomato mixture and continue cooking it over a low flame.

Grind the spices together dry and add them to the broth. When it comes to a boil, add the chopped meats and cook, to let them season, for a few minutes.

12 eggs
½ teaspoon salt

Beat the eggs together well with the salt. Lower the broth to a simmer and add the eggs gradually by pouring them around the edge of the dish.

Do not stir the eggs; they should form a rather solid but juicy mass. Gently slide a spatula around the edges of the dish and along the bottom so that they do not stick. Gently tip the dish to one side so that the eggs set and cook evenly.

Serve immediately with a *picante* sauce. The chili for the *picante* sauce used in Oaxaca is not generally available elsewhere, but Salsa de Chile Pasilla (page 304) would be suitable.

Vegetables *(Verduras)*

The Bounty of the Toltecs
They enjoyed great bounty;
there was an abundance of food, of the sustenances of life.

They say that the squash was so huge
that some measured six feet around
and that the ears of corn were as long as grinding stone mullers;
they could only be clasped in both arms.

—FROM "CODEX MATRITENSE DE LA BIBLIOTECA REAL PALACIO,"
TRANS. THELMA D. SULLIVAN

"One of the most interesting sights to an inquisitive stranger in Mexico is a ramble early in the morning to the canal which leads to the Lake of Chalco. There hundreds of Indian canoes, of different forms and sizes, freighted with the greatest variety of animal and vegetable productions of the neighbourhood, are constantly arriving; they are frequently navigated by native women accompanied by their families. The finest cultivated vegetables which are produced in European gardens, with the numberless fruits of the torrid zone, of many of which even the names are not known to us, are piled up in pyramids and decorated with the most gaudy flowers."

—FROM *Six Months Residence and Travel in Mexico,*
BY W. H. BULLOCK

252

If you give a Mexican peasant a few square meters of land, in no time at all he will have built himself a little shack and hung the outside walls with a hundred little tin cans full of trailing plants and colorful flowers. In summer the little plot of ground will be bursting with growth: tall, strong cornstalks twined with wandering vines of pumpkins, squash, green beans, and *chayotes*. The peas will be in flower and the wild greens will be crowding themselves in wherever they can, exuberantly celebrating the arrival of the welcome rains.

Although Mexico City has grown so immense and unwieldy, even the supermarkets in the more sophisticated residential areas offer bunches of pumpkin flowers and *huitlacoche*—the fungus that makes gray-black deformities of the kernels—cheek by jowl with the more commonplace cauliflowers, spinach, and potatoes. And the large entranceways attract peasant women with their little piles of avocados, peanuts, or sweetmeats, for anywhere in the city, whether in the poor barrios or outside the homes of the rich, somebody has something to sell and another little curbside market is born.

But no longer do the canoes come into the city with their fresh produce; instead, for blocks around Merced market—the central wholesale market of Mexico City—there is a thick mass of slowly moving trucks from all over the republic, jostling for a place to stop and unload. The younger men have invested in small trolleys to haul the produce to the stands inside, but there are still many wrinkled old men bent under the weight of enormous, overflowing hampers, attached by thick leather bands around their heads. They weave through the crowd, gently nudging people out of their way and saying in a low monotonous tone that can be heard, miraculously, above the din, their warning, "*Golpe . . . golpe . . . bulto . . .*"

Despite their stark, concrete edifices, the modern markets still retain a character unique and Mexican. Take a walk through some of the smaller local markets: Santa Julia, Juárez, San Juan, or San Ángel. Some stands will be piled high with produce that overflows onto the floor while others have just a few little piles—*montoncitos*—of dried, richly hued chilies; small *tunas,* red and orange, some of them carefully peeled ready to eat; a few *colorín* flowers for *tortas;* or some tiny, pale-green limes. You wonder how the person sitting there manages to spin out the day, and at the end of it, how many pesos she will have made to spend.

San Juan and Santa Julia in particular have an amazing variety of mushrooms. From about the middle of August on through October, there are russet-colored cepes; the rich-brown, hooded morels; small white puffballs for salad, the spindly little *clavitos* for soups and *quesadillas* and the rich-orange *yemas* for stuffing. And once in a very great while, a few of the blue mushrooms from the sierras around Valle del Bravo.

There are tall bundles of *guauzoncles*—just like overgrown *epazote*—the ragged *romeritos* to cook with dried shrimp cakes in a *mole* for Easter and Christmas, the wild purslane that is cooked with pork, Swiss chard, cabbages, leeks, turnips—indeed, all the vegetables you can think of are there. If anything is new to you and you don't know how to cook it, within five minutes you will be given as many recipes as there are people to hear your question. And as you buy there will be that constant chorus of young voices . . . "*Le ayudo? Le ayudo?*" for everyone wants to earn a peso or two carrying your load.

Generally speaking in Mexico, vegetables are served as a separate dish, before the main course. They are made into *tortitas*—little fritters of light batter served in a tomato sauce; or cooked into rather solid *budines*—puddings of eggs, cheese, and flour; or cooked in a stew of meat and fish or in substantial soups like the *mole de olla* or the favorite from Sonora, *pozole de milpa.*

TORTA DE CALABACITAS [*Zucchini squash torte*]

The zucchini squash of Mexico, which are used a great deal there, are small, pale green, and have a very delicate, sweet flavor, quite unlike those in the markets here, which are so often inclined to be too large and too bitter. A round variety that is very popular, and especially good and convenient for stuffing, is also available there. I shall always remember going very early on Sunday mornings in October to the Xochimilco market to buy roses and plants for the terrace of our apartment and finding the new shoots of the zucchini plant, still with the flowers and half-formed little squash on them. I would steam them all together and then eat them with butter and pepper; a delicacy to rival the freshest green asparagus.

A saucepan

1½ pounds zucchini squash (see note below)

¼ teaspoon salt

Boiling water to cover

A colander

A 2-quart soufflé dish or casserole

2 tablespoons finely ground, toasted bread crumbs

⅓ recipe Rajas con Jitomate (page 261) (using 4 chilies, 10 ounces of tomatoes, ½ medium onion)

6 ounces Muenster at room temperature

A bowl and beater

3 eggs, separated

¼ teaspoon salt

The soufflé dish

The cooled squash

The cooled rajas con jitomate

The cheese

The beaten eggs

3 tablespoons softened butter

Clean and trim the squash and cut them into rounds about ⅛ inch thick. Cover them with boiling water, add the salt, and cook them until they are just tender—from 3 to 5 minutes, depending on the squash. They should not be allowed to become too soft.

Drain the squash and set it aside to cool.

In the meantime, preheat the oven to 350°. Butter a 2-quart soufflé dish or casserole, and sprinkle it with finely ground, toasted bread crumbs.

Make the rajas con jitomate, cool them, then slice the cheese thinly, and cut it into small pieces.

Beat the egg whites stiff, then add the salt and the egg yolks, one by one, beating well after each addition.

Put a layer of the squash over the bottom of the dish, pour one-half of the rajas over it, put one-third of the cheese onto the sauce, and cover with one-third of the beaten eggs. Dot with butter. Repeat in the same order and finish off the torte with a layer of squash, the rest of the beaten egg, butter, and cheese.

Cook the torte in the top of the oven until

(continued)

it is well heated through and the egg set—
about 25 to 30 minutes. Serve immediately.

In Mexico this would be served alone as a separate vegetable course
before the main dish. It makes a very good supper or luncheon dish
followed by a salad.

Some of the squash on the market here has rather a strong and bitter
flavor, so I sprinkle the cut squash with plenty of salt about 2 hours before
using and then rinse it well before adding it to the boiling water.

Make sure that the zucchini and the *rajas* are cool before you start putting
the torte together or the eggs will become a little watery and not set as well.
The cheese should be out of the refrigerator for some time before using.
Everything that makes up this dish can be prepared ahead of time and then
the eggs beaten and the torte assembled at the last moment.

CALABACITAS RELLENAS DE ELOTE
[*Zucchini squash stuffed with fresh corn*]

6 servings

This is such a colorful and attractive dish with the pale-green squash and
yellow corn topped with the tomato sauce. It has a subtle medley of flavors,
too, and can very well stand alone as a separate course.

Have ready:

Salsa de Jitomate Cocida (*page 302*)

*1½ pounds zucchini
    squash (choose 6 fat
    ones)*

Preheat the oven to 350°.

Clean and trim the squash. Cut them into
halves lengthwise and scoop out the inner
flesh, leaving a shell about ½ inch thick. Discard the pulp or reserve for another use.

*A shallow ovenproof dish,
    just large enough for
    the squash to fit in
    one layer*

Place the squash in the dish and set aside
while you prepare the filling.

A blender

About 2 cups corn (1 10-ounce package)

2 medium eggs

2 tablespoons milk

¼ teaspoon salt, or to taste

Blend the corn, eggs, milk, and salt to a coarse puree. Do not add more liquid unless absolutely necessary to release the cutting blades.

6 ounces grated mild Cheddar or Muenster cheese

Mix about three-quarters of the cheese into the corn puree, saving the rest for the topping.

The zucchini shells

The stuffing

The reserved cheese

3 tablespoons butter, softened

Fill the zucchini shells with the corn stuffing, which will be quite runny. Sprinkle with the remaining cheese and dot with the butter.

The Salsa de Jitomate Cocida

Cover the dish with foil and bake until the squash is tender—about 50 minutes. Serve covered with the tomato sauce.

In Mexico a soft cream cheese is used in the filling; you could use farmer cheese in it here, but sprinkle the top with Cheddar.

This is a dish that is far better eaten fresh rather than left to stand around. However, the filling, the zucchini, and the sauce can be prepared ahead of time, ready to assemble for the oven.

CALABACITAS PICADAS CON JITOMATE
[*Chopped zucchini and tomato*]

6 servings

*A saucepan or fireproof
serving dish*
*3 to 4 tablespoons peanut
or safflower oil*
*1½ pounds zucchini
squash*
1½ pounds tomatoes

*1 clove garlic, peeled and
finely chopped*
*1 medium onion, finely
chopped*
2 whole chiles serranos
*½ teaspoon salt, or to
taste*

Heat the oil until it just begins to smoke. Let it cool off a little while you prepare the vegetables.

Clean and trim the squash and cut roughly into ½-inch squares. Peel, seed, and roughly chop the tomatoes, straining the juice from the tomato seeds (page 43). Add the squash, tomatoes, juice, and the rest of the ingredients to the pan.

Cover the pan, and cook the vegetables over a medium flame for 10 minutes, then uncover and cook until the squash is tender—about 40 minutes in all. Scrape the bottom of the pan and stir the mixture well from time to time so that it does not stick. Serve hot.

When the squash is cooked there should not be any liquid in the pan.

This is probably the simplest way of cooking zucchini in Mexico. It is a very versatile dish, going admirably with poultry, meat, or fish. It can be prepared well ahead of time and is even better reheated the following day.

The same recipe can be used for cooking *verdolagas* (purslane), *acelgas* (Swiss chard), *quelites* (wild greens, *Chenopodium mexicanum*), and *espinacas* (spinach).

CALABACITAS CON CREMA [*Zucchini squash with cream*]

6 servings

There are hundreds of ways of cooking squash in Mexico, and every cook has her own method and seasoning. This was our maid Godileva's way of preparing them, and the dish frequently appeared on our dinner table. It has an exotic flavor, and is quite unlike any other squash dish I have come across.

A saucepan or flameproof
    serving dish
1½ pounds zucchini
    squash
2 medium tomatoes (¾
    pound)
6 peppercorns
4 sprigs fresh coriander
2 sprigs mint, fresh if
    possible
½-inch stick cinnamon
4 whole cloves
2 whole chiles serranos
½ cup thin cream
½ teaspoon salt, or to
    taste

Clean, trim, and dice the squash; skin, seed, and chop the tomatoes (page 43). Put them into the pan together with the other ingredients.

Water if necessary

Cover the pan with a tightly fitting lid and cook the mixture over a low flame, scraping the bottom of the pan and stirring the mixture well from time to time so that it does not stick. If the vegetables are drying up too much, add a little water. It will take about 30 minutes to cook.

When cooked the zucchini should be very soft, the cream completely absorbed, and no liquid remaining in the pan. The chilies should remain whole and just flavor the squash—it should not be *picante*.

This is a very good vegetable dish with meat or fish. It can be prepared well ahead of time and it is perhaps even better heated up the next day.

RAJAS DE CHILE POBLANO [*Chile poblano strips*]

6 servings

In the central and northern part of Mexico, where the *chile poblano* is used a great deal, to ask for *rajas* most commonly means strips of *chile poblano* cooked in this way. It makes an excellent accompaniment for broiled meats (see for instance, Carne Asada a la Tampiqueña, page 181).

8 chiles poblanos, *roasted and peeled* (*page 44*) *or 12 canned, peeled green chilies*

Remove the seeds and veins from the chilies and cut them into strips about 1½ inches long and ½ inch wide. If the chilies seem too *picante*, soak them in salted water for about 30 minutes.

A small frying pan
6 tablespoons peanut or safflower oil
1½ medium onions, thinly sliced

Heat the oil and fry the onions gently, without browning them, until they are soft.

The chili strips
½ teaspoon salt, or to taste

Add the chili strips and salt to the onions in the pan, cover, and cook gently for about **8 minutes for *poblanos* and 4 minutes for canned chilies.**

You can always prepare these ahead of time and they will keep in the refrigerator for several days. They are inclined to get a bit soggy if you freeze them. (See also page 45.)

PAPAS FRITAS CON RAJAS [*Potatoes fried with chili strips*]

6 servings

This is an excellent accompaniment for roasted and broiled meats, especially if you want something more substantial than the *rajas* alone.

I shall never forget the wonderful smell of the chilies frying as we would walk in very hungry at lunch time. Sometimes our maid Rufina would use strips of the long, thin, dark green *chile chilaca,* which can bite your stomach as well as your mouth quite fiercely.

Prepare the recipe for Rajas de Chile Poblano (page 260). After frying the onion, add, with the chili strips, 2 pounds cooked red bliss or other waxy potatoes, cut into small cubes. (Be careful not to cook the potatoes too much; they should be *al dente,* or they will disintegrate during the frying.) You will need to add about 2 more tablespoons oil, and 1 teaspoon of salt. Without covering the pan, fry the potatoes until they are nicely browned, stirring the mixture from time to time, as the chili and onions are apt to stick to the bottom of the pan.

RAJAS CON JITOMATE [*Chili strips with tomatoes*]

6 servings

Prepare the recipe for Rajas de Chile Poblano (page 260). To the onions in the pan, add, along with the chili strips, 2 pounds of peeled, seeded, and chopped tomatoes (page 43) and ½ to ¾ teaspoon salt, or to taste. Cook uncovered, over a fairly high flame until the vegetables are well seasoned and the liquid has evaporated—about 10 minutes.

This is excellent served like a thick sauce over Torta de Elote (page 272). It also makes a very good accompaniment to plain broiled meat, fish, or chicken.

CHILE CON QUESO [*Chilies with cheese*]

6 servings

I had always thought of *chile con queso* as a Texas dish until I went to Chihuahua. It is eaten there as a vegetable with broiled meats, and it is also served as an appetizer with hot tortillas. The light green Anaheim chili with which it is made is grown extensively in the north of Mexico and southwestern United States. It is used a great deal in the cooking of Chihuahua and Sonora.

Two of the best Mexican cheeses come from Chihuahua—the *queso Chihuahua* made by the Mennonites, living there in settlements, and the *queso asadero,* a very creamy, slightly acidy cheese that is layered like a mozzarella. It is always used cooked, and gives the lovely creamy stringiness that the Mexicans hold in high esteem. It is curious that in some parts of the State they use a wild plant to coagulate the milk instead of the more usual rennet. I have not yet been able to find out what this is—possibly a type of thistle that I have seen mentioned in the same connection in an old Spanish cookbook.

20 fresh Anaheim chilies or 20 canned, peeled green chilies

If you have fresh chilies, roast and peel them as you would *chiles poblanos* (page 44). Cut the chilies into strips without removing the seeds.

A frying pan or flame-proof serving dish
5 tablespoons peanut or safflower oil
1 medium onion, thinly sliced

Heat the oil and cook the onion, without browning, until it is soft.

1 medium tomato (6 ounces), skinned (page 43)
The rajas

Slice the tomato thinly and add it with the *rajas* to the onions in the pan. Cover and cook over a medium flame for about 8 minutes.

¾ cup milk
3 tablespoons water

Add the milk and water and let the mixture cook for a few minutes more.

½ pound Muenster or mild Cheddar cheese
1½ teaspoons salt, or to taste

Just before serving, cut the cheese into thin slices and add, with the salt, to the chili mixture. Serve as soon as the cheese melts.

CHILES RELLENOS [*Stuffed chilies*]

6 servings

This dish consists of large chilies or bell peppers stuffed with meat or cheese, coated with a light batter, and fried. They are served in a light tomato broth.

There is always an exclamation of pleasure and surprise when a *cazuela* of golden, puffy *chiles rellenos* sitting in their tomato broth is presented at the table. If you have eaten those sad, flabby little things that usually turn up in so-called Mexican restaurants in the United States as authentic *chiles rellenos,* you have a great surprise in store. Here is yet another prime example of the fine feeling the Mexicans have for texture in their food: you bite through the slightly crisp, rich *chile poblano* to experience the crunch of the almonds and little bits of crystallized fruits in the pork filling. Then there is the savory broth to cut the richness of the batter.

Chiles poblanos are imported in great quantities to large centers of Mexican population here in the States but very few find their way to the East. I am afraid the bell pepper is about the only suitable substitute for appearance and size—you can always spike them with a little *chile serrano.*

Assembling the chilies may seem like a long laborious task, but it is no more complicated and time consuming than most worthwhile dishes, and this dish is certainly worthwhile.

THE PICADILLO

A large saucepan
3 pounds boneless pork
   (*see note*)
½ onion, sliced
2 cloves garlic, peeled
1 tablespoon salt, or to
   taste
Cold water to cover
A colander

Cut the meat into large cubes. Put them into the pan with the onion, garlic, and salt and cover with cold water. Bring the meat to a boil, lower the flame and let it simmer until just tender—about 40 to 45 minutes. Do not overcook. Leave the meat to cool off in the broth.

Strain the meat, reserving the broth, then shred or chop it finely and set it aside. Let the broth get completely cold and skim off the fat. Reserve the fat.

(*continued*)

A large frying pan
6 tablespoons lard or the
*   fat from the broth*
½ medium onion, finely
*   chopped*
3 cloves garlic, peeled and
*   finely chopped*
The cooked meat (about
*   3 cups)*
A molcajete
8 peppercorns
5 whole cloves
½-inch stick cinnamon
3 heaped tablespoons
*   raisins*
2 tablespoons blanched
*   and slivered almonds*
2 heaped tablespoons
*   acitrón or candied*
*   fruit, chopped*
2 teaspoons salt, or to
*   taste*
1¼ pounds tomatoes,
*   peeled and seeded*
*   (page 43)*

Melt the lard and cook the onion and garlic, without browning, until they are soft.

Add the meat and let it cook until it begins to brown.

Crush the spices roughly and add them, with the rest of the ingredients to the meat mixture. Cook the mixture a few moments longer.

Mash the tomatoes a little and add them to the mixture in the pan. Continue cooking the mixture over a high flame for about 10 minutes, stirring it from time to time so that it does not stick. It should be almost dry.

THE TOMATO BROTH

A blender
1¼ pounds tomatoes,
*   peeled and seeded*
*   (page 43)*
¼ medium onion, roughly
*   chopped*
2 cloves garlic, peeled and
*   roughly chopped*

Blend the tomatoes, with the juice extracted from their seeds, with the onion and garlic until smooth.

A large flameproof dish at
    least 3 inches deep
¼ cup lard or reserved
    fat from the broth
4 whole cloves
6 peppercorns
2 small bay leaves
2 ½-sticks cinnamon
Scant ¼ teaspoon dried
    thyme

Melt the lard and fry the tomato puree over a high flame for about 3 minutes, stirring to prevent sticking. Add the rest of the ingredients and cook them over a high flame for about 5 minutes, stirring.

3 cups reserved pork broth

Salt as necessary

Add the pork broth and continue cooking the broth over a medium flame for about 15 minutes. By that time it will be well seasoned and reduced somewhat—but still a broth rather than a thick sauce. Add salt as necessary.

THE CHILIES

6 chiles poblanos *or bell*
    peppers

A damp cloth or large
    plastic bag

Put the chilies straight onto a fairly high flame or under the broiler—not into the oven —and let the skin blister and burn. Turn the chilies from time to time so they do not get overcooked or burn right through.

Wrap the chilies in a damp cloth or plastic bag and leave them for about 20 minutes. The burned skin will then flake off very easily and the flesh will become a little more cooked in the steam.

Make a slit in the side of each chili and carefully remove the seeds and veins. Be careful to leave the top of the chili, the part around the base of the stem, intact. (If the chilies are too *picante,* let them soak in a mild vinegar and water solution for about 30 minutes.) Rinse the chilies and pat them dry.

(continued)

The picadillo
Chopped chile serrano, *if*
necessary
Paper toweling

Stuff the chilies until they are well filled out. If you are using bell peppers, add some chopped fresh chili to make them a little *picante.* Set them aside on paper toweling while you make the batter.

THE BATTER

A heavy frying pan
Peanut or safflower oil (at
least ¾ inch deep)
A bowl and beater
4 eggs, separated
¼ teaspoon salt
The stuffed chilies
A little flour
The batter

Heat the oil until it starts to smoke.

Meanwhile, beat the egg whites until they are stiff, but not too dry. Add the salt and egg yolks one by one, beating well after each addition.

Pat the chilies completely dry (or the batter will not adhere) and sprinkle them lightly with flour. Coat them with the batter.

Fry the chilies in the hot fat, turning them from time to time, until they are an even gold all over.

Paper toweling
The tomato broth

Drain the chilies on the paper toweling and place them in the tomato broth—it should come about halfway up the chilies—to heat through over a low flame. Serve immediately.

Canned tomatoes are acceptable in this recipe, but if you have plenty of fresh ones available, then peel, seed, and mash them before using (page 43). And don't forget to strain the seeds to extract the juice for the broth.

In Puebla during the fruit season peaches, pears, or even apples are cut up into little pieces and used in the *picadillo.*

It is quite unnecessary to buy an expensive cut of pork for *picadillo.* I buy shoulder and cut off the meat, then cook it with the bone and skin to give the broth added richness.

Some chilies and peppers have thinner flesh than others, and some look a bit tattered when you have roasted and cleaned them; it really doesn't matter, since the batter will seal in the stuffing and juices.

You can prepare the stuffing and the sauce the day before, and skin and clean the chilies. But do not put the stuffing into the chilies until about 2 hours before cooking. You can coat and fry them just before your guests arrive and leave them on paper toweling in a warm spot until the last moment, when they can be just warmed through in the tomato broth. In Mexico they are served by themselves, just before the main course. But in fact they make a very good main course—in which case you could serve two small chilies, one filled with cheese (see below) and the other with the pork *picadillo*, accompanied by some white rice and hot tortillas. If you have any *picadillo* left over it will freeze very well; reheated, it makes a very good filling for *tacos*. The tomato broth, too, will freeze and can be used for *tortitas*.

CHILES RELLENOS DE QUESO [*Chilies stuffed with cheese*]

Follow the instructions for Chiles Rellenos (page 263), but stuff the chilies with slices of mozzarella or mild Cheddar cheese instead of the *picadillo*. In Mexico the braided *queso de Oaxaca* is generally used.

CHILES EN NOGADA [*Chilies in walnut sauce*]

6 servings

This is one of the famous dishes of Mexico: large, dark green *chiles poblanos* stuffed with a pork meat *picadillo* and covered with a walnut sauce. It is decorated with red pomegranate seeds and the large-leafed Italian parsley.

The recipe is said to have been concocted by the grateful people of Puebla, who were giving a banquet in honor of Don Agustín de Iturbide's saint's day, August 28 in 1821. He and his followers had led the final revolt against Spanish domination; as self-proclaimed emperor he had just signed the Treaty of Córdoba. All the dishes at the banquet were concocted of ingredients of the colors of the Mexican flag; in this dish were the green chilies, the white sauce, and the red pomegranate seeds.

It is almost worth a special journey to Mexico City or, better still, to Puebla toward the end of August. By then it is well on in the rainy season, and the fresh crop of walnuts will have been gathered. The peasants come in from the country with them, and you can see them sitting on the sidewalks at every street corner selling little piles of a dozen walnuts. Sometimes they are crammed into small paper bags, but the top one will always be cracked open so that you can see its quality. The flesh is tender, almost milky, with a very delicate flavor, and the papery skin around it can be peeled off easily. Practically every restaurant will have *chiles en nogada* on the menu, and no family fiesta will be complete without them during their short season.

THE STUFFED CHILIES

6 chiles poblanos	Prepare the chilies as for Chiles Rellenos (page 263).
The picadillo	Prepare the *picadillo* as for Chiles Rellenos (page 263) with these few minor changes: chop the meat finely and add a chopped pear and peach to the stuffing.

THE NOGADA (**WALNUT SAUCE**)

One day ahead:

A small dish	Cover the nuts with boiling water and leave
20 to 25 fresh walnuts, shelled, or ¼ pound canned walnut meats	them to soak for about 5 minutes. (If you leave them soaking too long the skin will become too soft and will be more difficult to
Boiling water to cover	remove.) Remove the thin papery brown skin—it should come off quite easily.
Cold water to cover	Cover the walnuts with cold water and leave them to soak overnight.

On serving day:

A blender	Blend all the ingredients until they are smooth.
The soaked and drained nuts	
1 small piece white bread, without crust	
¼ pound farmer cheese	
1½ cups Thick Sour Cream (page 20)	
½ teaspoon salt or 1½ tablespoons sugar (see note below)	
A large pinch of powdered cinnamon (optional)	

ASSEMBLING THE DISH

The chilies	Cover the chilies with the sauce and garnish with parsley leaves and pomegranate seeds.
The sauce	
A small bunch of Italian parsley	
The seeds of one small pomegranate	

You really have to use *chiles poblanos* for this dish. Bell peppers or the canned, peeled green chilies are no substitute. The walnuts should be very fresh, but in a pinch you could use the commercially packed walnuts, which soften and swell when soaked in water overnight.

Many people like a slightly sweet sauce, while others prefer it a little salty—it is entirely a matter of taste.

One of the points most vehemently discussed among Mexican cooks is whether the chilies for this dish should be *capeados* (covered with beaten egg and fried) or not. I agree with those who say no; I think the rich sauce and batter together is too much. They are served warm with the cold sauce poured over them at the last moment. But if you personally prefer them *capeados,* then do it that way.

TORTITAS DE PAPA [*Potato cakes*]

6 servings

A food mill
1½ pounds Idaho potatoes (5 small ones), cooked and peeled

Pass the potatoes through the fine disk of a food mill.

A garlic press
1 clove garlic, peeled
½ pound farmer cheese, crumbled
1 teaspoon salt
Freshly ground pepper

Crush the garlic and add it, with the rest of the ingredients, to the potatoes.

2 small eggs

Beat the eggs together well and work them well into the potato mixture. Form the mixture into 12 small cakes, each about 2½ to 3 inches across and ½ inch thick.

Flour or some finely ground, toasted bread crumbs

Pat a little flour or bread crumbs on the outside of the cakes.

A frying pan
Peanut or safflower oil (½ inch deep)
The potato cakes
Paper toweling

Heat the oil until it is very hot, but do not let it get so hot that it smokes. Fry the potato cakes for about 3 to 5 minutes on each side, depending on how browned and crisp you like them. Drain them on the paper toweling and serve them immediately with Salsa de Jitomate Cocida (page 302).

After the cakes have been fried, you can keep them hot in a 400° oven for about 15 to 20 minutes—after that they will dry out. If you put them in a slower oven they will get too soft.

To test the heat of the fat, put a wooden spoon into it, and if the fat sizzles around it then it is hot enough to put in the potato cakes. If the fat is too hot the outside of the potato cakes will start to crumble away and they will color too quickly on the outside without heating right through.

ELOTE CON CREMA [*Fresh corn with cream, chilies, and cheese*]

6 servings

Again, there are so many variations of corn-chili-cream dishes that it is hard to know just which recipe to choose. For a change, the chilies could be left whole, stuffed with corn and cheese, and cooked in cream. But this combination is delicious any way.

Preheat the oven to 350°.

A 2-quart flameproof dish
¼ cup butter
½ medium onion, finely
    chopped
1 clove garlic, peeled and
    finely chopped

Melt the butter and cook the onion and garlic, without browning, until they are soft.

5 chiles poblanos,
    roasted and peeled
    (page 44) or 7
    canned, peeled green
    chilies

Cut the chilies into *rajas* (strips), add them to the pan, and cook them, covered, **8 minutes for *poblanos*, 5 minutes for canned chilies.**

About 4 cups corn (1½
    pounds frozen corn or
    kernels from 5 ears)
¼ pound mild Cheddar
    cheese in small cubes
1 teaspoon salt, or to taste
Thick Sour Cream (page
    20)

Add the corn, cheese, and salt to the chili mixture. Cover tightly with foil or a lid and let it bake for 20 minutes for frozen corn. If you use fresh corn, cook for 40 minutes, adding the cheese after the first 20 minutes of cooking time.

Serve the vegetables hot, with the sour cream.

This is a very rich dish, and is very good served as a separate course with hot tortillas. It is best eaten right after it's cooked, as the cheese gets tough when reheated.

TORTA DE ELOTE [*Fresh corn torte*]

6 servings

Preheat the oven to 350°.

Have ready:

An ovenproof dish (approximately 9 × 9 × 2 inches), well greased and sprinkled with toasted, finely ground bread crumbs

A baking sheet, put into the oven about ⅔ of the way down

A blender
6 ears of corn—as old as you can find (see note below)
A little milk

Cut the kernels from the ears of corn, as near to the core as you can.

Put about one-third of the quantity into the blender, adding only sufficient milk to loosen the cutting blades of the blender and blend the corn to a rough consistency. Add the rest of the corn by degrees and keep stopping the machine frequently to release the cutters. Set the mixture aside.

An electric mixer
¼ pound butter, softened
½ cup granulated sugar
4 eggs, separated
¼ to ½ teaspoon salt
The corn mixture

Beat the butter and sugar together until they are fluffy.

Add the egg yolks one at a time to the creamed mixture and keep beating until they are well mixed in. Add the salt and the corn mixture and beat again.

A bowl and beater
1 teaspoon baking powder

Beat the egg whites until they are stiff and fold them into the mixture with the baking powder.

The ovenproof dish
The baking sheet

Pour the mixture into the prepared dish. Place the dish on the hot baking sheet in the oven and bake for 1 hour.

Serve immediately with Thick Sour Cream (page 20) and salt or Rajas con Jitomate (page 261).

It is so much easier to make this in Mexico, where the local white corn has a much higher starch content. I have experimented with using "fillers," like cornstarch, but I don't like the texture. I have obtained the best results from buying the corn and keeping it for a few days in the kitchen to dry out. It is well worthwhile trying, since it makes a very interesting and colorful first course with the *rajas con jitomate* sauce. It could very well accompany plainly roasted meat, too.

They make a very good *torta de elote* in my favorite Veracruz restaurant, and quite often they add raisins and serve it as a dessert.

CHAYOTES RELLENOS [*Stuffed vegetable pears*]

6 servings

This makes a very good first course, or accompaniment to some plainly broiled or fried fish—or serve it alone as a supper dish.

Have ready:

An ovenproof serving dish
12 small strips of Muenster or mild
  Cheddar cheese

12 tablespoons Thick Sour Cream
  (*page 20*), *or more to taste*

A saucepan
3 chayotes (*between ¾*
    and 1 pound each)
2 teaspoons salt
Boiling water to cover

Cover the whole *chayotes* with boiling water, bring them to a boil, and then let them cook over a medium flame until they are tender but not too soft—about 1 hour.

Drain them and let them cool off. When they are cool enough to handle, cut them into halves and remove the pithy core and almond-like seed. Scoop out the flesh carefully, leaving the outside skin intact. Mash the flesh well and leave it to drain in a colander for a few minutes, since the *chayotes* here are very watery. Put the *chayote* shells upside down to drain.

A colander

(*continued*)

A small frying pan
2 heaped tablespoons
    butter
½ medium onion, finely
    chopped
2 cloves garlic, peeled
    and finely chopped

Melt the butter and cook the onion and garlic gently, without browning, until they are soft.

4 eggs, well beaten with
    salt and pepper
The mashed chayote flesh

Add the eggs and stir them as you would for scrambled eggs until they are just set. Add the mashed *chayote* flesh and let the mixture dry out a little for a minute or so over a low flame.

6 ounces farmer cheese,
    crumbled
The reserved chayote
    shells
The ovenproof dish

Stir the crumbled cheese into the mixture, and stuff the reserved *chayote* shells. Place on the ovenproof dish.

Preheat the oven to 400°.

The cheese strips
The sour cream

Put the strips of cheese and sour cream on top of the filling and heat them through in the oven for about 15 minutes, then serve. (Do not attempt to eat the shell.)

For a change, do not top with the cheese and sour cream, but serve them covered with Salsa de Jitomate Cocida (page 302).

CHAYOTES EMPANIZADAS
[*Sliced vegetable pears, breaded and fried*]

Allow about 6 ounces per person. Cook the *chayotes* as in Chayotes Rellenos (page 273), skin them, and cut them into slices about ¼ inch thick (eat the delicious "almond" in the center—that's the cook's privilege). Dip the slices in well-beaten egg and then coat them with finely ground, toasted bread crumbs that have been seasoned with salt and pepper. Fry the slices in a mixture of butter and oil until they are crisp and well browned. Serve with Salsa de Jitomate Cocida (page 302) or Salsa de Chile Serrano Seco (Japonés) (page 304). Serve immediately.

These are very good served as a separate course or with plainly broiled meat.

GUAUZONCLES

During the rainy season in central Mexico, you will see in the markets tall bunches of greens, spiked on top and thick with small, green seeds that look like overgrown *epazote*—they are *guauzoncles* (*Chenopodium nuttalliae*), delicious and interesting to eat.

The stalks will be about 3 feet tall. Cut off the bushy tops and any full and leafy side stems into lengths that will fit into a large saucepan. Cook them in well-salted water until they are tender (about 10 minutes) and drain them. When they are cool enough to handle, cut off the tops and small stems into lengths of about 4 inches and make small bunches, 4 or 6 to a bunch. Gently squeeze out the excess water and put a small wedge of cheese (Cheddar or Muenster) between the stems. Dust the bunches lightly with flour and dip them into an egg batter (see Chiles Rellenos, page 263). Fry them in hot oil until they are a golden color and drain them on paper toweling. You can eat them just as they are, eating off the tender leaves and seeds with the runny cheese in between—but you will be left with the rather woody stems in your hand. Or, you can make smaller *tortitas* of the fleshy stem ends stuffed with cheese, fry them in batter and heat them through in a tomato broth (again, see Chiles Rellenos, page 263).

BUDÍN DE CHÍCHARO [*Pea pudding*]

6 servings

One of the curiosities of the Mexican kitchen is the vegetable pudding. Some of the simpler ones resemble the Italian *sformatos*, but the more complicated ones, like this one with peas, are really vegetable cakes, baked with sugar, rice flour, butter, and eggs. They can be served either as a separate vegetable course, or with the main meat dish.

Have ready:

A buttered Pyrex dish (8 × 8 × 2 inches)

A baking sheet, placed on a shelf two-thirds of the way down in the oven

A sauce made by combining 2 cups fresh orange juice with ¾ cup finely chopped walnuts

Preheat the oven to 500°.

A food mill
2 pounds frozen peas, cooked

Pass the peas through the medium disk of the food mill.

6 ounces unsalted butter
A mixer
3 eggs, separated
½ cup granulated sugar
6 ounces rice flour, sifted
The melted butter
The pea pulp
1 teaspoon salt
¼ pound mild Cheddar cheese, grated
1½ teaspoons baking powder

Melt the butter and set it aside to cool.
Setting the egg whites aside, beat the egg yolks until they are thick. Add the sugar and continue beating until it is well incorporated. Beat in the rice flour alternately with the butter.
Stir in the pea pulp, salt, and cheese, mix well, and last of all add the baking powder.

A bowl and beater
The reserved egg whites

Beat the egg whites until they are stiff and fold them into the mixture.

The Pyrex dish	Pour the mixture into the prepared dish.
The baking sheet	Place the dish on the baking sheet and bake **for 10 minutes.** Then lower the oven temperature to 350° and continue cooking for
The budín *mixture*	about 55 minutes. The *budín* should be soft and spongy to the touch—the top and sides nicely browned, but the inside moist.
The orange and walnut sauce	Serve immediately, with the orange and walnut sauce to accompany it.

BUDÍN DE ELOTE [*Corn pudding*]

6 servings

This *budín* is made with *uncooked* corn, unlike the others, which are made with cooked vegetables.

Defrost 2 pounds of corn kernels and blend them with as little milk as necessary to release the cutting blades of the blender. Follow the recipe for Budín de Chícharo (page 276) and serve with coarsely ground salt and Thick Sour Cream (page 20).

BUDÍN DE ZANAHORIA [*Carrot pudding*]

6 servings

Cook 2 pounds of sliced carrots until they are very soft. Drain them well and pass them through the medium disk of a food mill.

Follow the recipe for Budín de Chícharo (page 276) and serve with coarsely ground salt and Thick Sour Cream (page 20). This can also be served as a dessert (page 328).

Beans *(Frijoles)*

"The gentlemen Creoles or natives of Chiapa are as presumptuous and arrogant as if the noblest blood in the Court of Madrid ran through their veins. It is a common thing amongst them to make a dinner only with a dish of *frijoles* in black broth, boiled with pepper and garlic, saying it is the most nourishing meat in all the Indies; and after this so stately a dinner they will be sure to come out to the street-door of their houses to see and to be seen, and there for half an hour will they stand shaking off the crumbs of bread from their clothes, bands (but especially from their ruffs when they used them), and from their mustachios. And with their tooth-pickers they will stand picking their teeth, as if some small partridge bone stuck in them—and they will be sure to vent out some non-truth, as to say 'O Sir, what a dainty partridge I have eaten today,' whereas they pick out nothing from their teeth but a black husk of a dry frijol or Turkey bean."

—FROM *Travels in the New World,*
BY THOMAS GAGE

Beans are an indispensable part of the Mexican meal, and there is an astonishing variety to choose from: the black *veracruzanos*, the purple-mottled *flor de mayo*, the deep yellow *canarios*, the brownish *bayos* or *sabinos*, the white *aluvias* and big green and white *habas*—to name a few—overflowing the big woven baskets or poured into piles like small slag heaps in the marketplaces. The stands selling them are usually grouped together at one side of the market, and there the peasant women will come and choose with great care and discussion, running the beans through their fingers to make sure their few *centavos* are well spent. Or on market days in the small towns and villages, canvas awnings like huge square umbrellas are set up along the streets by those with produce to sell: small bunches of fresh herbs, a basket of squash, or a new crop of beans—*frijoles nuevos*—still in their pods, with just a few shucked ones at the side so that you can be assured they are full and fresh.

Each type of bean has its special flavor and quality. To savor them, they should be cooked in the simplest of ways—*de olla*—very slowly in an earthenware pot with a little onion, lard and salt—and, if they are black, with a good sprig of *epazote*, the pungent flavor of which complements them. They are served in their broth in a small bowl, like soup, but usually after the main course of the meal. You can add a little cheese to melt and string into them, or a pungent, pickled chili, and scoop it all up with a tortilla—if you can manage it. Occasionally a few *nopales*—tender cactus pieces—are cooked in with them, or some *chicharrón*—pork cracklings. In the north, in Nuevo León for instance, they can become more complicated. Take, for instance, *frijoles a la charra*, with pieces of pork rind and some fried tomato, onion, and coriander; add some beer and they become *borrachos*, and slightly different still, with a strong flavor of cumin, the *rancheros*, to accompany the plainly roasted *agujas* or *cabrito* (ribs of beef or kid).

For a change they can be fried—but in their broth, so that all the flavor is absorbed. They can be lightly fried to a loose paste—no onion, nothing, just beans—and accompanied, as they were once served to me in a modest restaurant in Tacámbaro in Michoacán, with some thick, slightly sour cream. In Veracruz the black beans are fried with chopped onions and a small, dried red chili, and further east in Yucatán, the beans are sieved to a smooth paste and then fried with onion and the whole, fiery *chiles habaneros;* they must not break open but simply impart some of their flavor. They are used for the *panuchos, pan de cazón, garnachas,* and *huevos motuleños* of the southeast. There are the rich *maniados* of Sonora and the north of Sinaloa cooked with milk, butter and a rich cream cheese, and further south the *puercos,* fried up into a stiff roll with *chorizo,* bacon, and olives. But for every day I would choose the simple well-fried beans, rolled out of the pan like a stiff, sizzling omelet, sprinkled with crumbled white cheese and stuck like a porcupine with crisp *totopos*.

Beans are not only the food of the poor; they are everybody's food. Beans are served with *almuerzo*, the hearty midmorning breakfast; always after the main course of the *comida*, the heavy midday meal, and again at supper —this time perhaps just a few fried beans with cheese. No wonder an Englishman traveling across Mexico in 1864 wrote: ". . . but for the frijoles which followed, and which come in at the conclusion—like God Save the Queen at the end of a concert—we should have gone to bed famishing."

Notes on Cooking Beans

If you want the best-flavored beans:

1. Don't soak them overnight.

2. Cook beans very slowly, covered. The cooking time can vary considerably, from 1½ to 2½ hours, depending on how dry the beans are. If more water is necessary, add boiling water.

3. Do not add the salt until the beans are soft. The Mexicans say it hardens the skins.

4. Mexican cooks say that you should never stir the beans with a metal spoon or they will stick and burn. I obey them implicitly, and I really don't want to know what the home economist would say to that.

5. Beans have a much better flavor if cooked in an earthenware pot.

6. Beans are much better eaten a day or two after they have been cooked. Put them into the refrigerator when they are cool, as they very quickly turn sour—especially in hot, muggy weather. Just bring them up to a boil for a few minutes each day. The bean broth will become thick and soupy and delicious.

FRIJOLES DE OLLA [*Beans cooked in a pot*]

10 servings

Frijoles de olla are traditionally served, beans and broth together, in small earthenware bowls, after the main course and before the dessert. They are often just scooped up with a tortilla, although for the uninitiated this is a rather noisy and messy business, so it is permissible to compromise and use a spoon. Sometimes small pieces of good cream cheese, which melt and string invitingly, are dropped into the hot broth. Or you may add a little piquancy, a little *chile serrano* or *jalapeño en escabeche*. They are much better a day or so after being cooked.

1 pound beans—black turtle, pink, or pinto
An earthenware bean pot
10 cups water (see note below)
¼ onion, roughly sliced
2 tablespoons lard

Rinse the beans and run them through your hands to make sure that there are no small stones or bits of earth among them.

Put the beans into the pot and cover them with the cold water. Add the onion and lard and bring to a boil.

As soon as the beans come to a boil, lower the flame and let them barely simmer, covered, for about 2 hours for black beans and 1½ hours for the other varieties, or until they are just tender but not soft. **Do not stir during this time.**

1 tablespoon salt, or to taste
2 large sprigs epazote (only if black beans are used)

Add the salt and *epazote*, if you are using it, and simmer for another 30 minutes. Set aside, preferably until the next day. There should be plenty of soupy liquid.

10 cups water should be enough for the black beans, but more like 12 to 14 cups will be needed for the pinto or pink beans, since these seem to absorb more. Of course much will depend on such considerations as the size of the pot, what it is made of, and how tightly fitting the lid is, so it is difficult to be exact.

FRIJOLES REFRITOS [*Well-fried beans*]

6 servings

During all my years of living in Mexico and teaching Mexican cooking in New York, I (like everyone else) have thought of *frijoles refritos* as refried beans. Several people have asked me why, when the beans are fried, they are called *re*fried. Nobody I asked in Mexico seemed to know until quite suddenly it dawned on me.

The Mexicans have a habit of qualifying a word to emphasize the meaning by adding the prefix *re-*. They will get the oil very hot (*requemar*), or something will be very good (*retebien*). Thus *refrito* means well fried, which they certainly are, since they are fried until they are almost dry. I am glad to say that Santamaría in his *Diccionario de Mexicanismos* bears this out, but I am embarrassed that it has taken so long for the light to dawn.

Have ready:

A warm serving dish
½ pound beans, cooked as for Frijoles de Olla (page 281) (3½ to 4 cups with broth)

2 ounces farmer cheese, crumbled
12 Totopos (page 139)
Some romaine lettuce leaves
6 radish roses

A 10-inch frying pan
6 tablespoons melted lard or pork drippings
¼ onion, finely chopped
The cooked beans

Heat the lard and fry the onion, without browning, until it is soft.

Add 1 cup of the beans and their broth to the pan and mash them well over a very high flame. Add the rest of the beans gradually, mashing them all the time, until you have a coarse puree.

When the puree begins to dry out and sizzle at the edges, it will start to come away from the surface of the pan. As you let it

Mashing and rolling fried beans

The serving dish
The beans
The crumbled cheese
The totopos
The lettuce leaves
The radish roses

continue cooking, tip the pan from side to side. The puree will form itself into a loose roll. This will take from 15 to 20 minutes.

Tip the roll, rather like folding an omelet, onto the serving dish and garnish with the cheese. Spike it with the crisp triangles of tortillas.

Decorate the dish with the lettuce and radishes. Serve immediately.

(continued)

You have to fry the beans almost dry to form the traditional bean roll, or *brazo*. The dark brown of the beans, sprinkled with the white cheese, looks very attractive against the green and red of the lettuce and radishes. They are served generally towards the end of the meal, as are *frijoles de olla*. Often they are just fried to a loose paste and served with breakfast eggs or with Chilaquiles (page 67) or *antojitos* at suppertime.

Any leftovers will freeze very well. To reheat, defrost the beans and then fry them in a little more lard. A little *chile serrano* or *jalapeño en escabeche* can be eaten with them. You may need to add a little water to make them less dry.

FRIJOLES COLADOS Y REFRITOS A LA YUCATECA
[*Yucatecan sieved and fried beans*]

About 2¾ cups

It is peculiar that only in this part of Mexico do they sieve the beans before frying them to form a smooth paste. The bean paste is then used for such dishes as Panuchos (page 126), Garnachas Yucatecas (page 128), Huevos Motuleños (page 248), and cooked beyond this stage to form a roll to serve with the meal. The very *picante chile habanero* is used—simply to give a good flavor to the beans, not to make them *picante*.

Have ready:

*½ pound black turtle beans cooked
    as for Frijoles de Olla (page 281)
    (about 3½ to 4 cups, depending
    on the amount of broth), with a
    lot of epazote*

A food mill

Pass the beans, together with their broth, through the medium disk of a food mill.

A large frying pan
3 tablespoons lard
*¼ medium onion, roughly
    sliced*

Melt the lard and wilt the onion.

The sieved beans
1 chile habanero or
    cayenne

Add the sieved beans and the chilies and cook the beans over a high flame until they form a loose paste that plops off the spoon— about 15 minutes, depending, of course, on the amount of liquid with the beans.

FRIJOLES A LA CHARRA [*Savory beans*]

6 servings

This is the Nuevo León version of *frijoles de olla*. Literally it means: beans cooked in the way the lady *charro* would prepare them (the *charros* are the elegant horsemen of Mexico).

The green chilies and coriander give the beans a unique and interesting flavor, making them a perfect complement to the simple broiled meats so popular in Monterrey, the capital of Nuevo León: the *agujas* (ribs of beef) and *cabrito* (kid) cooked over wood or charcoal. There are many variations of this recipe and the very similar *frijoles rancheros* and *frijoles fronterizos*—which may very well have been the forerunners of the Texas *chile con carne*.

A bean pot
¼ pound pork rind (see
    note below)
½ pound pink or pinto
    beans
¼ onion, sliced
2 small cloves garlic,
    peeled and sliced
6 cups water

Cut the pork rind into small squares and put them, together with the beans, onion, and garlic, into the bean pot.

Add the water and bring to a boil. Lower the flame, cover the pot, and let the beans cook gently until they are tender—about 1½ hours.

1¼ teaspoons salt

Add the salt and cook them, uncovered, for another 15 minutes.

(*continued*)

A frying pan
3 thick strips bacon (about
  ¼ pound)
2 tablespoons melted lard
  or pork drippings
2 medium tomatoes
  (about ¾ pound) or
  1 cup canned
  tomatoes
3 chiles serranos, finely
  chopped
2 large whole sprigs fresh
  coriander

Cut the bacon into small pieces and cook it gently in the lard until it is slightly browned.

Peel, seed, and chop the tomatoes (page 43); strain the seeds and add the juice. Add the tomatoes together with the rest of the ingredients. Cook the mixture over a fairly high flame for about 10 minutes, until it is well seasoned.

The beans

Add the tomato mixture to the beans and let them cook together, uncovered, over a low flame for about 15 minutes.

Serve in small individual bowls with broiled meats, or add some more liquid and serve as a soup.

You should be able to buy pork rind by the pound from the butchers specializing in pork. If not, the shoulder of pork recommended for so many of the recipes here usually has the rind left on. You can cut it off and freeze it for this or the occasional French recipe that calls for it.

FRIJOLES BORRACHOS

Monterrey is an important center for the beer industry—by adding ⅓ small bottle of beer to the above recipe they become *frijoles borrachos*, a very lusty plateful.

Rice Dishes   (*Sopas Secas*)

When their trade routes to the East were being threatened by the Turks and Portuguese in the 1560s, the Spanish opened up new trade routes between the Pacific ports of the New World and the Philippines. Manila was founded, and became the clearing house for Oriental spices, foods, silks and other luxuries. The *Nao de China,* a heavily armed galleon that was a match for any pirates lying in wait for it, plied between Manila and Acapulco. It was at that time that rice was introduced to Mexico and readily adopted into the cuisine.

Arroz is considered a "dry soup" (*sopa seca*) and is served as a course by itself, usually after the "wet soup" (*sopa aguada*). It is quite often served with a fried egg on top but more often than not by itself, eaten with tortillas and perhaps a little green tomato sauce, or *guacamole*.

In cooking the rice dishes that follow, I suppose I was partly influenced by the way the most delicious rice I have ever eaten was cooked. I was with a friend of mine who had gone to deliver CARE donations to a small village in the Sierra de Puebla. She was the guest of honor at a meal in the rustic and very simple home of the village judge. Only the men had been in evidence throughout the ceremonies, so we went to greet the women. They were all hard at work in the large, thatched-roof hut that was the kitchen. There was no furniture. Four large wood fires were burning on the earth floor; tortillas were puffing up on an earthenware comal set on one of the fires, on another an immense *cazuela* of bubbling *mole* was cooking, while a huge *olla* of foaming chocolate was being beaten on a third. But what caught my eye was another huge *cazuela* full of rice. The grains were standing apart, and there was just a little of the tomatoey broth—from fresh tomatoes roasted and ground with garlic and onion in *molcajetes*—still bubbling around the edges. When we tasted it its flavor was incomparable, with just a subtle touch of wood smoke.

Notes on Cooking Rice

1. Preparing a rice dish is one of the few occasions when I do break down and use canned tomatoes. Be careful that they are not too acidy (I prefer the Contadina round tomatoes).

2. If you have any rice left over, store it in the refrigerator or freezer in foil. To reheat it simply put the foil package straight into a 350° oven, whether frozen or not, until it is well heated through. This way it keeps all its flavor and moisture.

3. Many Mexican cooks say, "Don't stir the rice while it is cooking, or it will stick and burn." I obey them implicitly.

4. If you have cooked the rice correctly, according to the directions in the recipes themselves, every grain should stand apart and it should not be mushy. It is exactly how we used to cook it in Mexico City—although it does come out a little harder here, owing to the different quality of the rice. If you prefer it softer, then you can always cook it in a covered pan over a lower flame—a method that many cooks in Mexico use, too.

ARROZ A LA MEXICANA [*Mexican rice*]

6 servings

A large saucepan
1½ cups long-grain white rice
Hot water to cover
A sieve

Pour the hot water onto the rice and let it stand for about 25 minutes. Drain the rice and rinse it well in cold water. Shake the sieve and leave the rice to drain for a while.

A deep flameproof dish
(not larger than 8½
inches in diameter)
Just over ⅓ cup peanut
or safflower oil

Heat the oil well. Give the rice a final shake to get rid of any excess water. Stir the rice into the oil, making sure that the grains are well coated.

Fry the rice, stirring it from time to time until it is a pale gold color. This will take about 10 minutes or more, depending on the width of the pan.

Tip the pan to one side. Hold back the rice with the back of a large metal spoon and let the oil drain away from it. In this way you can drain off most of the excess oil.

A blender
1 large tomato (about ½
pound) peeled,
seeded, and chopped
(page 43) or ⅔ cup
canned tomatoes
⅓ medium onion
1 clove garlic, peeled
The tomato puree
The rice

Blend the tomato with the onion and garlic to a smooth puree—there should be 1 cup if fresh tomatoes are used and ⅔ cup if canned.

Add the tomato puree to the rice and cook over a high flame, stirring the mixture constantly, until it is almost dry—about 3 minutes.

3½ cups well-salted
chicken broth or
water containing 1½
teaspoons salt

Stir the broth or salted water into the rice— **do not stir again during the cooking period—** and cook the rice over a medium flame, uncovered, until most of the liquid has been absorbed (at this stage holes will appear in the surface). This will take about 10 minutes.

Cover the pan and let the mixture continue cooking over a very low flame for 5 minutes more.

Remove from the flame and set the rice

aside, still covered, in a warm place for 30 minutes—it will cook and soften more in its own steam.

This rice can be cooked ahead and heated through gently, tightly covered, in a 300° oven for about 40 minutes. Any left over can be heated through in the same way the next day—obviously, the length of time will be calculated depending on quantity.

The rice freezes very successfully, too. Wrap it in a foil package. To re-heat, place the package, still frozen, into a 350° oven and heat through for about 1 hour.

ARROZ BLANCO [White rice]

6 servings

A large saucepan
1½ cups long-grain white rice
Hot water to cover
A colander
A flameproof dish
⅓ cup peanut or safflower oil
The rice

⅓ medium onion, sliced
1 clove garlic, peeled and finely chopped

3½ cups chicken broth

Pour the hot water over the rice and let it stand for about 25 minutes. Drain the rice and wash it in cold water until the washing water is clear. Shake the colander well and leave the rice to drain for a while.

Heat the oil until it is very hot. Give the rice a final shake to get rid of any excess water. Stir the rice well into the oil, making sure that as many grains as possible get coated. Fry the rice over a high flame, stirring it from time to time until it is just beginning to color. Add the onion and garlic and continue frying until the rice is a pale gold—about 10 minutes altogether.

Tip the dish to one side and drain off some of the excess oil (page 289).

Stir the broth into the rice **and do not stir again during the cooking time.** Cook the rice over a medium flame—it should bubble fairly briskly—until almost all of the liquid has disappeared—about 10 minutes. Lower the flame, cover the dish with foil, and cook the rice for 5 minutes longer. Remove the dish from the flame and let it stand, still covered, for at least 30 minutes, so that it will continue to cook in its own steam.

VARIATIONS

1. Add 1 cup fresh or frozen—but not canned—corn to the rice at the same time as the broth, or
2. One-half carrot cut into thin slices and a small handful of peas, or
3. Serve the rice with slices of fried plantain (page 25).

ARROZ VERDE CON CHILES RELLENOS
[*Green rice with stuffed chilies*]

6 servings

This is a very popular Lenten dish in Mexico, and a substantial one. Canned chilies are rather a pale substitute both in color and flavor for the rich, dark *chiles poblanos,* which in Mexico are stuffed fat with Chihuahua cheese—so fat, in fact, that Margarita Sánchez, whose recipe this is, covered the slit of the chili with a piece of tougher Oaxaca cheese and then tied it up with a piece of thread so that none of the stuffing would seep out into the rice. I am afraid with the canned ones it does seep out, but nevertheless this is a worthwhile and delicious dish. Serve it as a separate course, 1 chili per person with the rice. It is particularly good before a main course of fish.

The rice is a good deal softer than in the other rice recipes.

1¼ cups long-grain white rice

A blender

A large bunch of Italian parsley

1 clove garlic, peeled

½ small onion

⅓ cup water

Soak and drain the rice as for the other rice recipes (pages 288, 290).

Wash the parsley well, remove the coarse stems, and put the leaves and sprigs into the blender with the rest of the ingredients. Blend to a smooth sauce. Set aside.

(continued)

A flameproof casserole
½ cup peanut or safflower
     oil

The rice

Heat the oil. Give the rice a final shake to get rid of any excess water. When the oil is very hot, stir in the rice, making sure that as many grains as possible get coated with the oil. Cook the rice over a high flame, stirring it from time to time, until it becomes a pale golden color—about 10 minutes.

Tip the dish to one side and drain off some of the excess oil (page 289).

The blended parsley

Stir the blended parsley into the rice and cook for 2 minutes more.

4 cups milk
2 teaspoons salt, or to
     taste

Stir the milk and salt well into the rice and let the mixture come to a boil. Lower the flame, cover the dish tightly, and let the rice cook very slowly for 15 minutes. (See note below.)

Meanwhile, prepare the chilies.

6 small chiles poblanos,
     roasted and peeled
     (page 44) or 6 large
     canned, peeled green
     chilies
½ to ¾ pound mild
     Cheddar cheese

Cut the chilies down one side and carefully remove the seeds. Cut the cheese into thick slices and stuff the chilies well.

The rice

Set the chilies well into the rice, the slit side up to prevent the stuffing from seeping out. Cover the dish and continue cooking the rice over a low flame for another 15 minutes.

Up to the point of adding the milk and cooking the rice slowly, the dish can be prepared ahead of time.

PASTEL DE LUJO [*"Luxury" cake*]

6 servings

This is a curious sweet/savory dish from Campeche and Yucatán that can be served either hot or cold. Some cooks insist the *pastel de lujo* have chicken, not pork, in the filling, and that it be sprinkled heavily with sugar and served cold, just like a cake—which is a little too bizarre for most tastes here, I think.

Have ready:

An ovenproof dish, at least 3 inches deep and preferably about 10 inches in diameter, buttered and sprinkled with finely ground, toasted bread crumbs

1 cup long-grain white rice cooked as for Arroz Blanco (page 290), which should make about 4 cups cooked

THE PICADILLO FILLING

Preheat the oven to 350°.

A large frying pan
6 ounces raw pork
¾ pound raw boneless chicken
⅓ medium onion
¼ green pepper
1 large tomato
12 small pitted green olives
1 tablespoon capers
1 tablespoon raisins
¾ cup water
1 teaspoon salt, or to taste
A pinch of granulated sugar

Finely chop the pork, chicken, onion, and pepper. Skin, seed, and mash the tomato (page 43). Chop the olives roughly. Add these with the rest of the ingredients to the pan.

(continued)

A mortar and pestle
2 whole allspice
1 whole clove
½-inch stick cinnamon
16 peppercorns
2 cloves garlic, toasted
    (page 43)
1 tablespoon vinegar

Grind the spices dry. Crush the garlic, with the vinegar, into the ground spices. Add to the mixture in the frying pan.

½ cup Madeira or sweet
    sherry

Cook the *picadillo*, uncovered, over a medium flame until the meat is tender and most of the liquid has evaporated—about 20 minutes.

Remove the pan from the flame and stir in the Madeira.

THE RICE MIXTURE

A blender
3 cups corn kernels
    (about 4 ears or 15
    ounces frozen corn)
½ cup milk
The cooked rice
The corn puree
2 eggs, well-beaten
2 tablespoons softened
    butter
1 tablespoon sugar
salt to taste

Put about one-third of the corn into the blender with the milk. Blend until smooth. Add the rest of the corn gradually and blend until smooth.

Remove the onion and garlic from the rice, add the puree of corn, and the rest of the ingredients. Mix them all together well.

THE PASTEL DE LUJO

The prepared ovenproof
    dish
The rice mixture
The picadillo
1 tablespoon finely ground
    toasted bread crumbs

Put half of the rice mixture into the dish, then the *picadillo*, and cover it with the remaining rice.

Sprinkle the top of the rice with the bread crumbs and bake for about 30 minutes.

You can prepare this well ahead of time, but put it together at the last minute so that the rice does not become too soggy underneath. It freezes very successfully, too.

If the rice is left plain, without the corn and butter, it is called *costrada de arroz*.

Sauces and Relishes (*Salsas*)

A dish of sauce or relish is as indispensable to the Mexican table as our salt, pepper, and mustard—or their little bowl of *chiles en escabeche*, chilies with herbs and slices of carrot and onion in oil and vinegar. But what a contrast there is between the gentle tomato sauce of Sonora and the fiery sauce made of *chiles habaneros* from Yucatán.

Of all the markets in Mexico, one of the sights, and smells, that stands out in my mind, is the piles and piles of dried fish and shrimps at the back of the central market of Oaxaca. It was here, in the same market, that a kindly old man selling little mounds of unhulled pumpkin seeds gave me the recipe for the regional dried shrimp sauce called *chiltextli*.* First of all everything is toasted on the comal: *the chiles pasillas de Oaxaca* (quite different from the *chiles pasilla de Mexico*), avocado leaves, dried shrimps, small, unhulled yellow pumpkin seeds, and the very tiny *tomates verdes* called *miltomatos*. Then they are ground. This sauce is eaten with roasted meats, rabbit, and armadillo.

There is no end to the variety of sauces; they just depend, very often, on what is available.

* A Nahuatl name, from *chil* (chili) and *textli* (something ground) (T. Sullivan)

SALSA MEXICANA CRUDA [*Fresh Mexican sauce*]

About 1½ cups

You will find this sauce on Mexican tables at any time of day, for it goes well with breakfast eggs, with roasted or broiled meats at lunchtime, or *tacos* at evening, and there are people who put a spoonful of it into their *frijoles de olla*. It is marvelously crunchy and refreshing served just with tortillas. The Sinaloa version calls for some scallions and lime juice in place of the onions and water, and the Yucatecan version, *x-ni-pec*, substitutes Seville orange juice for the water.

1 medium tomato (about 6 ounces)
½ medium onion
6 sprigs fresh coriander
3 chilies, preferably serranos
A bowl
½ teaspoon salt, or to taste
⅓ cup cold water

Chop all the ingredients finely—do not skin the tomato or seed the chili. Mix together in a bowl and add the salt and water.

Although this can be made up to three hours ahead, it is best made at almost the last minute, for it soon loses its crispness and the coriander its sharp flavor.

SALSA DE TOMATE VERDE CRUDA [*Mexican green tomato sauce*]

1¼ cups

This is one of the most important and uniquely Mexican table sauces. You may not take to it at first, but it will grow on you—and soon you may find yourself hankering after some of this refreshing and lovely green sauce.

A Mexican friend here in New York has just reminded me of how he used to eat this green sauce, topped with sliced avocado and slices of a fresh white cheese, at the Lincoln Grill in Mexico City. It was called Salsa de Albaniles (page 139) and served with a pile of hot tortillas—a very different and delicious idea for something to serve with drinks.

A molcajete *or mortar and pestle*

2 chiles serranos

¼ small onion

1 small clove garlic, peeled

2 large sprigs fresh coriander (optional)

¼ teaspoon salt, or to taste

Grind the ingredients together until almost smooth.

1 cup tomates verdes (½ pound), drained

A pinch of granulated sugar

Add the *tomates verdes* and grind them until you have a fairly smooth sauce.

⅓ cup water

Dilute the sauce with the water—it should have quite a loose consistency.

1 teaspoon fresh coriander, finely chopped (optional)

Sprinkle the coriander over the sauce and serve.

If you really have to use a blender, then don't overblend the sauce and give it that frothy, all-purpose texture with no character at all.

The sauce is best used the day it is made, for very soon the coriander loses its very special flavor and becomes soggy.

When the sauce has stood for a while its consistency becomes thin and jelly-like. Dilute it with a little water before using.

For those who can't stand coriander, it can be left out.

A point always under discussion by Mexican cooks is whether the chili should be cooked or not—sometimes boiled, sometimes toasted. I have decided to go along with those who say "raw for an uncooked sauce and cooked for a cooked sauce."

SALSA DE TOMATE VERDE COCIDA
[*Cooked green tomato sauce*]

Almost 2 cups

A blender

**2 cups tomates verdes,
    drained**

**1 clove garlic, peeled and
    roughly chopped**

**¼ medium onion, roughly
    chopped**

**2 or 3 chiles serranos,
    toasted (page 43)**

**¼ teaspoon granulated
    sugar**

¼ teaspoon salt, or to taste

Blend the ingredients together until smooth.

A small frying pan

**2 tablespoons peanut or
    safflower oil**

Heat the oil and cook the sauce for about 5 minutes, until it has thickened a little and is well seasoned.

This sauce is used in Budín Azteca (page 81) and Huevos Rancheros (page 246), and is good mixed with shredded meat as a filling for Tacos (page 116).

SALSA RANCHERA [*Country sauce*]

1 serving (about ½ cup)

A blender

**1 tomato (about ½
    pound), broiled
    (page 44)**

**1 or 2 chiles serranos,
    toasted (page 43)**

½ clove garlic, peeled

Blend the tomato, chilies, and garlic together to a fairly smooth sauce. Do not overblend.

(*continued*)

A small frying pan
1 tablespoon peanut or
    safflower oil
A thick slice of onion,
    finely chopped
⅛ teaspoon salt, or to
    taste

Heat the oil and cook the onion, without browning, until it is soft. Add the blended ingredients and salt and cook the sauce over a brisk flame for about 5 minutes, until it reduces and thickens a little.

This sauce is most commonly used for Huevos Rancheros (page 246), but it also makes a very good base sauce for a shredded meat filling for Tacos (page 116). You can always make it ahead of time, as it keeps very well and freezes quite satisfactorily.

SALSA DE JITOMATE YUCATECA [Yucatecan tomato sauce]

1 cup

A molcajete *or mortar and*
    pestle
3 medium tomatoes
    (1 pound), broiled
    (page 44)
A small frying pan
2 tablespoons peanut or
    safflower oil
¼ medium onion, finely
    chopped
The mashed tomatoes
¼ teaspoon salt
1 whole chile habanero or
    cayenne

Remove any very blackened pieces of the skin from the tomatoes and mash the tomatoes roughly.

Heat the oil and cook the onion, without browning, until it is soft. Add the mashed tomatoes, salt, and chili. Cook the sauce for about 8 minutes over a medium flame until it has reduced and thickened.

Some cooks in Yucatán prefer to boil the tomatoes (in which case the skins should be removed before mashing), while others prefer to roast or broil them. There is no doubt that the latter gives a better flavor to the sauce. Some prefer to slice rather than chop the onion but they all agree on one point: the *chile habanero* they use is left whole to flavor the sauce but not to make it *picante*. In their words, "The chili takes a walk through the sauce."

This sauce is used for Papa-dzules (page 70), Garnachas Yucatecas (page 128), and Huevos Motuleños (page 248). The sauce freezes well.

SALSA DE JITOMATE DEL NORTE [*Northern tomato sauce*]

2 cups

The people of Sonora are very proud of their local dishes. They say that they are very healthy and do not have the spices and hot chilies used in the rest of Mexico that irritate the stomach. This is certainly a rather soothing but delicious sauce to be found daily on the table, and a very good accompaniment to the typical Sonorense *carne asada*—a huge piece of steak cooked over a wood fire in one of the large open-air restaurants of Hermosillo. I have also had it served there with fresh clams and oysters from the nearby Gulf of California.

A blender
2 large tomatoes
   (1 pound), broiled
   (page 44)

Blend the tomatoes until you have a fairly smooth puree. Do not overblend.

A serving dish
The tomato puree
1 heaped teaspoon finely
   chopped fresh
   coriander
¼ medium onion, finely
   chopped
¾ teaspoon salt

Transfer the tomato puree to a serving dish and add the rest of the ingredients. The chilies should be cut into strips and added, together with their seeds.

Set aside to season for about 30 minutes.

(*continued*)

*2 canned, peeled green
    chilies (see note
    below)
1½ teaspoons mild white
    vinegar*

The canned, peeled green chili packed so well by Ortega is the *chile Anaheim,* used a great deal in Sonora and Chihuahua. The sauce does not freeze successfully.

This sauce is used with Gallina Pinta (page 161), and can be served with fried eggs, *frijoles,* or Burritos (page 131), roasted and broiled meats, and seafood.

SALSA DE JITOMATE COCIDA [*Cooked tomato sauce*]

About 2 cups

*A blender
3 medium tomatoes
    (1 pound), broiled
    (page 44)
¼ onion, roughly chopped
1 small clove garlic,
    peeled and roughly
    chopped*

Blend the ingredients to a fairly smooth sauce —it should have some texture.

*A small frying pan
2 tablespoons peanut or
    safflower oil
The sauce
¼ teaspoon salt, or to taste*

Heat the oil, add the sauce and salt, and cook over a medium flame for about 8 minutes until it has thickened and is well seasoned.

This is a simple sauce to use with Tortitas de Papa (page 270) and Calabacitas Rellenas de Elote (page 259).

SALSA DE CHILE CASCABEL [*Chile cascabel sauce*]

About 1½ cups

This is another of those very satisfying rustic sauces. The toasted *chile cascabel* has a rich, nutty flavor, and even though the seeds are ground up in it the sauce is not too *picante*. I first encountered it when we were visiting the archaeological zone and planning a trip into the *selva* to see the more remote ruins of Bonampak and Yaxchilán. It was served to us in a small restaurant, run by a family from Chihuahua, on the outskirts of Palenque. When I got home it was adopted by our household and has been a great favorite ever since.

A comal or griddle
10 chiles cascabel

Heat the comal and toast the chilies, turning them constantly so that they do not burn.

When they are cool enough to handle, slit them open and remove the seeds and veins. Separate the seeds from the veins and toast the seeds well, turning them constantly or they will burn.

A blender
2 medium tomatoes (about ¾ pound), broiled (page 44)
The toasted chilies and seeds
3 cloves garlic, peeled
½ teaspoon salt
⅓ cup water, more if necessary

Blend all the ingredients together for a minute or two, but be careful not to over-blend—the sauce must have some texture. (Add a little more water if necessary; the sauce should have quite a loose consistency.)

This is extremely good served with Tacos (page 116), or used on Sopes (page 115) with sour cream and chopped onion—and with plainly broiled meat.

SALSA DE CHILE PASILLA [*Chile pasilla sauce*]

About 1 cup

A griddle or comal
4 chiles pasilla
A blender
1 clove garlic, peeled
½ teaspoon salt
¾ cup cold water

Heat the comal and toast the chilies well (page 43). Do not soak them.

Blend the toasted chilies together with the rest of the ingredients. Do not overblend— the sauce should have some texture.

A sauce dish
1 tablespoon onion, finely
  chopped

Put the sauce into the dish and garnish with the onion.

This is a really earthy sauce. If it is too *picante* for your taste, remove the veins and some of the seeds of the chilies before toasting them. It is very good with *tacos* but even better with scrambled eggs (pages 242 and 243), as it is often served in Mexico.

It can also be fried in lard for a few minutes, and added to cooked and shredded meat as a filling for crisp Tacos (page 116).

The sauce freezes well.

SALSA DE CHILE SERRANO SECO (JAPONÉS)
[*Sauce of dried chiles serranos*]

1 cup

A comal or griddle
25 chiles serranos secos

A blender
2 small tomatoes
  (½ pound), broiled
1 large clove garlic, peeled
½ teaspoon salt
½ cup water

Remove the seeds and veins from at least half of the chilies. Toast the chilies lightly, turning them constantly so they do not burn, and transfer to the blender jar.

Add the rest of the ingredients and blend until almost smooth—the sauce must have some texture.

I have seen little bags of the small dried *chile serrano,* very often labeled *chile japonés,* in many Puerto Rican *bodegas* and stores carrying Indian spices. It makes a very good and *picante* sauce, but it is advisable to remove the seeds and veins from a number of the chilies or it will burn your palate. Use it for Tacos (page 116), broiled meats, and Sopes (page 115).

The sauce freezes well.

SALSA DE TÍA GEORGINA [*Aunt Georgina's sauce*]

About 1½ cups

A comal or griddle
8 chiles anchos

A serving dish
The chilies
1 small onion
4 small cloves garlic,
    peeled
½ cup olive oil
½ cup red wine vinegar
½ teaspoon salt
¼ cup crumbled cream
    cheese

Toast the chilies lightly, turning them constantly so they do not burn. When they are cool enough to handle, remove the veins and seeds.

Cut the chilies into small pieces and chop the onion and garlic finely. Mix them all well with the oil, vinegar, and salt. Set the sauce aside to season for at least 2 hours. To serve, sprinkle with the crumbled cheese.

This sauce will keep indefinitely, and it gets better as it matures. It has an interesting texture and provides a very earthy and crunchy accompaniment to broiled meats, Carnitas (page 112), and rice. This is a family recipe, a variation of several of its type; when *chiles pasilla* are used in the same way it is called *salsa de moscas. Salsa de los reyes* has the three chilies—*mulato, ancho,* and *pasilla*—mixed together. All of these sauces are used principally with barbecued meats.

SALSA BORRACHA [*"Drunken" sauce*]

About 1½ cups

Salsa borracha means, literally, "drunken sauce" and no *barbacoa* prepared in the Valley of Mexico is complete without it. It should, of course, be made with *pulque*, the fermented milky sap drawn from the maguey or century plant that thrives in the central plateau of Mexico in altitudes roughly between 6,000 and 7,000 feet, but tequila is an acceptable substitute. The more simple rustic version calls for *chiles pasilla*, or *chiles mulatos*, both a lovely chocolatey-brown color, soaked in *pulque* and cut into small pieces. Salt is added, and nothing else.

A small frying pan
½ cup peanut or safflower oil
6 chiles pasilla
A blender
1 cup orange juice
½ teaspoon salt

Heat the oil and fry the chilies, turning them constantly so that they do not burn—they will become a lighter color. Remove them with a slotted spoon, leaving the oil in the pan, and let them cool a little, then remove the stems and crush them a little. Put them into a blender jar and blend with the juice and salt to an almost smooth sauce.

1 small onion, finely sliced
The sauce

In the oil in the pan, cook the onion, without browning, until it is soft. Add the sauce and continue cooking, over a high flame, for about 5 minutes. Set the sauce aside to cool.

¼ cup tequila

Before serving, add the tequila.

This sauce will freeze well.

SALSA PICANTE A LA YUCATECA [*Yucatecan hot sauce*]

Almost 1 cup

A comal or griddle
12 chiles habaneros *or* 16 chiles cayennes

Heat the comal and toast the chilies lightly, turning them constantly until they are soft and cooked.

A blender
⅔ cup lime juice or mild
    white vinegar
½ teaspoon salt

Remove the stems from the chilies and blend them with the rest of the ingredients for a few seconds.

This is the really fiery sauce served in Yucatán with stuffed cheese, Bola de Queso Relleno (page 133). Just a very little is needed, since the *chile habanero*, of all the chilies, probably takes first place for piquancy. You can use the long, bright-green *cayenne*, which is readily available the year round. This amount of sauce will go a very long way; it also freezes well.

Of course, if you happen to be doing it in the traditional way, using a *molcajete*, you must *tamular*, as they say in Yucatán, the chilies while they are still hot. If you let them cool off they will become tougher to grind.

CEBOLLAS ENCURTIDAS [*Pickled onion rings*]

1 pint

A 16-ounce glass jar
1 large purple onion
    (½ pound), thinly
    sliced
10 peppercorns
¼ teaspoon oregano
2 cloves garlic, peeled and
    sliced
½ teaspoon salt
Mild white vinegar to
    cover (about ¾ cup;
    see note below)

Mix the onion, peppercorns, oregano, garlic, and salt together well. Cover with the vinegar and set aside in a cool place for at least 2 days before using.

This will last indefinitely, and is very useful to have on hand at all times for garnishing *antojitos*, cold meat dishes, and salads.

If strong commercial vinegar is used, dilute it 1 part vinegar to 2 parts water.

CEBOLLAS ENCURTIDAS A LA YUCATECA
[Yucatecan pickled onion rings]

About 1 pint

A colander
Boiling water
2 medium onions, finely
    sliced into rings
A glass or china bowl
¾ cup mild white vinegar
    (see note below)
1 teaspoon salt
⅛ teaspoon oregano,
    toasted (page 43)
1 chile habanero *or*
    cayenne, finely sliced,
    or some freshly
    ground pepper

Pour the boiling water over the onion rings. Drain well.

Cover the onions with the vinegar and the rest of the ingredients, and leave them to season for at least 1 hour.

The onions will keep for several weeks. They are the traditional garnish for Cochinita Pibil (page 169) or Pollo en Escabeche Oriental (page 209). In Yucatán a small piece of the very *picante chile habanero* would be used, but sometimes just freshly ground pepper.

If a commercial white vinegar is used, dilute it 1 part vinegar to 3 parts water.

Salads (*Ensaladas*)

The weekly Saturday morning visit to San Juan market in Mexico City was mouth watering and time consuming. Slim bunches of the most delicate scallions—*cebollitas de cambrai;* delicate little radishes, crisp and nutty; avocados of all shapes and sizes; watercress, cucumbers, and every type of lettuce imaginable. But often the freshest and most delicate were not to be found on the stands in the market but spread out in front of the peasant woman sitting on the floor in the entranceway. She would touch your skirt or make a little hissing sound of the word *marchanta* to gently attract your attention. She would have neat little bunches of freshly picked herbs, or squash blossoms, or some small, freshly shelled peas or broad beans, and very soon I would be carried away, completely forgetting what I had really come for, and return home laden with two huge baskets overflowing with lovely, delicate, perishable things that two people could never have disposed of before they wilted and lost their bloom.

But it was on Sunday mornings that there was a brisk run on the salads already prepared and displayed on large shallow wheels of trays, of *nopalitos* or green or broad beans mainly, elaborately garnished with tomato and onion rings and sprinkled with chopped green coriander.

A salad is not as indispensable a part of a Mexican meal as, for instance, beans are. But that is not to say that raw vegetables are not eaten much in Mexico. On the contrary, to have *antojitos* served without a wealth of shredded lettuce, sliced tomatoes, and little radishes either sliced or in roses, is inconceivable. And then there are the table sauces or relishes, *guacamole, salsa mexicana cruda* and its Yucatecan counterpart *xni-pec,* eaten in great quantities with *tacos* or just tortillas. During the summer months the wandering street vendors offer cucumbers, peeled and slashed so that they spread out like a flower, and as they hand you one it is liberally sprinkled with powdered *chile piquín,* salt, and a squeeze of lime juice. In wintertime their place is taken by the *jícama,* which is thinly sliced and seasoned in the same way.

In the past *ensalada* was the name given to practically any accompaniment to the main meat course, and it fascinates me to read of salads of raw pineapple and cooking apple liberally doused with sherry; of boiled, acidy prickly pears (*xoconostles*) cooked with cinnamon and sugar; and a salad for ladies—*ensalada de damas*—which was considered much more appropriate fare for them instead of the meats offered to men, because "they are not as strong and lead a more sedentary life." The ladies were to eat an incredible mixture of cooked vegetables—beets, green beans, peas, zucchini squash, cauliflower—chopped up with plantain, pineapple, sweet potato, apples, avocados, olives and pickled chilies.

It was also suggested that for more elegant occasions salads of plain greens should be presented more colorfully adorned with edible flowers: borage, nasturtiums, mallow, wild chicory, or orange flowers.

The influences from the United States and Europe are seen in the restaurants where Waldorf, Russian, and chef's salads are served, but in private homes you are much more likely to get a salad of cooked vegetables—zucchini, cauliflower, and green beans—dressed with oil and vinegar and sprinkled with dried oregano and onion rings.

I could never quite take the eye-catching Christmas Eve salad seriously—lettuce, beets, sugar cane, oranges, bananas, sweet limes, *jícamas,* peanuts, and small, hard sugar candies all mixed up. But two that always spring to mind as being just right, different, and very Mexican are the nopal and stuffed chili salads, for which the recipes are given, along with recipes for some cooked vegetable salads and one for a salad of that very unusual vegetable, the *jícama.*

ENSALADA DE CHILES RELLENOS [*Stuffed chili salad*]

6 servings

THE MARINADE

A glass bowl
6 tablespoons water
2 tablespoons vinegar,
preferably wine
1 clove garlic, peeled and
sliced
⅛ teaspoon marjoram
⅛ teaspoon oregano
½ bay leaf
¼ teaspoon salt, or to taste
3 tablespoons olive oil

Mix all the ingredients well together and set them aside.

THE CHILIES

6 small chiles poblanos,
roasted and peeled, or
canned, peeled green
chilies

Remove the seeds and veins if you use *chiles poblanos*, and if they are very *picante* leave them to soak in salted water for about ½ hour. Put the chilies into the marinade and leave them at least 2 days, turning them from time to time. If the marinade appears to be too *picante*, then replace it with fresh.

THE GUACAMOLE STUFFING

A molcajete or mortar and
pestle
¼ onion, finely chopped
1 large avocado (see note
below)
¼ teaspoon salt, or to
taste
¼ teaspoon lime juice

Crush the onion. Cut open the avocado and scoop out the flesh. Mash it with the rest of the ingredients.

(*continued*)

THE SALAD

The chilies	Drain the chilies and stuff them well with the
The guacamole	*guacamole.* Arrange on a bed of lettuce
A serving dish	leaves on a serving dish and decorate them
Lettuce leaves	with the pomegranate seeds or chopped
Pomegranate seeds or	coriander.
chopped fresh	
coriander (see note	
below)	

This is a very unusual and refreshing salad. Since it is rather rich, 1 chili should be sufficient per serving.

If *chiles poblanos* were used, you will need 2 medium avocados and a little more onion and lemon juice.

There is no real substitute for the pomegranate seeds, which give such a crunchy texture and a touch of sweetness to the chilies, but a suitable garnish would be some chopped coriander.

The pomegranate season seems to be limited to the fall and early winter months. But when they are available they keep well at the bottom of the refrigerator, and although their skins dry out, I have used one after four months' storage in this way and the seeds were still juicy and crisp.

ENSALADA DE NOPALITOS [*Salad of nopal cactus pieces*]

6 servings

This is a truly Mexican salad, and at its best when the very young cactus joints are used. I first learned to like it in a modest little restaurant in Tacámbaro, Michoacán. The joints were so small and delicate, as only those can be that come out after the first rains of the season.

A large bowl	Mix all the ingredients together well and set
2 cups nopal cactus pieces,	aside to season for about 1 hour.
fresh (page 24) or 2	
small cans nopalitos	
finos al natural	

*2 medium tomatoes,
    skinned, seeded, and
    chopped (page 43)*
3 tablespoons olive oil
*4 teaspoons red wine
    vinegar*
¼ teaspoon oregano
⅓ onion, finely chopped
½ teaspoon salt, or to taste
6 sprigs fresh coriander
Freshly ground pepper

A serving dish
Lettuce leaves
The salad
Strips of seeded chiles
    jalapeños en
    escabeche
*¼ pound cream or farmer
    cheese, crumbled*
1 small onion, sliced
1 medium tomato, sliced

Line the dish with the lettuce leaves, put the salad on top, and garnish with the rest of the ingredients.

ENSALADA DE EJOTE Y CALABACITA
[*Green bean and zucchini squash salad*]

6 servings

*¾ pound cooked green
    beans*
*¾ pound cooked zucchini
    squash*
1 small onion

Cut the squash into halves and then into quarters lengthwise. Cut the beans into three parts. Slice the onion thin and mix it with the rest of the vegetables.

(*continued*)

A well-seasoned oil and
   vinegar dressing
2 peaches, peeled and
   sliced
1 small avocado, peeled
   and cut into strips
Seeds of half a
   pomegranate, if
   available

Toss the vegetables in the dressing.

Garnish the salad with the peeled and sliced peaches, the avocado strips, and the pomegranate seeds.

ENSALADA DE CALABACITA [*Zucchini squash salad*]

6 servings

1½ pounds cooked
   zucchini squash,
   cauliflower, or
   chayote, *still slightly
   crisp*
A well-seasoned oil and
   vinegar dressing
½ teaspoon oregano
Cebollas Encurtidas
   (page 307) or
   avocado strips
Green olives
Strips of cream cheese

Cut the squash into halves and then into quarters lengthwise (divide the cauliflower into flowerets, cut the *chayote* into slices).

Mix the vegetables with the oregano and salad dressing and garnish them with pickled onion rings or avocado strips, olives, and strips of cream cheese.

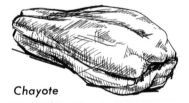

Chayote

ENSALADA MIXTA [*Mixed vegetable salad*]

6 servings

3 chiles poblanos, *roasted
    and peeled* (*page
    44*), *or canned,
    peeled green chilies*
1 large avocado
2 medium tomatoes
1 medium onion
A well-seasoned oil and
    vinegar dressing
Lettuce leaves
2 hard-boiled eggs, sliced

Remove the seeds from the chilies and cut them into strips. Slice the avocado, tomatoes, and onion and mix them together with the salad dressing.

Arrange the salad on a bed of lettuce leaves and decorate with the sliced hard-boiled eggs.

Jícama

ENSALADA DE JÍCAMA [*Jícama salad*]

6 servings

The *jícama* (*Pachyrrhizus erosus*) is the bulbous root of a leguminous plant indigenous to Mexico and other parts of Central and South America. It has a thin, patchy, light-brown skin and juicy, crisp, white flesh of a radish/potato consistency. It is mostly eaten by the Mexicans as a snack, peeled, thinly sliced, and seasoned with salt, a *picante* chili powder, and lime juice. In Campeche and Yucatán it is used for a salad. It is to be found in Mexican markets on the West Coast or in Chinese markets practically anywhere—it is called yam bean.

(continued)

*2 small jícamas or 1 large
 one (about 1½
 pounds)*

*1 heaped tablespoon finely
 chopped fresh
 coriander*

1 teaspoon salt

*¾ cup Seville orange juice
 (page 27)*

1 large sweet orange

Peel the *jícamas* with a potato peeler and cut them into about ¼-inch cubes. Add the coriander, salt, and Seville orange juice and set aside to season for at least 1 hour.

Peel and thinly slice the orange. Serve the salad garnished with the orange slices.

Desserts (*Postres*)

On a visit to a convent: "We came at length to a large hall, decorated with paintings and furnished with antique high-backed arm chairs, where a very elegant supper, lighted up and ornamented, greeted our astonished eyes; cakes, chocolates, ices, creams, custards, tarts, jellies, blancmanges, orange and lemon-ade and other profane dainties ornamented with gilt paper cut into little flags."

—FROM *Life in Mexico,*
BY FRANCES CALDERÓN DE LA BARCA

Almost every day when I am in Mexico City, I walk through Chapulte-pec Park to the metro station just in front of the statue of the Niños Héroes —is there anywhere else in the world that you would find, instead of the usual signs forbidding you to spit or loiter, one saying *Prohibir pasar con globos* ("It is forbidden to carry balloons into the subway")? For, if you have seen Chapultepec Park on a Sunday or holiday, with its clouds and clouds of brilliantly colored and bizarrely shaped balloons, you understand why.

From early morning to late afternoon, just outside the station, is a young woman selling *postres* from an ingeniously devised little cart. It has an enclosed glass top for the more delicate ones, and a folding extension with gently sloping ramps on which the little brightly colored jellies shiver. Some are brilliant and clear, red and green; others opaque and creamy looking, pinks, greens and browns; there are some with creamy bottoms and crystalline tops displaying a whole unhulled strawberry or some chopped walnuts, little cups of rice pudding or custards with caramel bottoms—the flavors, among others, pistachio, walnut, black currant, or wine. But you don't have to have such a complicated cart. On Saturday evenings in the streets of Puebla near the market little boys scurry along with trays of wobbling *natillas* and *jaleas* on their heads or in various artfully designed little cages with lots of shelves and glass sides that sit comfortably on the back of a bicycle.

I am not going to try and draw the impossible line between the candies and desserts of Mexico, because what we would call candies are so often served as *postre,* the end of a meal. Undoubtedly the nuns from Spain during the colonial period were the greatest innovators, and many of their sweetmeat creations still exist today in the same form and made with the same recipes.

You don't have to go to Puebla to see the varied "convent" *dulces.* When you are next in Mexico City, take a walk from the Palace of Fine Arts down Calle Cinco de Mayo towards the Zócalo. On the right-hand side you will come across a shop called Dulces de Celaya, owned by the same family who founded it in 1874. Its showcases, windows, fittings, and lamps, nearly everything about it is the same as it was then except for a background of constant, sharp traffic noises from the busy main street outside.

One window is usually filled with crystallized fruit—whole sweet potatoes, thick slices of pineapple, rich, dark-red watermelon, hunks of the whitish *chilacayote* with its black seeds, and whole shells of orange peel. On the opposite side are the *gaznates*—cornets of a thin, fried dough filled with a pineapple and coconut paste; thin triangles of almond *turrón* between layers of rice paper, and thick disks of chocolate ground on the *metate* with almonds and sugar and perfumed with vanilla and cinnamon. Inside the shop those that specially catch my eye are the small, brilliant green limes stuffed with coconut; almond paste miniatures of earthenware milk pitchers about one inch high, a *mamey* with a piece of its light-brown skin curled back to display the rich, salmon-pink fruit inside; or the papaya, also in miniature, with a slice cut out of it to see the flesh and small seeds inside. There are large rectangular *jamoncillos* of Puebla decorated with pine nuts and raisins; the acid-sweet tamarind candies from Jalisco and small fudge-like rolls covered with pecan halves from Saltillo. The variety is overwhelming, and I always want to try everything—just once more.

For the present-day traveler who accepts what is on the menu of the average hotel and restaurant there is very little to choose from beyond the usual ice creams and canned fruit (there are some excellent Mexican commercial brands on the market), canned *chongos*, and the inevitable flan of very varied quality. But if you are traveling around the country, look for some of the regional specialties.

In San Luis Potosí there is a dark preserve of prickly pears—*queso de tuna*—served with slices of the very good local cream cheese or the dried pressed peaches—*duraznos prensados*. Go into one of the many shops selling the pastes or thinly rolled *láminas* of guava, quince, or crab apple under the arches of the buildings around the central Plaza of Morelia; in the supermarket of La Paz in Baja California I bought some delicious paste of mango a few summers ago. After a good meal of *cabrito* and *frijoles rancheros* in Monterrey, the industrial capital of the north, make sure that you get with your coffee the round candies of crystallized goat's milk *cajeta—bolitas de leche quemada*—a specialty of the little town of General Zuazua. Irapuato and Zamora are great centers for strawberries, and besides some of the most delicious jams, they sell little packages of pressed crystallized strawberries.

On my first visit to Alcolmán, a lovely convent and a very early one of the colonial period, situated on the road out to the pyramids of Teotihuacán, I was rather astounded to see carved on the stone arch over the main door an unmistakably round and solid flan, along with grapes and other fruits and vegetables. Dairy cattle were introduced by the Spaniards as early as 1530, and the nuns lost no time reproducing their favorite sweetmeats and desserts, combining what they had brought with them from Spain with local products.

There are no really hard and fast rules about flans, and you can make them as solid or soft as you like, increasing or decreasing the amount of eggs in proportion to the milk used. Although it is not supposed to be the thing to do, you can even have air bubbles in them like those served in the Yucatecan restaurant in Mexico City, El Círculo del Sureste. Of course, these days if you are eating in Mexican restaurants you have to make sure that you are not going to get a flan made from a package from the supermarket shelf.

As far as flans go in Yucatán and Campeche, it is safer to choose the solid, sweet *queso napolitano,* made with condensed milk and occasionally with ground almonds, than the rather wishy-washy little custards that pass for flan.

Just as I suppose most people make a beeline when they are traveling for a famous church or museum, I head first of all for the market. It's the key to my eating for the next few days. It seems to me that the most interesting part of Mérida's market is spread outside its walls for about a block on either side. Under the covered arches of the buildings nearby are the candy vendors. Most of their candies seem to be based on coconut, and my favorite of all, though death to one's fillings, is the *coco melcochado:* finely grated coconut in a well-burned caramel brittle.

Quite by accident I came across the *marañón*—the fleshy fruit of the cashew nut—in a supermarket in Campeche. The nut grows on the outside of its red and yellow fruit, which ripens in May. There is quite an industry in Campeche bottling them in alcohol and syrup. But try those preserved in syrup—*en almíbar*—they need the sweetness; those preserved in alcohol are curiously bitter. I remember seeing in the bus station, of all places, a small, sealed plastic bag containing what looked like a large, fleshy prune— it was a dried *marañon.* The flavor is subtle, and although I ate it every day for the best part of a week, I simply can't relate it to anything else.

The "pickled" peaches and quinces, as they are called (and they are pickled in every sense of the word in a sugar-cane spirit called *aguardiente*), are the specialty of the Chiapas highlands. The air is damp up in San Cristóbal, and as in England, from time to time you need to stoke up to drive out the penetrating cold. It was in the Dulcería Santo Domingo where I saw the fruit in huge glass jars. What a find the Dulcería was! They had the freshest, richest *pan dulce* that I have ever found in Mexico, and if you happen to be there about five o'clock in the afternoon, the lightest, flakiest *empanadas* arrive hot from the oven with a slightly sweet pork filling.

Yes, there is a tremendous variety of wonderful sweetmeats to eat in Mexico, but you have to be prepared to look for the really good ones.

TORTA DE CIELO [*Almond sponge cake*]

I had eaten this cake—literally "cake of heaven"—many times in the Casa Chalam Balam in Mérida and loved it. In Yucatán it is served at weddings and first communion receptions. I was told that the recipe was kept a secret by the old ladies who made it for the hotel. After many experiments I think this recipe comes as close as possible to the version I like so much. The soaking of the almonds keeps the cake rich and moist; it is sometimes also flavored with anise.

Preheat the oven to 325°.

A 9-inch spring-form pan
Parchment paper
Butter
All-purpose flour
A bowl
Hot water to cover
½ pound almonds

Line the bottom of the pan with parchment paper. Butter the paper and sides of the pan well, and dust with flour.

Pour hot water over the almonds so that they are well covered and leave them to soak for at least 6 hours. (Remove the skins—they should slip right off—if they are not already skinned.)

A blender or spice grinder

Chop the nuts roughly and grind them a little at a time. They should be neither too coarse nor too fine. Set aside.

A bowl and beater
5 eggs, separated
A good pinch of salt

Beat the egg whites until they are fluffy. Add the salt and continue beating until they are stiff. Add the yolks one by one and continue beating until they are all incorporated.

The ground almonds
½ pound granulated sugar
¼ teaspoon baking powder
1 tablespoon all-purpose flour
The beaten eggs

Mix the dry ingredients together and, beating at a low speed, gradually add them to the eggs.

(*continued*)

The prepared pan
1 tablespoon brandy
A drop of almond extract

Add the brandy and almond extract and pour the batter into the prepared pan.

Bake for 1¼ hours in the middle level of the oven. Let the cake get cold before removing it from the pan.

This moist, textured cake keeps almost indefinitely if stored in a cool, dry place—preferably not the refrigerator.

GUAVAS RELLENAS CON COCADA
[Guavas stuffed with coconut]

Have ready:

12 guava shells (see note below)

A heavy saucepan
½ pound granulated sugar
½ cup water, preferably the water from the coconut

Melt the sugar in the water over medium heat, then bring the syrup to a boil. Let it boil fast until it forms a thin thread—225° to 230°F. on a candy thermometer.

½ pound finely shredded coconut (approximately ½ fresh coconut) (see note below)

Add the coconut to the syrup and cook it until it is transparent but not too soft—about 5 minutes. Set aside to cool.

2 egg yolks, lightly beaten
Finely grated peel of 1 orange
6 tablespoons orange juice
½ teaspoon lime juice

Add the rest of the ingredients and continue cooking the mixture over a medium flame for about 15 minutes, until the mixture is almost dry, scraping the bottom of the pan continuously. Set it aside to cool.

The guava shells
The cocada

Fill each guava shell with a large tablespoon of the *cocada*, covering the top of the guava shell completely.

Place the filled shells under the broiler and

let the *cocada* brown a little. **Take care: it will burn very quickly.** Set them aside to cool before serving.

Ripe guavas, either those with yellow or pinkish flesh, have a subtle and delightful flavor to which you can very easily become addicted. For a short period each year they find their way into the American markets but the ones I have tried have certainly not been worth the very high price. If you are lucky enough to find some good ones, they should be peeled, cut into halves, and poached in a light syrup. When they are tender, you can easily remove the soft seedy part in the center, leaving the shell ready to fill. The canned varieties are generally far too sweet and tasteless, with the exception of the Clemente Jacques label.

If you are using desiccated coconut, 4 ounces is plenty but moisten it first with ⅔ cup very hot water. If the coconut you are using is not finely shredded, grind it in the blender. On no account should sweetened coconut be used.

DULCE DE CAMOTE [*Yam dessert*]

Serves 6

This is a recipe given to me some years ago by Elizabeth Borton de Treviño, whose book, *My Heart Lies South,* about her early married life in Monterrey, Nuevo León, gives a fascinating picture of a provincial town.

Three days ahead:	Preheat the oven to 375°.
2 pounds orange yams	Wrap the yams in foil and cook them until they are quite soft—about 2 hours. Set them aside to cool. Remove the skin and press the
A food mill	pulp through the medium disk of the food mill. There should be about 2 cups of pulp.
A thick saucepan *½ cup granulated sugar* *¼ cup water*	Put the sugar and water into the saucepan and set over a low flame until the sugar has dissolved. Turn the flame up and boil the syrup until it threads—225° to 230° F. on a candy thermometer.

(continued)

The yam pulp

1 teaspoon vanilla extract
1 teaspoon ground
    cinnamon
½ cup coarsely chopped
    walnuts or pecans
½ cup mixed candied and
    dried fruits, chopped
    (see note below)
1 ounce dark rum
1 ounce tequila
    (preferably añejo)

On serving day:

A serving dish
Unsweetened whipped
    cream or Thick Sour
    Cream (page 20)

Add the yam pulp to the syrup and mix well together.

Mix in the rest of the ingredients. Cover the mixture and leave it to ripen for at least 3 days at the bottom of the refrigerator.

Turn the mixture into a serving dish and serve with unsweetened whipped cream or sour cream.

This is a very concentrated dessert, so this quantity should make 6 good portions.

How good it is depends very much on the quality of the candied fruits, so don't on any account use those packets of oversweet, innocuous fruits put out at Christmastime. I suggest the best candied citron, orange and lemon peel, angelica, and candied pineapple. You should also add some chopped dried pear and apricot, which are less sweet.

CHONGOS ZAMORANOS [*Curds in syrup*]

Serves 4

Chongos zamoranos are small rolls of custardlike curds in a thin syrup formed by the sugar and the whey.

According to Spanish dictionaries, one of the meanings of the word *chongo* in Mexico is "topknot." The Mexican *Diccionario de Cocina* published in 1878 describes it as "a sweet soup made of bread or dried cake with cheese—made in innumerable ways . . ." Going down the list I find that the "whey *chongos*" or "whey conserves" are just like those of today.

Those most generally known and popular in Mexico are the canned *chongos zamoranos*. The curd of these is very rubbery and squeaks just a little as your teeth bite into it; and they are overly sweet. I have followed Mexican recipes, vague as they are, and careful instructions from Mexican friends, to the letter; I have tried every brand of milk that I can lay my hands on; varied the shapes and sizes of the dishes; used different amounts of rennet and longer cooking times. In all, I would say, without exaggeration I have tried a hundred variations to try and get them more like the Mexican version. And then I stop and wonder why, when the *chongos* made here are far more delicious.

A saucepan
1 quart milk
A bowl and beater
2 egg yolks
4 rennet tablets
½ tablespoon cold water
A flameproof dish—ideally
    a round dish at least
    3 inches deep and
    between 8 and 10
    inches in diameter

Heat the milk gently to 110°—a little hotter than lukewarm.

Beat the egg yolks lightly and mix them well into the milk.

Crumble the tablets and let them dissolve in the water.

Pour the milk mixture into the dish and stir in the rennet solution. Set the dish in a warm place until the milk has set—about 30 minutes. Then, with a pointed knife, carefully cut across the junket, dividing it into 4 equal segments.

½ cup dark brown sugar
2 1-inch sticks cinnamon

Put the dish over a low flame, and as soon as the curds and whey start to separate, sprinkle the sugar between the segments of the curd. Break up the cinnamon sticks a little and put the pieces into the whey.

An asbestos mat, if
    necessary

Leave the dish over the lowest possible flame for 2 hours. Watch it carefully to see that it does not come to a boil. If necessary, put an asbestos mat under the dish. The curds will get firmer as the cooking time lengthens and the sugar and whey will form a thin syrup.

(continued)

At the end of the cooking time, remove the dish from the flame and set it aside to cool.

Cut each segment of curds into halves. Then starting from the pointed end of each piece, roll the curd up carefully.

A small serving dish

Put the rolled pieces onto a serving dish and pour the syrup, with the cinnamon pieces, over the *chongos*.

Serve at room temperature.

If the syrup has little pieces of curd in it, pour it through a fine strainer or cheesecloth. For a change, omit the egg yolks and put a few small pieces of fresh pineapple into the syrup for the last hour of cooking time.

Chongos will last for several days in the refrigerator, but they get sweeter as they absorb the syrup.

If you use raw milk you can reduce the rennet by half but they are rarely as creamy-tasting. Some brands of milk will simply not set to a curd that is tough enough and will disintegrate almost entirely at the slightest bubble in the syrup. Of the many brands I have tried in the New York area, Gold Medal and Sealtest work the best—in the case of the latter probably because it is carefully held at the pasteurization temperature for a very short time, thereby perhaps increasing the free calcium that encourages clotting. The type of milk and consistency of the curd changes enormously with the type of cattle, their feed and water, so there, with the added factor of pasteurization, lies the difference in results between the United States and Mexico—although my Mexican friends complain that since pasteurization they cannot make the same *chongos*.

HUEVOS REALES [*Egg sponge in syrup*]

4 servings

Huevos reales, literally "royal eggs," are segments of egg "sponge," sweetened and moistened with a syrup with which they are saturated. This is one of the so-called convent desserts, which for the most part are concentratedly sweet. With them I like to serve strong black coffee.

Have ready:

A well-buttered flan mold

Preheat the oven to 350°.

A bowl and beater
5 egg yolks
A pinch of salt
½ tablespoon water
The flan mold

At high speed, beat the egg yolks together with the salt and water until they are very thick and mousselike—about 4 to 5 minutes.

Pour the mixture into the prepared mold. Cover the mold and set it into a warm water bath on the lowest shelf in the oven. Cook until the mixture is firm—about 40 minutes.

Let the mixture cool off, still covered. For easy removal, cut it into four portions and remove them carefully from the mold. The "sponge" should be about ¾ to 1 inch thick if you have beaten the yolks sufficiently.

A saucepan
½ cup granulated sugar
¾ cup water
2 1-inch sticks cinnamon

Put the sugar and water together into the pan and set it over a low heat until the sugar has dissolved. Bring the syrup to a boil, add the cinnamon, and let it continue boiling fast for 5 minutes.

The sponge pieces
1 tablespoon raisins

Place the sponge pieces and the raisins in the hot syrup and let them heat through gently for about 3 minutes.

A shallow serving dish
2 tablespoons rum
1 heaped teaspoon pine
   nuts or blanched and
   slivered almonds

Transfer the pieces to a shallow serving dish. Pour the remaining syrup over them. Sprinkle with the rum and nuts and let them cool off before serving.

This dessert can be prepared well ahead of time, and will keep well for several days.

BUDÍN DE ZANAHORIA [*Carrot pudding*]

6 servings

Follow the recipe for Budín de Zanahoria (page 277), omitting the cheese and adding ½ cup raisins.

This can either be eaten hot as a coffee cake or served as a dessert with a thin syrup (made as for Huevos Reales, page 326, the quantity doubled and with the addition of ¼ cup rum) poured over it just before serving.

MANGOS FLAMEADOS [*Mangoes flambées*]

This recipe was invented in Mexico for Mexican products (a very acceptable Triple Sec is being made there now). I have included it because I think it will become a classic—and besides, it is absolutely delicious.

For each serving:

A chafing dish
1 tablespoon butter
1 tablespoon granulated sugar
½ orange
½ lime
1 ounce Triple Sec or Cointreau
Juice of ½ orange
Juice of ½ lime

2 mango halves, canned or fresh (see note below)
1 ounce tequila

Melt the butter in the pan, and when it is very hot, add the sugar and stir until it has dissolved.

Thinly pare the orange and lime and add the parings to the chafing dish.

Add the Triple Sec and flame it.

When the flames have died down, add the juices and cook the mixture until it has reduced a little and is just turning brown. Remove the fruit parings.

Add the mangoes, and as the syrup starts to bubble add the tequila and flame again.

Serve immediately, either as it is or over
coconut ice cream, or with unsweetened
whipped or sour cream.

If you are a bit of a showman with pyromaniac tendencies, you can make
an impressive display with the chafing dish at the table. You can pare the
lime and orange carefully so as to make complete spirals of the rinds. You
can douse them with tequila and set them afire over the dish so that the
flames circle around for quite a while. That's how it was done when I tried
them for the first time in the company of the man whose recipe it is,
Howard Brown of the Ramada Inn in Monterrey. But if you prefer to do
things quietly, and alone, and ahead of time, then cook them up to the final
flaming. Just before serving, heat them up and flame the tequila.

The yellow *manila* mango of Mexico is best, as it has just the right combination of sweetness and acidity. You could try the big green mangoes
that come onto the market in the early summer but if you ever tried to
peel and remove the pits from one mango—let alone six—you will be happy
to read that I think you should use canned. But most of the canned mangoes
are far too sweet: sweet to begin with, they are then canned in heavy syrup.
Again, you need the mango halves and not the mango slices. The best imported product is the *manila* mango packed in a light syrup from Mexico.

BUÑUELOS [*Fritters in anise-flavored syrup*]

12 small buñuelos

Most countries have their version of *buñuelos*, or fritters, either sweet or
savory, and they are certainly great favorites throughout Spain and Latin
America.

In many parts of Mexico *buñuelos* are made of a stiffer dough, which is
rolled out thin anywhere up to 12 inches in diameter and then fried crisp
and stacked up ready for use. In Uruapán I have wandered around in the
evenings under the *portales* of the central plaza looking for the crispest and
freshest to eat with a cup of hot chocolate. There they are broken into
small pieces and heated quickly in a thick syrup of *piloncillo*, the raw sugar

of Mexico. These of Veracruz are very much like the *churros* of Spain, but flavored with aniseeds, and served with a syrup.

Thirty eggs went into the batch that were being made in the Brisas del Mar Restaurant, in a small village a few miles south of Veracruz. Srita. Duarte, whose recipe this is, showed me how to make them, and I must say everyone was very good humored about the bizarre shapes that some of their customers had to eat that day.

THE SYRUP

A saucepan
3 cups water
1½ cups dark brown sugar
¼ scant teaspoon
    aniseeds

Put all the ingredients together into the saucepan. Set the pan over a medium heat until the sugar has melted, and then bring it quickly to a boil. Let the syrup boil for about 20 minutes; by then it should have reduced to about 1¼ cups. Set it aside to cool.

THE DOUGH

A saucepan
1 cup water
¼ teaspoon salt
¼ teaspoon aniseeds
3 tablespoons lard
¼ pound sifted flour

Put the water, salt, aniseeds, and lard into the saucepan and bring to a boil.

When the lard has completely melted and the mixture is still boiling, stir the flour into it quickly. Beat the mixture, while continuing to cook it, until it shrinks away from the sides of the pan. Set it aside to cool.

When the dough is cool enough to handle, knead it until it is quite smooth.

3 medium eggs (about 2
    ounces each)

Beat the eggs lightly and stir them into the mixture, a little at a time, reserving some of the egg until you have tested the dough. You should be able to roll it into a soft ball that will **just hold its shape.** Add the rest of the egg if necessary.

A pinch of baking powder

Mix the baking powder into the dough.

THE BUÑUELOS

A frying pan
Peanut or safflower oil
    (½ inch deep)
A bowl of cold water
The dough

Heat the oil until it smokes. Wet your hands well, take a piece of the dough, and roll it into a ball about 1½ inches in diameter.

Place the ball on your fingers—**not on your palm**—and flatten it to make a cake about ¾ inch thick. Make a large hole in the center of the dough and drop it into the hot fat. Cook it on both sides until it is a golden brown, and well puffed up.

Remove the *buñuelos* from the fat with a slotted spoon and drain them on the paper.

Paper toweling
The syrup

Pour ¼ cup syrup over each serving of two *buñuelos,* and serve immediately.

These can be cooked several hours ahead and doused with syrup just before serving, but they do not keep successfully from one day to another.

CAJETA DE CELAYA [*Goat's milk dessert*]

About 1 quart

Cajeta was the name originally given in Mexico to the small wooden boxes especially made to store sweetmeats, although it has come to mean the sweetmeat itself: a paste made of fruits, nuts, or thickened milk. Evolved presumably to preserve these products before the days of refrigeration, the present-day *cajeta de leche*—known in other parts of Latin America as *dulce de leche*—is now sold in glass jars; indeed, it would be a frustrating job to keep it in a box, as it would ooze out.

The *cajeta de Celaya,* which takes its name from the small bustling town in the Bajío where the making of it has become quite a large industry, can be bought in different flavors: wine, caramel, strawberry (strawberries grow in abundance in that part of the country). Like many other products all over the world, the demand has become so great that poor-quality *cajetas* are selling in great quantities, even though they have lost the characteristics of the original through the addition of too much cane syrup. Still the best is the musky goat's milk *cajeta* from San Luis Potosí that I first came across in Mexico.

I have seen it made commercially in huge vats in San Luis, and I thought that the dark color was due to the long cooking time—but when I made it at home I found out that it wasn't so. None of my friends could tell me how to get that rich, dark brown of the San Luis *cajeta,* and no cookbook mentioned it, but in the same little book that told me about the pineapple and banana *cajeta* I came across the rather obvious method that I have included in this recipe.

Traditionally in Mexico it is eaten by itself, and that is how I think it is best. However, it has come to be used over vanilla ice cream, which I personally think is not a good combination. In Argentina apparently it is used ad nauseum—on breakfast toast instead of marmalade, to fill éclairs and other French pastries.

There are unfortunately no import licenses available for foreign goat's milk products from Mexico at the present time. But this *cajeta*—as well as the ones on the following pages—is well worth the trouble of making; goat's milk can be obtained in limited quantities, particularly at health food stores.

A large, heavy saucepan
1 quart goat's milk
3½ cups cow's milk

Put the milks into a saucepan and bring to a boil.

A small bowl
¾ teaspoon cornstarch
¼ scant teaspoon baking soda
½ cup cow's milk

Mix the cornstarch, soda, and milk together and stir the mixture into the boiling milk.

1½ cups granulated sugar

Stir the sugar gradually into the saucepan and keep stirring until it has dissolved. Continue cooking the mixture. Meanwhile prepare the coloring.

A small frying pan
½ cup granulated sugar

Caramelize the sugar (see Notes on Making Flans, page 336). Remove the milk mixture from the flame and very gradually add the hot caramel. Take care as it will foam up alarmingly.

Continue boiling the mixture until it is just beginning to thicken—about 40 to 50 minutes depending on the depth of the cajeta in the pan. Then continue to cook, stirring it all the time, until it forms a thread and coats the back of a wooden spoon.

Pour the *cajeta* into a dish to cool before using. From start to finish it will take about 1½ hours to cook.

A shallow serving dish

Cajeta de Celaya will keep indefinitely in screw-top jars outside the refrigerator.

CAJETA DE LECHE ENVINADA
[*Cow's milk dessert with wine and almonds*]

6 servings

A large, heavy saucepan
6 cups milk
1 pound granulated sugar
A pinch of baking soda

Put the milk, sugar, and soda into the pan and set it over a medium flame until the sugar has melted. Then raise the flame and boil it as fast as possible for 30 minutes.

Put ¾ cup of the milk-sugar mixture aside to cool.

A small bowl and beater
3 egg yolks

Beat the egg yolks until creamy and add them to the cooled milk.

Continue boiling the rest of the milk mixture until it becomes thick, like condensed milk. As it thickens, stir the mixture continually or it will stick to the pan. This should take about 30 minutes.

The egg mixture

Remove from the flame and add the egg mixture to the thickened milk, stirring all the time. Continue cooking the mixture over a medium flame until it starts to come away from the bottom and sides of the pan.

(*continued*)

⅓ cup almonds, blanched
   and slivered
½ cup medium-dry sherry
   or Madeira

Stir the almonds and sherry into the mixture.

A shallow serving dish

Pour the mixture into the serving dish and let it get thoroughly cool before serving.

CAJETA DE PIÑA Y PLÁTANO [*Pineapple and banana dessert*]

6 servings

This is a thick, dark paste of fruit with an unusual and refreshing flavor.

Whenever I make it I think of Luz, our first Mexican maid. Although she only came to clean for a few brief periods each week, somehow she managed to give me my first Mexican cooking lessons. At that time I didn't think to ask her where she had first come across this recipe, and I had never been able to find it in any cookbook, or find anyone else who knew of it, at least in Mexico City. But one day I was reading through a book I had just acquired, *Recetas Prácticas para la Señora de Casa* published in Guadalajara in 1895, and there it was.

And I shall remember her also for sentimental reasons, for she was our maid when Paul decided he would take the plunge and get married again. It was the day of our civil wedding, and when we returned home Luz was standing at the entrance of the apartment house, almost blocking the door with the biggest flower arrangement I have ever seen. She was beaming, and in her excitement had apparently told everyone she could find about the wedding, for she was surrounded by the caretaker and his family, various maids, and curious onlookers. Indeed she had informed everyone, for that evening as I went into the bathroom—and I must explain that our bathroom window was extremely large and low and opened into a well immediately opposite the bathroom window of our French neighbor's—with true Gallic courtesy M._____ rose, threw open his arms, and exclaimed: "*Felicidades, señora,* I hear that you and the *señor* are getting married." And with that he shut the window.

Unfortunately for us Luz couldn't stay. She went off to her first independent business venture, a concession for providing meals for an army barracks, which, we heard later, ended in financial disaster.

Preheat the oven to 325°.

A saucepan
1½ cups brown sugar
4 cups water
2-inch stick cinnamon

Bring the sugar, water, and cinnamon to a boil and let them continue to boil fast for about 20 minutes. The liquid will have reduced to **about** 2½-3 cups. Remove the cinnamon stick.

A blender
1 pineapple (3½ to 4 pounds)
2 pounds bananas

Clean and dice the fruit and blend it with the syrup to a **coarse** puree. It is best to blend it in three lots.

A shallow ovenproof dish, ideally not much more than 3 inches deep
2 1-inch sticks cinnamon
Juice and peel of ½ lime

Pour the mixture into the dish and add the cinnamon and lime peel and juice. Set the dish in the oven and let the fruit puree cook for about 5 to 6 hours (see note below). From time to time, scrape the mixture from the sides of the dish and stir it well. This is particularly important toward the end of the cooking period.

A small serving dish

When the mixture is thick, sticky, and a rich, dark brown, transfer it to a small serving dish and glaze it quickly under the broiler.

Set it aside to cool.

Serve the *cajeta* with cream cheese or Thick Sour Cream (page 20).

This should keep for about 10 to 15 days in the refrigerator—but I doubt whether that will be necessary. I'm afraid I always dip a finger into it each time I open the refrigerator door.

Cooking time, of course, will very much depend on the depth of the mixture in the oven dish. The deeper it is the longer it will take.

Notes on Making Flans

Here are the general rules for making all types of flan:

1. To make the caramel: first heat a small heavy frying pan. Add ½ cup granulated sugar and leave it over a medium flame for a few minutes until the sugar on the bottom has melted and is transparent. Raise the flame and stir the sugar with a wooden spoon until it turns a deep brown and starts to froth up. The color will depend on how dark you like the caramel, but be careful not to let it burn too much. Pour the caramel into the flan mold and turn the mold around quickly, tipping it from side to side until there is an even coating of the caramel over the bottom and halfway up the sides of the mold.

2. Let the caramel get cool before adding the flan mixture.

3. Always cover the mold with a lid; it helps the cooking of the flan and prevents a hard skin from forming. For the almond and coconut flans the mixture will rise up to the top of the mold, so be sure to grease the inside of the lid well with butter.

4. Always set the mold in a water bath of hot water that comes about halfway up the outside of the mold.

5. Always set the mold on the lowest shelf in the oven.

6. To test to see if the flan is cooked through, insert the blade of a knife or a skewer well into the flan. The knife should come out clean. Take care not to pierce the flan at the bottom or it will spoil the appearance of the top when it is unmolded.

7. It is not essential to make the flan the day before, but it makes serving easier.

8. Always serve a flan at room temperature to enhance the flavor.

9. A flan is delicate, so take special care when you are unmolding it. If the caramel was cooked to a very high point, it will harden while standing in the refrigerator. Do not attempt to unmold it unless you are absolutely certain that the caramel is melted. The flan should slither around easily as you tip the mold. If you are not certain, place the mold in a pan of warm

water for about 5 minutes and then test again. Do not attempt to loosen the flan with a knife.

10. Unmold the flan onto a dish or plate that has a little bit of depth so that none of the caramel is lost.

FLAN A LA ANTIGUA [*Old-fashioned flan*]

6 servings

A very solid version of a caramel custard, this cuts better if made the day before. To make it, follow Notes on Making Flans (pages 336–337).

Have ready:

A flan mold coated with caramel

Preheat oven to 350°.

A saucepan
1 quart milk
½ cup granulated sugar
A vanilla bean or a stick of cinnamon (about 2 inches)
A pinch of salt

Heat the milk, add the sugar, vanilla bean or cinnamon, and salt and let it simmer briskly for about 15 minutes. The milk should be reduced by about ½ cup. Set it aside to cool.

4 whole eggs
6 egg yolks
A fine cheesecloth or strainer

Beat the eggs and egg yolks together well. Add them to the cooled milk and stir well.

Pour the mixture through the strainer into the coated mold. (Rinse the vanilla bean, let it dry, and store it for use again.)

A water bath

Cover the mold and set it in a water bath on the lowest shelf in the oven. Cook the flan for 2 hours and test to see if it is done. When it is done, set it aside to cool.

QUESO DE NÁPOLES [*Neapolitan cheese*]

6 servings

There are many variations of *queso de Nápoles*, or *queso napolitano*. If you ask for it in Yucatán, you will be given a very solid flan made with canned condensed milk, with or without ground almonds. And it may also be cooked without the caramel. I have chosen this version because I think it is by far the best: a white, delicate flan, with a spongy, nutty layer at the bottom. It is also a marvelous way of using up those egg whites which always have a way of accumulating. Whenever I have leftover egg whites, I put four at a time into a polyethylene bag and freeze them for the next *queso* or batch of meringues.

To make this, follow Notes on Making Flans (pages 336–337).

Have ready:

A flan mold coated with caramel

Preheat the oven to 350°.

A saucepan
2 cups milk
¼ cup granulated sugar
¼ cup finely ground almonds (about 1½ ounces)

Bring the milk to a boil and let it simmer for 5 minutes.

Add the sugar and the almonds to the milk and let the mixture simmer for another 5 minutes. Set it aside **until it is cool.**

A bowl and beater
4 egg whites
A pinch of salt
The milk mixture
The prepared mold

Beat the egg whites until frothy, add the salt, and continue beating until they are stiff.

Fold the beaten whites into the milk mixture. Pour the mixture into the prepared mold.

A water bath

Cover the mold with a well-greased lid and set it in the lowest part of the oven in a water bath. Cook for 1½ hours, then test to see if the *queso* is cooked. When it is done, set it aside to cool.

COCADA IMPERIAL [*Imperial coconut flan*]

6 servings

Have ready:

A flan mold coated with caramel

Preheat the oven to 350°.

A heavy saucepan
2 cups milk
¾ cup granulated sugar

Melt the sugar in the milk over a low flame, then raise the flame and boil it briskly. Take care that it doesn't boil over. As soon as it begins to thicken, stir the mixture so that it does not stick to the bottom of the pan. After about 30 minutes, it should be the consistency of a thin condensed milk and should have been reduced to about 1 cup (see note below).

A saucepan
1 small coconut

Pierce a hole through two of the "eyes" of the coconut and drain the water from it. Set the water aside.

Put the whole coconut into the oven for about 8 minutes. Crack it open; the flesh should come away quite easily from the shell.

Pare the brown skin from the flesh with a potato peeler and grate the flesh finely. (2¼ cups, loosely packed, will be needed for the flan.)

A saucepan
The grated coconut
The reserved coconut
   water
The condensed milk

Add the grated coconut to the coconut water and boil it over a brisk flame for about 5 minutes, stirring it all the time.

Add the condensed milk and continue cooking for another 5 minutes. Set the mixture aside to cool.

A bowl and beater

Beat the egg yolks together until they are

(*continued*)

5 *small eggs, separated*

creamy and stir them well into the coconut mixture.

A clean bowl and beater
The egg whites
A pinch of salt

Beat the egg whites until they are frothy, add the salt, and continue beating until they are stiff. Fold them into the mixture.

The prepared mold

Pour the mixture into the prepared mold. Cover the mold with a well-greased lid and put it into a water bath.

A water bath

Cook the flan on the lowest shelf in the oven for about 1½ hours, then test to see if it is done. When it is done, set it aside to cool.

Of course, you can use shortcuts by substituting 1 cup of slightly thinned canned, sweetened condensed milk for the milk and sugar and pre-grated but unsweetened coconut. Use milk instead of the coconut water: the flavor will just not be quite as good.

Don't think you have done something wrong when you see that the custard and the coconut have separated. That is how it is meant to be. And the caramel will nearly all have been absorbed by the spongy layer of coconut.

If you are using a fresh coconut there will almost certainly be some left over. It will keep perfectly well if it is frozen.

Beverages (*Bebidas*)

Mexico is justly famous for such diverse drinks and beverages as tequila, *pulque, aguas frescas,* chocolate, *atole,* and its beer and coffee, all of which, discussed in detail later, are readily accessible to the visitor. Many of the regional drinks are much more difficult to come by. Usually made at home, they are often produced from the fermented juice of local, often wild fruits. There is the pineapple *tepache* of Jalisco; the *sangre de Baco* (blood of Bacchus) made of wild grapes from Guerrero; *teshuino,* maize fermented with raw sugar from the mountainous regions of Chihuahua and Nayarit. On the coast of Colima and Guerrero the sap from the trunk of the coconut palm is made into *tuba,* and there are innumerable other concoctions based on sugarcane or flavored with wild cherries; there are the mescals of Oaxaca; the much-esteemed *bacanora* of Sonora; the anise-flavored liqueur made of flowers and called *Xtabentun,* from Yucatán—and, of course, the world-famous Kahlúa.

The central plateau of Mexico, besides, is rich in mineral springs. There are small spas dotted here and there, and the thermal, therapeutic waters attract people from all over the Republic. Some of the larger ones bottle and distribute quite widely the naturally gaseous and still mineral waters.

TEQUILA

Tequila is distilled from the fermented liquid of the crushed, pineapple-like bases of a much smaller agave, the *Agave tequilana*. It is named after the small town, not too far from Guadalajara, in Jalisco, which is the principal tequila-producing state. The Spaniards introduced the process of distillation to Mexico, and it is generally believed that tequila was first made around the middle of the eighteenth century, although it was not until a hundred years later that it became an industry set up by two of the best-known families in the industry today, Cuervo and Sauza.

There are various types of tequila. The ordinary whites, best for mixed drinks; the pale-gold tequilas, which have usually been aged for one year, and the much heavier *añejos*, which have been left to mature for six to eight years. There is one very special tequila, Centenario, which is brought out every six years to coincide with the inauguration of each new presidential term. The label is designed with miniature portraits of the preceding presidents.

If you are drinking tequila by itself you may wish to have an aged one, *añejo,* which has a very pale, gold color and more body and flavor. The Mexican way of drinking it is with a piece of lime and some salt. Hold a quarter of a lime in your left hand and place a little salt in the well at the base of the thumb and index finger of the same hand. Hold the tequila glass in the other hand. Lick the salt, swallow some tequila, then suck the lime.

Sangrita glass   Tequila glass

MARGARITA

1 serving

Hardly anyone would disagree that the *margaritas* at Carlos Jacott's El Parador are the lustiest in New York. He has given me the following recipes for his margaritas, as well as for his Tequila Cocktail (below).

Since limes are sometimes scarce and very expensive, freshly squeezed lemon juice can be substituted for the lime juice. The ordinary white tequila is the one most suitable for these cocktails.

A large cocktail glass
A slice of lime or lemon
A little salt, either ordinary
*   table salt or finely*
*   ground rock salt*
1½ ounces white tequila
½ ounce Triple Sec
1 ounce fresh lime or
*   lemon juice*
A few ice cubes, crushed
The prepared glass

Chill a large cocktail glass well. Rub the rim with a slice of lime. Put the salt onto a plate. Press the rim of the glass into it, giving it a turn to make sure that the rim is ringed with salt.

Put the tequila, Triple Sec, lime juice, and ice cubes into a cocktail shaker. Cover and shake together well. Pour the mixture through a strainer into the prepared glass.

TEQUILA COCKTAIL or TEQUILA SUNRISE

1 serving

A large cocktail glass
A blender
2 ounces white tequila
1½ ounces fresh lime or
*   lemon juice*
1 tablespoon grenadine
*   syrup*
1 teaspoon egg white
Some ice cubes, crushed

Chill a large cocktail glass well.

Put the tequila, lime juice, grenadine syrup, and egg white into a blender with the ice cubes. Blend the mixture until frothy and pour into the prepared glass.

SANGRITA

My friends in Jalisco say that *sangrita* was originally made with the juice of sour pomegranate—they gave me brandy made of the sour pomegranates that had been aged for some years; it was a deep amber color, perfectly smooth and delicious—but since they are more and more difficult to come by the Seville orange juice and grenadine syrup make a good substitute.

*1¼ cups Seville orange
    juice (page 27)*
*3½ tablespoons grenadine
    syrup*
Salt to taste
*A good pinch of powdered
    red chili,* **pequín** *or*
    cayenne
*½ ounce tequila per
    person*

Mix all the ingredients except the tequila together well and chill. Serve in small glasses, about 2 ounces per person. Serve the tequila in separate glasses.

PULQUE

"Another bullfight last evening! It is like pulque, one makes a wry face at first and then begins to like it."

—FROM *Life in Mexico,*
BY FRANCES CALDERÓN DE LA BARCA

The tall, stately maguey or *Agave*—century plant, so much a part of the landscape of the central plateau of Mexico—like many other succulents throughout history has sustained wandering tribes. No wonder it was held in such high esteem, and gods and goddesses of it created in pre-Hispanic mythology. The milky substance drawn off from the center of the plant, just before it thrusts up a main trunk crowned with flowers, provides a highly nutritive liquid that can be converted to honey, crystallized to a sugar, or fermented to make the highly alcoholic drink *pulque,* a yeastlike rising agent, or even vinegar. In fact the properties of this *aguamiel*—literally "honey-water"—has always fascinated and still fascinates scientists, who have written hundreds of learned treatises on the subject. The large pointed leaves—*pencas*—were converted into paper and cord, and are still used today to line barbecue pits; while the membranelike skin stripped from the leaves wraps the chili-seasoned barbecued lamb called *mixiote*. The thorns were used as needles. The thick white maggots that feed on the plant are fried crisp and eaten with great relish, and the eggs of the ants sheltering under its broad base are made into a stew called *escamole*.

If you happen to pass peasants in the countryside drawing off the *aguamiel* with their long gourds, stop and try it. It is curiously refreshing and slightly sweet. The fermented *pulque* is a much more acquired taste and packs an unexpected and sudden punch. To really appreciate it, either plain or cured with fruits and almonds, it is best drunk fresh at some reputable ranch where it is produced.

BEER

Beer is no late-comer. The first license for the sale of "beer"—a concoction of barley, lemon, tamarind, and sugar—was issued in 1544. Toward the middle of the nineteenth century the first breweries were established by Swiss and German residents, and beer was produced based on parched Mexican barley and *piloncillo*. Another decade or so later hops were introduced, and the first lager-type beer, more as we know it today, came into being.

It is such an appropriate accompaniment to a Mexican meal, and Mexican beers can hold their own against, and more often than not surpass, those brewed in other parts of the world. Two of the more local beers, not widely distributed in the republic, are the canned American-type Tecate made in Baja California and Cruz Blanca from Chihuahua. From breweries established in Monterrey as far back as 1890 come the much-exported and well known Carta Blanca and Bohemia and the dark, rich Noche Buena, which appears only around Christmastime. And one should never pass through Monterrey without drinking a well-chilled stein of draught beer with a meal of *cabrito* or *agujas*. From Orizaba in the State of Veracruz come the light Superior, the slightly heavier Dos XX and the Bock-type Tres XXX—in both a light and dark version. There is the ubiquitous Corona made in Mexico City and its dark, heavier version, Negro Modelo. In Yucatán to the southeast there are the justly touted pilsner- type Carta Clara; Montejo, more like a Munich brew; and León Negro, a very dark porter-type beer—to mention just a few.

AGUA FRESCA DE FLOR DE JAMAICA
[*Jamaica flower water*]

4 cups

"Great quantities of earthenware are also exposed in the markets, and the stranger will be pleased to observe the beautiful way in which Indian women produce a variety of liquors of every colour and flavour. A vase, much larger than any made in Europe, of red earthenware resembling the Etruscan, is filled with water, and nearly buried in wet sand. A variety of flowers, principally poppies are stuck in, among which stand the glasses containing the showy coloured beverages, which, with chocolate, pulque, and ices are served out for a trifle."

—FROM *Six Months Residence and Travel in Mexico,*
BY W. H. BULLOCK

Despite the tremendous popularity of commercial bottled drinks all over the country from the capital to the smallest mountain hamlet, the red watermelon, pale-green lime, or orangey-brown tamarind waters, sweetened and kept cool with huge chunks of ice, are sold from huge glass or earthenware containers in the marketplaces, by the street vendors, or in a few of the more traditional restaurants. This is one of them: acidy and refreshing, it is colored by the deep red of the Jamaica flower (*Hibiscus sabdariffa*).

A saucepan
⅔ cup Jamaica flowers
(*see note below*)
1½ cups cold water

Put the flowers and water together into the saucepan and bring them to a boil. Continue boiling the flowers for about 3 minutes over a brisk flame.

Water as necessary to
    make 4 cups of liquid
⅓ cup granulated sugar,
    or to taste
A colander
A jug (at least 1 quart
    capacity)
Granulated sugar, if
    necessary

Add the rest of the water and the sugar and set it aside for at least 4 hours or overnight (see note below).

Strain the liquid into the jug. Add more sugar if necessary. Serve well chilled.

The dried flowers, labeled "sorrel," are obtainable in Mexican markets in the South and Southwest and in West Indian markets. The Jamaicans use a syrup made of the flower for their rum punches.

Because of its acid quality, do not leave the drink standing in any receptacle with a surface that is attackable by acid—i.e., poorly glazed earthenware, enamel, copper, aluminum.

CHOCOLATE

"Here are also two cloisters of nuns [in the Dominican convent in Oaxaca], which are talked of far and near, not for their religious practices, but for their skill in making two drinks, which are used in those parts, the one called chocolate and the other atole, which is like unto our almond milk, but much thicker, and is made of the juices of the young maize or Indian wheat, which they so confection with spices, musk and sugar that is not only admirable in the sweetness of the smell, but much more nourishing and comforting to the stomach. This is not a commodity that can be transported from thence, but is to be drunk there where it is made. But the other, chocolate, is made up in boxes, and sent not only to Mexico [City] and the parts thereabouts, but much of it is yearly transported into Spain."

—FROM *Travel in the New World,*
BY THOMAS GAGE

When I am in Oaxaca, I love to go to the grind-it-yourself place. The townswomen and the peasants from the countryside buy their kilos of cacao beans, and a certain quantity of sugar and almonds to go with them, depending on what they can afford—if they are very poor, then they buy fewer cacao beans and almonds and more sugar. Each woman picks up a zinc tub, which she places under one of the several grinding machines around the store. The cacao and almonds are poured into the hopper, and very soon a satiny, tacky chocolate sauce oozes out of the spout—which has been sprinkled with sugar so that none will stick and be wasted—and falls onto the pile of sugar in the tub below. The women have brought with them two large wooden spoons to mix it all well together, and some even have brushes so that not one speck of the valuable chocolate is left sticking to the metal. Then the chocolate is carried to another machine for a second grinding—this time with the sugar—and it is at this point that you persuade someone to let you stick your finger in and try. It is then carried home and set to dry in small molds in the sun.

The subject of chocolate is inexhaustible, and certainly fascinated all the early writers about Mexico. Sahagún tells us that it was drunk only by the rich and noble, and even then in moderation, for it was thought to have deranging qualities like the mushroom. There was orange, black, and white chocolate; it was made with honey or mixed with purple flowers and served at the end of a feast with great ceremony. The distinguished men drank from painted cups, or black cups on a base covered with jaguar or deer skin. Perforated cups were used as strainers and the spoons were tortoiseshell. All this equipment was carried in special net bags.

Thomas Gage devotes a lot of space to chocolate in *Travels in the New World,* and tells how the women of Chiapas flouted the bishop and were excommunicated because they would not give up their comforting cups of chocolate to sustain them during Mass. Only the British seemed to scorn chocolate; when they captured a Spanish ship on the high seas laden with cacao they threw it overboard in disgust, calling it sheep's dung.

The name itself is derived from the Nahuatl words *xocotl* ("fruit"), and *atl* ("water").

The drinking chocolate of Mexico is quite different from the cholocate available here. It is lighter bodied, and it has a definite texture. Luckily, several varieties of Mexican chocolate are available here, because there is really no substitute for it.

To make the beverage in the authentic way:

1 serving

An earthenware pot
1 cup water
1 1½-ounce tablet of
    Mexican chocolate
A molinillo *or blender*

Heat the water in the pot. As it comes to a boil, break the chocolate into it and stir until the chocolate has melted. Let it boil gently for about 5 minutes so that all the flavor comes out, then beat it until it is frothy.

Traditionally, this is the perfect accompaniment for Tamales de Dulce (page 95–96).

ATOLE

A whole chapter could be devoted to the pre-Columbian beverage called *atole,* still much esteemed in Mexico. Though there are many variations, basically *atole* is a gruel thickened with *masa,* sweetened with raw sugar, and flavored with crushed fruits—such as pineapple and strawberries—or seasoned with chili. Some are made with a base of ground rice; others with fresh corn. For the Mexicans *atole,* too, is a natural accompaniment for *tamales.* For non-Mexicans, however, it is really not the sort of beverage that would be generally accepted, no matter how authentic, so I am giving only one recipe—for the *atole* flavored with chocolate and called *champurrado.*

CHAMPURRADO [*Chocolate-flavored atole*]

3 servings

An earthenware pot, if possible

Bring the 1½ cups water to a boil.

1½ cups water
½ cup masa harina
1 cup water

Mix the *masa harina* with the 1 cup water and strain into the boiling water, stirring it well so that it is completely smooth.

1 1½-ounce tablet of Mexican chocolate
1-inch stick cinnamon
Brown sugar to taste

Add the chocolate, cinnamon, and brown sugar. Keep stirring the mixture until it thickens and is well flavored—about 5 minutes.

COFFEE

So many mornings in Mexico I was awakened by the gentle swish of brooms. Some of the maids in the street would be sweeping sidewalks, terraces, or patios, slowly, rhythmically, while they gossiped, and others scuttled off into the cool morning air to bring back crisp *bolillos* and hot *pan dulce* from the *panaderías*. The time to go is either early morning or late afternoon, just as the baker is sending out his huge trays of freshly baked goods. You pick up a small, round metal tray and a pair of tongs, and wander around trying to decide what you really want from dozens of varieties: *triangulos, yoyos, kekis, suspiros, besos, yemas*, among so many others. I always choose the sugar-glazed flaky *campechanos*, or the rich, yeasty *puros* ("cigars"), which are so good with a large glass of *café con leche*.

And then my mouth waters as I remember my breakfasts in the Hermosillo market. Cele's scrupulously clean concession was always doing a roaring trade from huge pans of freshly brewed coffee and milk covered with a thickly matted skin of deep yellow cream: at intervals the baker next door would send fresh batches of *pan dulce*. Or sitting outside under the arches in Veracruz, where the waiter fills your glass halfway with strong, rich coffee and then hits it sharply so that its ringing tone summons with a sense of urgency his helper, who is scurrying to keep up, with a jug of steaming milk. Driving back to Mexico City, once more in the mountains, you stop at Córdoba—the coffee center of Mexico—to sit in a streetside café and drink a thick, black espresso with the smell of roasting coffee heavy in the air.

We hear very little about it, but Mexico is among the leading producers of excellent coffees. It is served in every way—Italian, Austrian, American— but a few traditional restaurants still have *café de olla* on the menu. It is served in small pottery mugs.

CAFÉ DE OLLA

1 serving

An earthenware pot
1 cup water
3 tablespoons dark-
    roasted, coarsely
    ground coffee
1-inch stick cinnamon
Dark brown sugar to taste
    (see note below)

In an earthenware pot, bring the water to a boil. Add the dark-roasted coffee, the cinnamon stick, and the dark brown sugar to taste. Bring to a boil twice, then strain and serve.

Piloncillo is used in Mexico.

PART THREE

Supplementary Information

Sources for Mexican Ingredients

Albuquerque

Valley Distributing Co.
2819 2nd Street N.W.
Albuquerque, New Mexico 87107
A wide variety of dried chilies and
Mexican ingredients; mail orders

Chicago

La Casa del Pueblo
1810 Blue Island
Chicago, Illinois 60608
A large Mexican supermarket stocking
fresh and dried chilies and other
ingredients

Casa Esteiro
2719 West Division
Chicago, Illinois 60622
Dried and fresh chilies and many other
Mexican ingredients

Los Angeles

El Mercado
First Avenue and Lorena
East Los Angeles, California 90063
Just like a Mexican open market, with
many stands selling fresh and dried
chilies, cooking utensils, canned goods

New York City (Manhattan)

DOWNTOWN

Casa Moneo
210 West 14th Street
New York, New York 10014
(Tel. 212 929-1644)
Large variety of Mexican ingredients,
canned goods, dried chilies, corn
husks, *chorizos*, spices, Mexican beer,
and cooking equipment; mail orders

MIDTOWN

Trinacria Importing Co.
415 Third Avenue
New York, New York 10016
(Tel. 212 LE2-5567)
Mexican canned goods, occasionally fresh
green chilies, fresh coriander, spices

H. Roth and Son
968 Second Avenue,
New York, New York 10022
(Tel. 212 593-3140)
Mexican canned goods (chilies and green
tomatoes), spices, etc.; for mail
orders write H. Roth and Sons, 1577 First
Avenue, New York, New York 10028
(Tel. 212 RE4-1110)

UPTOWN (West)

Perello, Inc.
2585 Broadway
New York, New York 10025
(Tel. 212 MO6-0901)

Masa harina, canned chilies, Seville
oranges, Mexican beer, fresh coriander

The Magic Carpet West
201 West 98th Street
New York, New York 10025
(Tel. 212 222-2189)
Open for retail trade Fridays and
Saturdays, 10 A.M. to 6 P.M.

Mexican canned chilies, guava shells,
dried chilies, cactus pieces, plus a
large range of spices, sesame seeds,
pepitas, flor de jamaica; mail orders

Max's Market
2603 Broadway, between 98th and 99th
Streets
New York, New York 10025
(Tel. 212 AC2-8351

Coriander, fresh chilies, green (unripe)
tomatoes, plantains and other ingredients

UPTOWN (East)

La Marqueta
Park Avenue between 112th and 116th
    Streets

    Stand 499, at 114th Street
(no telephone)

Nearly always has fresh green chilies
from Mexico—*serranos* or *jalapeños*—
and *very* occasionally *poblanos.*

    Stand 492, between 114th and 115th
    Streets
(Tel.: 212 369-1083)

Banana leaves, canned
chilies, cactus pieces, occasionally
dried chilies, *flor de Jamaica*

    Fresh green chilies, often Mexican *se-*

rranos and *jalapeños,* are carried by fruit
stores all over Manhattan and Brooklyn:
Cassaro Bros., 390 Third Avenue (corner
28th Street), New York, New York 10016,
(Tel. 212 889-4496), import for wholesale
and retail. The fresh *chiles cayennes*
are carried by many fruiterers throughout
the year in Chinatown, and also at
Jimmy's, 79 Bayard Street, New York,
New York 10013 (Tel. 212 WO2-0077);
Trinacria; the Magic Carpet; Ninth
Avenue Markets; Ann's Market

There are probably many small pork
butchers that carry sausage casings or
will order them for you—like Joe Esposito,
Italian Pork Store, 516 Ninth Avenue
(between 38th and 39th Streets)
New York, New York 10018
(Tel. 212 BR9-5096). He also
carries homemade lard, pork blood, etc.

Mexican cooking equipment

Casa Moneo (see previous listing) carries
tortilla presses, some *molcajetes* and
metates, comals

Cooking equipment general

Bridge Company
212 East 52nd Street
(between Second and Third Avenues),
New York, New York 10022
(Tel. 212 688-4220).

Carries a large range of cooking equipment at very reasonable prices.

San Antonio

Frank Pizzini
202 Produce Row
San Antonio, Texas 78207
(Tel. 512 CA7-2082)

Dried and fresh chilies, spices, dried
herbs, corn husks, etc.; mail orders

San Francisco

La Palma
2884 24th Street
San Francisco, California 94110
(415) MI8-5500

Fresh and dried chilies, fresh *tomate verde*, corn husks, canned goods, *flor de Jamaica*, spices

Santa Fe

Theo. Roybal Store
Rear 212, 214, 216 Galisteo Street
Santa Fe, New Mexico 87501

Herbs, lye, corn, corn husks, cooking utensils, spices, many Mexican ingredients; mail orders

Washington, D.C.

Safeway International
1110 F. Street N.W.
Washington, D.C. 20004
(Tel.: 202 628-1880)

Washington, D.C. (*continued*)

A large variety of basic ingredients for Mexican cooking, canned and dry goods, fresh chilies, *jícama*, etc.

Casa Peña
1636 17th Street N.W.
Washington, D.C. 20009
(Tel. 202 462-2222)

and a branch of Casa Peña

What in the World
5441 McArthur Blvd. N.W.
Washington, D.C.
(Tel.: 202 632-6500)

A large variety of dried and fresh chilies, fresh *tomate verde,* and Mexican canned and dry ingredients

Giant Food, Inc., supermarkets in Washington, Bethesda, and in Virginia carry a smaller selection of Mexican foods and ingredients, but most of all some *chiles anchos.*

Vocabulary and Pronunciation Guide

The list of words and their pronunciations that follows is intended to help those readers unfamiliar with the languages of Mexico to find their way around the world of Mexican cooking, especially in the markets both in this country and in Mexico. Toward that end I have included only what I consider the most important words and terms to be found in the book, as well as a few culinary terms I haven't used elsewhere.

aceituna	*olive*	ah-seh-ee-TOO-nah
achiote	*seeds of the annatto tree*	ah-chee-OH-teh
acitrón	*candied biznaga cactus*	ah-see-TRON
adobo, adobado	*name given to a rather sour seasoning paste made of ground chilies, herbs, and vinegar; seasoned with such a paste*	ah-DOH-boh, ah-doh-BAH-doh
agrio	*sour*	AH-gree-oh
agua, aguado	*water, watery*	AH-gwah, ah-GWAH-doh
aguardiente	*name given to an alcohol made of sugar cane*	ah-gwar-DYEN-teh
agujas	*name given to ribs of beef eaten in the north*	ah-GOO-hahs
ajonjolí	*sesame*	ah-hohn-hoh-LEE
albóndigas	*meat balls*	ahl-BON-dee-gahs

358

alcaparras	*capers*	ahl-kah-PAH-rrahs
almeja	*clam (general name for many species)*	ahl-MEY-hah
almendra	*almond*	ahl-MEHN-drah
almíbar	*light syrup*	ahl-MEE-bahr
almuerzo	*brunch*	ahl-MWER-soh
ancho	*name given to a variety of chili (lit. "wide")*	AHN-choh
añejo	*aged*	ah-NYEH-hoh
antiguo	*old, ancient*	ahn-TEE-gwoh
antojito	*appetizer (lit. "little whim")*	ahn-toh-HEE-toh
arroz	*rice*	ah-RROS
asadero	*type of cheese made in states of Chihuahua and Michoacán, Mexico*	ah-sah-DEH-roh
asar, asado	*To roast or broil; roasted or broiled*	ah-SAHR, ah-SAH-doh
barbacoa	*barbecued meat*	bahr-bah-KOH-ah
birria	*name given to a dish of seasoned meat, steamed or barbecued*	BEE-rryah
blanco	*white*	BLAHN-koh
bola, bolita	*ball, a little ball*	BOH-lah, boh-LEE-tah
bolillo	*small, elongated roll of bread*	boh-LEE-yoh
borracho	*drunk*	boh-RRAH-choch
botana	*name given to an appetizer served with drinks*	boh-TAH-nah
budín	*pudding*	boo-DEEN
buñuelo	*fritter*	boo-nyoo-WEH-loh
burrito	*name given to a taco made with a wheat-flour tortilla*	boo-RREE-toh
cabrito	*kid*	kah-BREE-toh
cacahuazintle	*corn with very large, white kernels*	kah-kah-wah-SEEN-tleh
cajeta	*a dessert usually of fruit or milk, cooked with sugar until thick*	kah-HEH-tah

calabacita	*zucchini squash*	kah-lah-bah-SEE-tah
calabaza	*pumpkin*	kah-lah-BAH-sah
caldo	*broth*	KAHL-doh
callo de hacha	*pinna clam*	kah-yoh deh AH-chah
camarones	*shrimps*	kah-mah-ROH-nehs
camote	*yam, sweet potato*	kah-MOH-teh
campo	*the country*	KAHM-poh
cantina	*bar*	kahn-TEE-nah
capeado	*covered with batter and fried*	kah-peh-AH-thoh
carbón	*charcoal*	kahr-BOHN
carne	*meat*	KAHR-neh,
carnitas	*name given to a dish of little pieces of cooked pork*	kahr-NEE-tahs
cascabel	*name given to a round chili (lit. "rattle")*	kahs-kah-BEL
cazón	*dogfish*	kah-SOHN
cazuela	*earthenware casserole*	kah-SWEH-lah
cebiche	*name given to fish marinated in lime juice*	seh-BEE-cheh
cebolla	*onion*	seh-BOH-yah
cecina	*name given to thin strips of dried meat*	seh-SEE-nah
cena	*supper*	SEH-nah
chalupa	*name given to an oval or boat-shaped piece of tortilla dough, pinched up around the edge and filled*	chah-LOO-pah
charro	*gentleman horseman*	CHAH-rroh
chayote	*vegetable pear*	chah-YOH-teh
chícharo	*pea*	CHEE-chah-roh
chicharrón	*name given to crisp-fried pork rind*	chee-chah-RROHN
chilaca	*name given to a long, thin, dark-green chili*	chee-LAH-kah
chilaquiles	*name given to a dish that uses up stale tortillas*	chee-lah-KEE-lehs
chile	*chili, hot pepper*	CHEE-leh

chilorio	*name given to cooked and shredded meat, fried with a paste of ground chilies and other seasoning*	chee-LOH-ryoh
chilpachole	*name given to a crab soup from Veracruz*	cheel-pah-CHOH-leh
chipotle, chipocle	*name given to a smoked chili*	chee-POT-tleh, chee-POH-kleh
chiquihuite	*name given to a woven basket for tortillas*	chee-kee-WEE-teh
chongos	*name given to a dessert of cooked milk curds*	CHOHN-gohs
chorizo	*a spicy pork sausage*	choh-REE-soh
chuleta	*a chop*	choo-LEH-tah
cielo	*sky*	see-EH-loh
cilantro	*fresh coriander*	see-LANH-troh
claveatado	*spiked or studded with cloves*	klah-beh-ah-TAH-thoh
clavo	*clove*	KLAH-boh
cocada	*name given to a coconut dessert*	koh-KAH-thah
cochinita	*a small pig*	koh-chee-NEE-tah
cocido	*cooked*	koh-SEE-thoh
cocina	*kitchen*	koh-SEE-nah
coco	*coconut*	KOH-koh
colado	*strained*	ko-LAH-thoh
comal	*thin plate of earthenware or metal for cooking tortillas*	ko-MAHL
comida	*the main meal of the day*	koh-MEE-thah
comino	*cumin*	koh-MEE-noh
corunda	*name given to a small cushion-shaped* tamal *wrapped in the long leaf of the corn plant*	koh-ROON-dah
crema	*cream*	KREH-mah
crudo	*raw*	KROO-thoh
cuaresmeño	*another name for* chile jalapeño (*lit. "lenten"*)	kwah-rehs-MEH-nyoh
cuchara	*spoon*	koo-CHAH-rah

cuchillo	*knife*	koo-CHEE-yoh
cuitlacoche	*see* huitlacoche	kwee-tlah-KOH-cheh
desayuno	*breakfast*	deh-sah-YOO-noh
deshebrar	*to shred*	deh-seh-BRAHR
dulce	*sweet*	DOOL-seh
durazno	*peach*	doo-RAHS-noh
elote	*ear of fresh corn*	eh-LOH-teh
enchilada	*name given to a tortilla dipped into a chili sauce and filled, generally with cheese or meat*	ehn-chee-LAH-thah
encurtido	*pickled, preserved*	ehn-koor-TEE-thoh
ensalada	*salad*	ehn-sah-LAH-thah
envinada	*wine added*	ehn-vee-NAH-thah
epazote	*herb used in Mexican cooking* (Chenopodium ambrosioides)	eh-pah-SOH-teh
escabeche	*pickle*	ehs-kah-BEH-cheh
estilo	*in the style of*	ehs-TEE-loh
estofado	*stew*	ehs-toh-FAH-thoh
faisán	*pheasant or name given to many game birds*	fay-SAHN
fiambre	*name given to cooked meats served cold*	FYAHM-breh
fingido	*false, ersatz*	feen-HEE-thoh
flameado	*flambé (served flaming)*	flah-meh-AH-thoh
flan	*caramel custard*	flahn
flor	*flower*	flohr
fresco	*fresh*	FREHS-koh
frijoles	*beans*	free-HOH-lehs
frito	*fried*	FREE-toh
gallina	*hen*	gah-YEE-nah
garnacha	*name given to a round antojito of tortilla dough*	gahr-NAH-chah
gordita	*name given to a thick cake of maize dough and lard*	gohr-DEE-tah
grano de elote	*corn kernel*	grah-no deh eh-LOH-teh

guacamole	name given to a "concoction" of crushed avocado	gwah-kah-MOH-leh
guajillo	name given to a long, thin dried chili	gwah-HEE-yoh
guajolote	wild turkey	gwa-hoh-LOH-teh
guiso	a stew	GHEE-soh
haba	a large bean	AH-bah
habanero	name given to a fiery chili used in the states of Campeche and Yucatán, Mexico	ah-bah-NEH-roh
harina	flour	ah-REE-nah
hígado	liver	EE-gah-thoh
hoja santa	a large leaf used in cooking in the south of Mexico (Piper sanctum)	OH-hah SAHN-tah
huachinango	red snapper	wah-chee-NAHN-goh
huauzoncle, guauzontle	a wild green with thin serrated leaves and spiky seeded tops	gwow-SOHN-tleh
huevo	egg	WEH-voh
huitlacoche	fungus that grows on corn	wee-tlah-KOH-cheh
jaiba	small, hard-shelled crab	HAHY-bah
jalapeño	name given to a small fat green chili (lit. "from Jalapa")	hah-lah-PEH-nyoh
jícama	brown bulbous root, sliced and used as an appetizer or salad (Pachyrrhizus erosus)	HEE-kah-mah
jitomate	tomato	hee-toh-MAH-teh
leche	milk	LEH-cheh
licuadora	blender	lee-kwah-DOH-rah
lima agria	a bitter lime used in Yucatán (Citrus limetta)	lee-mah AH-gree-ah
limón	lime	lee-MOHN
lujo	luxury	LOO-hoh
machacado	name given to a dish of scrambled eggs and shredded dried meat	mah-chah-KAH-thoh
maíz	dried corn	mah-EES

mano	muller used with the metate (lit. "hand")	MAH-noh
masa	name given to a dough of ground dried corn and water	MAH-sah
manteca	lard	mahn-TEH-kah
menudo	name given to a hearty soup of tripe	meh-NOO-thoh
metate	flat, rectangular tripod of basalt used for grinding corn and chilies, etc.	meh-TAH-teh
milpa	cornfield	MEEL-pah
mochomos	name given to roasted or cooked meat, shredded and fried crisp	moh-CHOH-mohs
molcajete	mortar of basalt for grinding chilies and sauces	mohl-kah-HEH-teh
mole	concoction or mixture	MOH-leh
mulato	name given to a dark black-brown dried chili	moo-LAH-toh
Nahuatl	the lingua franca of the peoples of the central highlands of Mexico; it was spoken by the Toltecs and people before them; still spoken today in a degenerated form (T. Sullivan)	NAH-wahtl
natilla	name given to a custard-like dessert	nah-TEE-yah
negro	black	NEH-groh
nogada	walnut sauce	noh-GAH-thah
nopal	fleshy oval joint of the Opuntia cactus	noh-PAHL
norte, norteño	north, of the north	NOHR-teh, nohr-TEH-nyoh
nuevo	new	NWEH-voh
ocote	small strips of resinous pine used to kindle a fire	oh-KOH-teh

olla	*a round earthenware pot*	OH-yah
pachola	*name given to a thin, half-circle-shaped piece of ground meat*	pah-CHOH-lah
pámpano	*pompano*	PAHM-pah-noh
pan	*bread*	pahn
pan dulce	*sweet roll*	pahn DOOL-seh
pancita	*stuffed sheep's stomach*	pahn-SEE-tah
papa	*potato*	PAH-pah
papa-dzul	*name given to a Yucatecan specialty*	pah-pah-DZOOL
pasilla	*name given to the dried* chile chilaca	pah-SEE-yah
pastel	*cake*	pahs-TEHL
pato	*duck*	PAH-toh
pechuga	*(chicken) breast*	peh-CHOO-gah
pellizcada	*name given to an* antojito *of tortilla dough pinched up around the edge and filled*	peh-yees-KAH-thah
pepita	*pumpkin seed*	peh-PEE-tah
pescado	*fish*	pehs-KAH-thoh
pib, pibil	*Yucatecan pit barbecue; barbecued*	peeb, pee-BEEL
picadillo	*name given to a mixture of ground or shredded meat and other ingredients usually used as a stuffing*	pee-kah-DEE-yoh
picante	*hot spicy as opposed to hot in temperature*	pee-CAHN-teh
piloncillo	*name given to a cone of dark-brown unrefined sugar*	pee-lohn-SEE-yoh
pimienta	*pepper*	pee-MYEHN-tah
piña	*pineapple*	PEE-nyah
pipián	*name given to a sauce of ground nuts or seeds and spices*	pee-PYAHN
plátano	*banana*	PLAH-tah-noh

plátano macho	plantain	PLA-tah-noh MAH-choh
plaza	market or central square	PLAH-sah
poblano	name given to a large green chili (lit. "of Puebla")	poh-BLAH-noh
pollo	chicken	POH-yoh
postre	dessert	POHS-treh
pozole	name given to a filling soup of meat and cacahuazintle corn	poh-SOH-leh
puchero	stew	poo-CHEH-roh
puerco	pork	PWEHR-koh
puesto	a stand in the market or on the street	PWEHS-toh
pulque	name given to the distilled milky sap obtained from the century plant	POOL-keh
quelite	a wild green	keh-LEE-teh
quemar, quemado	to burn, burned	keh-MAHR, keh-MAH-thoh
quesadilla	name given to a filled turnover of tortilla dough	keh-sah-DEE-yah
queso	cheese	KEH-soh
raja	name given to a strip of something, usually of chili	RAH-hah
ranchero	country-style (lit. "of the ranch")	rahn-CHEH-roh
real	royal	reh-AHL
recado	seasoning (Yucatecan usage)	reh-KAH-thoh
relleno	stuffing	reh-YEH-noh
robalo	snook	roh-BAH-loh
rojo	red	ROH-hoh
sal	salt	sahl
salpicón	shredded or finely cut	sahl-pee-KOHN
salsa	sauce	SAHL-sah
seco	dry	SEH-koh
sencillo	simple	sehn-SEE-yoh

serrano	name given to a small green chili (lit. "of the sierra [mountain area]")	seh-RRAH-noh
sesos	brains	SEH-sohs
sopa	soup	SOH-pah
sopes	name given to little round antojitos of tortilla dough	SOH-pehs
taco	name given to a tortilla wrapped around a filling, sometimes fried	TAH-koh
tamal	name given to a piece of dough or corn beaten with lard and steamed in a corn husk or banana leaf	tah-MAHL
tarasco	of the Tarascan Indians in the state of Michoacán	tah-RAHS-koh
tejolote	pestle for the molcajete	teh-hoh-LOH-teh
tenedor	fork	teh-NEH-dohr
tierno	tender	TYEHR-noh
tierra	land or earth	TYEH-rrah
tlalpeño	of Tlalpán, a small town now part of Mexico City	tlahl-PEH-nyoh
tomate verde	Mexican green tomato	toh-MAH-teh BEHR-deh
torta	name given to a sandwich made with a round roll	TOHR-tah
tortilla	name given to a thin, unleavened pancake of ground, dried maize	tohr-TEE-yah
tostada	name given to a tortilla fried crisp and garnished	tohs-TAH-thah
totopos, tostaditas	name given to small triangular pieces of crisp-fried tortilla	toh-TOH-pohs, tohs-tah-THEE-tahs
trigo	wheat	TREE-goh
tuna	the prickly pear, fruit of the nopal cactus	TOO-nah

uchepos	name given to the fresh corn tamales of Michoacán	oo-CHEH-pohs
uva	grape	OO-bah
verde	green	BEHR-theh
vinagre	vinegar	bee-NAH-greh
xoconostle	the acidy, green prickly pear	soh-koh-NOHS-tleh
yema	yolk	YEH-mah
Yucateco	of the state of Yucatán	yoo-kah-TEH-koh
zanahoria	carrot	sah-nah-OH-ryah

Bibliography

Bourchier, E. M., and Roldán, José. *Herbs for Pot and Body*. Mexico City: privately printed, 1962.

Bullock, W. H. *Six Months Residence and Travel in Mexico*. London: John Murray, 1824.

———. *Across Mexico*. London, 1864.

Calderón de la Barca, Frances. *Life in Mexico*. Edited and annotated by Howard T. Fisher and Marion Hall Fisher. New York: Doubleday, 1966.

Díaz del Castillo, Bernal. *The Discovery and Conquest of Mexico, 1517–1521*. Translated by A. P. Maudsley. Mexico City: Ediciones Tolteca, 1953.

Farga, Amando. *Historia de la Comida en México*. Mexico City: Costa-Amic, 1968.

Gage, Thomas. *Travels in the New World*. Edited by Eric J. Thompson. Norman: University of Oklahoma Press, 1958.

Halliday, Evelyn G., and Noble, Isabel. *Hows and Whys of Cooking*. Chicago: University of Chicago Press, 1957.

Latrobe, Charles Joseph. *The Rambler in Mexico*. London, 1836.

Martínez, Maximino. *Plantas Útiles de la Flora Mexicana*. Mexico City: Ediciones Botas, 1959.

Nuestra Cocina. Comité de Damas Pro Beneficencia Española. Mexico City: Impresiones Modernas, 1962.

Nuevo Cocinero Mexicano. Paris: Librería de Ch. Bouret, 1878.

Novo, Salvador. *Cocina Mexicana*. Mexico City: Editorial Porrua, 1967.

Ramos Espinosa, Alfredo. *Semblanza Mexicana*. Mexico City: Editorial Bolívar, 1948.

Recetas Prácticas para la Señora de Casa. Guadalajara: Imp. de J. A. Rodríguez, 1895.

Sahagún, Bernadino de. *"Historia General de las Cosas de Nueva España, 1547–1582."* Unpublished translation by Thelma D. Sullivan.

———. *Nahuatl Proverbs, Conundrums, and Metaphors*. Translated by Thelma D. Sullivan. Estudios de la Cultura Nahuatl, vol. IV, México, 1963.

Sánchez, Mayo Antonio. *La Cocina Mexicana*. Mexico City: Editorial Diana S. A., 1964.

Stephens J. L. *Incidents of Travel in Yucatán*. Dover Publications, Inc., 1963.

Ward, ———. *Ward's Mexico*, vol. II: *Personal Narrative* and appendices. London, n.d.

Zavaleta, Carmen. *Cocina Michoacana*. Mexico City: 1965.

Index

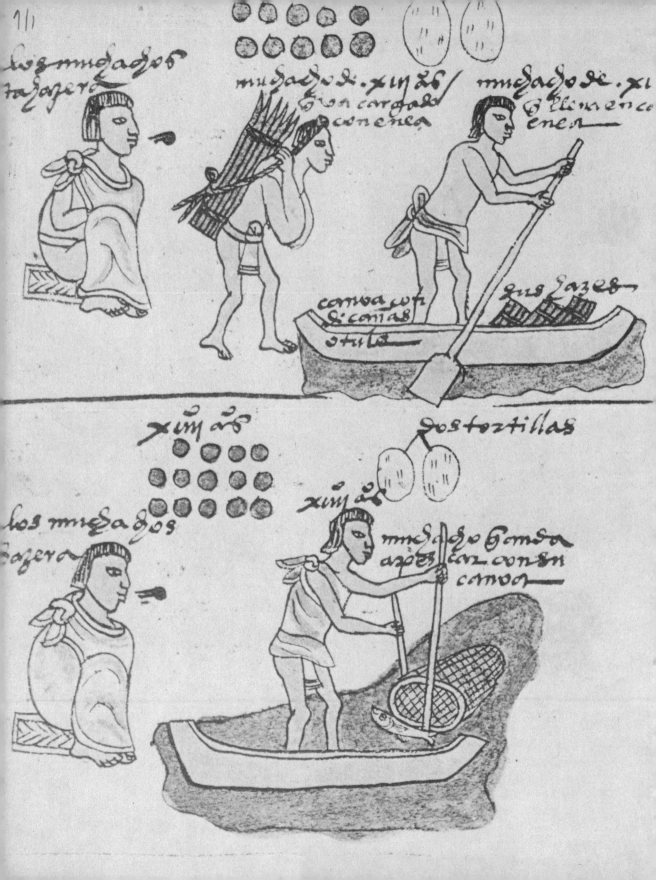